AFFIRMATIVE PSYCHOTHERAPY
AND COUNSELING
FOR
LESBIANS
AND
GAY MEN

AFFIRMATIVE PSYCHOTHERAPY AND COUNSELING

FOR

LESBIANS

AND

GAY MEN

JEFFREY N. CHERNIN

MELISSA R. JOHNSON

SAGE Publications
International Educational and Professional Publisher
Thousand Oaks ▪ London ▪ New Delhi

For information:

Sage Publications, Inc.
2455 Teller Road
Thousand Oaks, California 91320
E-mail: order@sagepub.com

Sage Publications Ltd.
6 Bonhill Street
London EC2A 4PU
United Kingdom

Sage Publications India Pvt. Ltd.
M-32 Market
Greater Kailash I
New Delhi 110 048 India

Printed in the United States of America

Library of Congress Cataloging-in-Publication Data

Chernin, Jeffrey N.
Affirmative psychotherapy and counseling for lesbians and gay men / Jeffrey N. Chernin and Melissa R. Johnson.
    p. cm.
Includes bibliographical references and index.
ISBN 0-7619-1768-3 -- ISBN 0-7619-1769-1 (pbk.)
    1. Counseling. 2. Psychotherapy. 3. Lesbians-Counseling of. 4. Gays-Counseling of. 5. Bisexuals-Counseling of. I. Johnson, Melissa R. II. Title.
BF637.C6 C395 2002
616.89'14'08664--dc21

                                                    2002013028

02 03 04 05 10 9 8 7 6 5 4 3 2 1

Acquiring Editor:	Margaret H. Seawell
Editorial Assistant:	Alicia Carter
Production Editor:	Claudia A. Hoffman
Copy Editor:	Meredith L. Brittain
Typesetter:	C&M Digitals (P) Ltd
Cover Designer:	Janet Foulger

Contents

Acknowledgments

We would like to acknowledge John Barry, Carolyn Solis, and Marty Perry for their support, friendship, and advice throughout this project. Better colleagues are not to be found!

Thanks to Andrew Kallimachos and Chris Emerson for their help early on in the project.

Special appreciation goes to Meredith Brittain, our copy editor, who went above and beyond our expectations. Her comments helped to strengthen and sharpen the book. We are also grateful to the staff at Sage.

From Jeff

Thanks to my partner and friend, Peter Nardi, for his unwavering support and encouragement. To my mom and dad, my sisters and their families, and my extended family: I value your love and your believing in me. My gratitude goes to the Counseling professors at the University of North Texas—in particular, Jan Holden, Robert Berg, and Cynthia Chandler—who have always been generous with their time, shown commitment to students, and offered invaluable assistance. Also, thanks to Veta Bailey, David Collier, Djinni and Mark Field, Jack Johnston, Sherry Larkins, Jay Newberry, Dewey Nichols, Ellen Nover, Jeanne Reyer and Mary Franklin, Scott and Hillary Schneider, and Jodi Wichman, who have always been there for me.

From Melissa

To the Dean of Education at The Art Institute of Dallas, Leslie C. Baughman: Thanks for your flexibility and consideration with my time during the many hours I spent in research and drafting the manuscript.

To my friends and family and, most of all, my partner, Edwina, and our son, Cameron: You provide me with the best life imaginable. Finally, to my coauthor, Jeff: We had no idea where this project would lead, and I am grateful that we have survived it relatively unscathed.

Preface

We have heard clinicians tell us in all sincerity that there is no difference between providing psychotherapy for gay/lesbian clients and heterosexual clients. Although the message these practitioners were trying to send was that they are not homophobic, they didn't realize that they were also conveying to us that they did not understand the complexities and nuances involved in working with issues unique to lesbians and gay men.

We have also spoken with clinicians who experience discomfort working with lesbian and gay clients, and two studies point to a need for more education. Avery, Hellman, and Sudderth (2001) surveyed lesbian, gay, bisexual, and transgender (LGBT) individuals with a mental illness to assess their level of satisfaction with mental health services. They found that the rate of dissatisfaction among LGBT respondents was twice as high as that of a heterosexual control group. Among the LGBT respondents who were women or members of ethnic minority groups, dissatisfaction rates were four times higher than for the respective control groups.

In the second study, Eliason (2000) surveyed 242 substance abuse counselors in Iowa about their knowledge and attitudes toward lesbian, gay, bisexual, and transgender clients. She found that, as a whole, substance abuse counselors had little formal education on lesbian and gay issues, as evidenced by misunderstanding the concepts of domestic partnership and internalized homophobia. More troubling, nearly half the respondents had negative or ambivalent attitudes toward lesbians and gay men.

We do not believe that clinicians who have difficulty working with lesbians and gay men purposely provide less than quality mental health services for lesbians and gay male clients. Rather, most clinicians try their best to offer affirmative treatment, but they have not had access to enough information. To help rectify this situation, we present practical and usable information about how to provide affirmative therapy to lesbians and gay men. Two questions should come to mind when reading a book such as this one: What is affirmative therapy for lesbians and gay men? How do you provide it? To answer the first question, Clark (2000) sums up the meaning of affirmative psychotherapy fittingly by describing a gay-affirmative clinician:

> Such a counselor may or may not be primarily homosexual in orientation, but if she or he is gay-affirmative by declaration, she or he believes that homosexuality is not merely to be accepted but must be appreciated—not as good as, but rather a gift accepted at some cost in a world still far from free of prejudice. The gay-affirmative counselor knows that while there is no need to address the question of whether or not to *be* gay, there may be some need to help a client find the way to be the best person he or she can be. (pp. 218-219)

The second question, regarding how to provide affirmative treatment for lesbians and gay men, is more difficult. Throughout this book, we supply information to facilitate providing competent, sensitive, and caring therapy for lesbian and gay male clients. You are indirectly, and sometimes directly, recognizing that gay and lesbian clients' sexual orientation is a valid and significant aspect of their overall identity when you provide affirmative therapy. As important, you are willing to empathize, understand, and learn from them. This book shows you how to treat issues unique to lesbians and gay men; it also enables you to treat other issues that are influenced by the fact that your client is lesbian or gay. We discuss treatment of same-gender couples and families, delve into ethnic minority issues, discuss HIV/AIDS, and review ethical and legal issues.

To complement the text, we include several case studies in each chapter that act as a bridge from theoretical information to application. We present fictional case studies—more than 30 in the book—as a way to stimulate thought and discussion. In Chapter 7, we offer therapist case studies to encourage consideration with respect to legal and ethical issues. To get the most out of the case studies, mull them over and answer the questions after each case. Compare the cases to clients in your practice, and notice any thoughts and feelings that arise as you read them.

To make this process more useful, instead of continually introducing you to new case studies in each chapter, we primarily present several cases in the first chapters and follow them throughout the book. To give you an example, we introduce you to Angela, who is struggling with her identity.

Preface Case Study (Angela)

Angela is a 31-year old African American who was referred to you by one of her acquaintances. Her sessions with you are her first experience in therapy. During the assessment, Angela informed you that she has been feeling unhappy and has uncontrollable crying spells. Angela also stated that no particular incident precipitated her depression. During the intake, Angela detailed her work and family history but, when she discussed her relationship, she referred to the person she is living with as "this person" or "them."

In today's session, her third, Angela admits that, "this person I've been telling you about is a woman I met at work. Jodi and I have been living together for 2 years. I haven't told anyone about the relationship, and only Jodi's friends know about it." Angela is quick to add, "I am not a lesbian, but I fell for Jodi."

To get the most from this and other case studies, think about general themes, ways to work with the client, and the impact of their current situation on their lesbian/gay identity. Among questions to consider for the previous case study are: Where would you start your work with Angela? How would you treat someone like Angela, given her gender, ethnicity, age, and uncertainty about her sexual orientation? How would you treat Angela differently from the way you treat clients who are out to their families, have a circle of friends, and are sure of their sexual orientation? What does it mean that she revealed the nature of her relationship to you?

Throughout the book, we provide the context in which to consider questions that pertain to lesbian/gay identity development, coming out, gender differences, and being in an ethnic minority. But we also ask questions after the case studies so that you will think about these scenarios on a deeper level and so that you will have the experience of contemplating treatment decisions. Usually, we do not answer the questions posed in the case studies because the questions are seeds for discussion and there is generally no one "right" answer.

If you are using this book as a classroom text, these case studies can be the basis for discussions about effective ways to treat these clients. If any uncomfortable thoughts or feelings come up for students, have them talk about their feelings, visit the Web sites in the appendix, and encourage them to see what the gay community offers. In your discussions, be sure that your class is a safe place to discuss discomfort. A safe place is a class atmosphere in which students who are uninformed or uncomfortable are given the opportunity to express their views without judgment or condemnation.

Another reason we want to introduce you to Angela is that many lesbians and gay men have their first therapeutic experience without revealing their sexual orientation to their therapists. Indeed, you may encounter some clients who are so deeply uncomfortable with their sexual orientation that you will learn about their orientation only after many months, or perhaps not at all. In such cases, you should provide clients with a good therapeutic experience so that when they are ready to address these issues later on, they will feel comfortable enough to do so. In the meantime, what you consciously or unconsciously reveal about your own level of comfort about lesbian/gay and sexual issues will have an impact on clients' level of trust and ability to deal with their sexual orientation. On the other hand, many clients enter therapy feeling comfortable about being lesbian or gay. Their presenting issues and course of treatment may have little to do directly with coming out or being attracted to people of the same gender.

Wherever clients fall on the coming out spectrum, and no matter how much or how little they feel comfortable about their sexual orientation, you will most likely hear their coming out stories, their histories, and their beliefs about having a same-gender sexual orientation. As a clinician, it is important to distinguish between issues that relate to living in a heterosexist culture and those that relate to personal difficulties; interventions that are appropriate for lesbians and gay men who are out of the closet and interventions for individuals who are struggling with their sexual orientation; and issues that are universal and those unique to lesbian and gay clients.

To provide affirmative treatment for lesbians and gay men, you should be familiar with relevant terminology and the context in which lesbians and gay men live. Chapter 1 provides definitions of many important terms, and Chapter 2 offers information on several lesbian and gay subcultures.

Furthermore, when you work with this population, you should develop an understanding of the coming out process and identity formation, and how younger lesbians and gay men, who sometimes prefer to call themselves queer, differ from older lesbians and gay men. You should be sensitive to related issues involved with treating this population, including the physical environment of your therapy office, the impact of heterosexist language in intake forms and psychological assessments, and referrals. Chapter 3 covers all of these areas.

In Chapter 4, we offer information on individual psychotherapy treatment, and we discuss universal themes as they apply to lesbian and gay clients, as well as issues unique to lesbians and gay men. Chapter 5 deals with couples therapy, and we present information on relationship stages, assessment and treatment issues, parenting, and HIV/AIDS in the context of dating and relationships. In Chapter 6, we discuss group psychotherapy and support groups. In particular, we discuss how Yalom's (1995) therapeutic factors apply to lesbian and gay male group clients. We also provide information and program outlines for facilitating support groups—including coming out groups, sexual orientation growth groups, HIV/AIDS groups, and groups for HIV-negative gay men—and comment on bereavement and substance abuse treatment groups.

Finally, the mental health field, more than any other, requires that we be aware of and work on our own issues while treating clients. To aid you in the process of examining your own issues, Chapter 7 addresses ethical and legal issues with respect to lesbian and gay clients. We focus on ethical issues about sexual orientation, such as countertransference, boundaries, research, HIV/AIDS, and reparative therapy.

Our primary focus is on how to create a physical and psychological environment that is conducive to providing affirmative psychotherapy for lesbian and gay clients. So, most of the book is geared toward issues directly related to being lesbian or gay. Furthermore, our focus is almost exclusively on lesbians and gay men because people who identify as lesbian or gay have many concerns that are different from those of bisexuals and transgender individuals. Nonetheless, much of what we discuss is applicable to these populations.

We made a special effort to include an appendix filled with resources for lesbian and gay clients, including organizations, books, and Web sites. Contact the authors in care of JNChernin@aol.com to receive updated Web site links.

Part I

Lesbian and Gay Life

*Definitions, Coming Out,
and Identity Development*

❖   ❖   ❖

1

Terminology and Identity Development

❖ ❖ ❖

To provide a starting point for treating lesbians and gay men, certain terms require definition. People may debate the exact meanings of these terms, which should serve to spur additional reading and discussion. In this chapter, we devote sections to the following sets of definitions:

1. Sexual orientation

2. Lesbian, gay, homosexual, and bisexual

3. LGBT, MSM, and WSW

4. Coming out

5. Gender role, gender identity, and transgender

6. Heterosexism and homophobia

After becoming familiar with these definitions, the next step is to understand lesbian/gay identity development. To that end, we present three models. The first two models, the Cass model and the Troiden model, are considered the standards in gay literature because they are popular and widely accepted. The third model, a social identity model, emphasizes sociological phenomena, setting it apart from the other lesbian/gay identity models.

❖ DEFINITIONS

Sexual Orientation

To provide affirmative therapy for lesbian and gay clients, it is important to make the distinction that the terms *lesbian* and *gay* reflect a social and sometimes political identity, as opposed to merely expressing same-gender sexual behavior. Moreover, *sexual orientation* is not just a cluster of sexual behaviors; rather, it involves thoughts, fantasies, and attraction in addition to sexual activities. In fact, some people self-identify as lesbian or gay and rarely, if ever, engage in same-gender sexual activity, and some individuals engage in repeated sexual acts with the same sex, yet do not self-identify as lesbian, gay, or bisexual (Laumann, Gagnon, Michaels, & Michaels, 1994). Self-definition is important because many clients enter therapy confused about their sexual orientation and do not link their behavior to self-definition, as illustrated by Case Study 1.1.

In contrast to Tom's situation, some lesbians and gay men do not develop a lesbian or gay identity solely because they engage in same-gender behavior without self-identifying labels (see Weinberg, 1978, for a discussion on self-definition). Some lesbians, such as Angela (introduced in the Preface), enter into relationships with other women, perhaps living with them for years, without seeing themselves as lesbian. Lesbians and gay men may avoid self-identification as lesbian or gay by limiting the terms to people with stereotypical characteristics or by their sexual roles, as in Case Studies 1.2 and 1.3.

Likewise, because contexts influence the way people view their sexual orientation, same-gender sex in various social contexts can be used as a way to avoid self-identification as lesbian or gay. Many heterosexuals have same-gender sex in social environments such as prison, the military, and boarding schools; lesbians and gay men use these same

---

Case Study 1.1 (Tom)

Tom, a 52-year old Caucasian, has a wife, Elizabeth, and three children. Tom has occasional sex with his wife to orgasm, and he has not had a sexual encounter with another man since he was in his teens. However, Tom has self-identified as gay since he was in his twenties, and he has lived his "gay life" by relying exclusively on fantasy.

Case Study 1.2 (Brian)

Brian, a self-identified gay Chinese American male, is 20 years old and struggles with being gay. In this session, Brian talks about seeing his first openly gay man 2 years ago; the man was presenting information on a sexuality panel to Brian's high school class. The gay man on the panel was effeminate, and Brian clearly remembers thinking to himself, "This femmy guy says he's gay, and if that's what being gay is, I couldn't possibly be like him."

Brian avoided defining himself as gay by believing that to be gay is to be effeminate and, because Brian did not see himself as effeminate, he was able to stave off self-labeling. Since that time, however, he has struggled with his sexual orientation. He has never dated, knows only a few gay people, and has never been to a gay bar. What interventions would you be making at this point? Would you try to stay a step ahead of him, perhaps suggesting he reveal his sexual orientation to his friends and family? How would you consider his Chinese American identity when suggesting that he come out to others?

---

social contexts to explain away their same-gender attraction, as with Tom in Case Study 1.4.

Case Study 1.3 (Roberto)

A 26-year old Latino client, Roberto, came out 2 years ago. In today's individual therapy session, Roberto tells you that, before he came out, he had sex with other men and considered himself heterosexual because "I always took the masculine role, while the bottoms were gay." In other words, because Roberto was the insertive partner, he had his "masculinity" and heterosexual orientation intact.

Case Study 1.4 (Tom, continued from Case Study 1.1)

Tom reports that he had sexual encounters as a teen, but that "the other guys at the (boarding) school kept talking about girls and what they did with them over summer, and there was no mention of sex between us guys. Well, I'm sure that some of them were basically straight, and I guess that I convinced myself that I was, too. Y'know, I just wasn't ready (to come to terms with being gay) for several years after I graduated."

In his twenties, despite realizing that he was gay, Tom decided to marry. Although he has never been sexually attracted to his wife, he grew to love and care for her. In his current situation, it is important to understand that Tom feels torn between a loving relationship and being true to himself. He has struggled with this issue for years before coming to see you. How will he adjust to what may be a long, arduous process of leaving his marriage? How will he deal with HIV and other sexually transmitted diseases? What feelings or judgments of your own would you, as his therapist, have to deal with during this process? What will you do if he asks to be in session with you when he comes out to his wife?

Lesbian, Gay, Homosexual, and Bisexual

Considering the almost limitless possibilities of sexual feelings, activities, and social contexts that may confuse individuals with respect to sexual identity (some of which you've seen in the case studies in the previous section), you can appreciate the barriers to ascribing meaning to sexual acts and coming to terms with being gay or lesbian. The terms *lesbian* and *gay* imply a developing or developed same-gender orientation, where thoughts, fantasies, and behavior act in concert, whereas the term *homosexual acts* refers to a cluster of same-gender behaviors.

Although this book focuses on lesbians and gay men, we would like to briefly define *bisexuality*. Bisexuals have thoughts, fantasies, and attraction to both men and women. Paul, Hayes, and Coates (1995) note that recognition of bisexuality as a distinct category by both the general public and the lesbian and gay community coincided with the development of a more organized bisexual movement. Bisexual people began protesting the invisibility and stereotyping of bisexuals and were upset that bisexuality was delegated to an errant form of heterosexuality or was considered a step on the way to coming out as lesbian or gay.

LGBT, MSM, and WSW

LGBT stands for *lesbian, gay, bisexual, and transgender*. Often, when you hear about the "gay community," people are referring to individuals who are LGBT. Many community organizations in the gay community have changed their names and mission statements to include lesbians, bisexuals, and transgender individuals. Throughout the text, we are encompassing LGBT individuals when we use the terms *gay community* or *lesbian/gay community*.

More and more, particularly in research studies focused on sexual behavior and HIV transmission, the term *MSM*, or men who have sex with men, has started to replace the term *gay and bisexual males*, and *WSW*, or women who have sex with women, is starting to appear in place of *lesbians and bisexual women*. This is happening because many subjects who responded "no" to being lesbian or gay would engage in same-gender behavior, and researchers found that they could more accurately capture data when asking people about their behaviors instead of their orientation.

Coming Out

The term *coming out* is not as simple as it appears. Does it mean coming to terms with a lesbian/gay sexual orientation, or is it revealing one's orientation to family and friends? Is it when someone goes to a gay bar for the first time? Or is it when someone has a first same-gender date or first same-gender sexual encounter?

Before we discuss these questions, we need to differentiate between coming out and lesbian/gay identity development. We discuss a coming out model in this section, and we present three identity development models later in the chapter. While reading about these models, keep in mind that individuals do not progress in an orderly, distinct fashion, and coming out is one aspect of lesbian/gay identity development. Thus, you can view the stages as places that people generally visit and revisit in varying degrees and for different lengths of time.

Kus (1990) offers a four-stage coming out model. Kus refers to the period before coming out as "stage zero" and calls it "life before the coming out process" (p. 31). Kus states that boys who are gay later in life tend to exhibit obedience, high levels of achievement, and heightened sensitivity to adult expectations. Girls who are lesbian later in life tend to be more assertive, outgoing, and shed traditional "feminine" roles to participate in nontraditional female interests.

The first stage, *Identification*, is the time when lesbians and gay men identify their attraction to members of the same sex and make their first attempts at self-labeling as gay or lesbian. Self-labeling arises from sexual experiences, identification with lesbian/gay role models or fictional characters, and emotional and sexual attraction. Kus compares the second stage, *Cognitive Changes*, to going to school. At this time, lesbians or gay men living in rural areas learn about gay culture by moving to larger cities, exploring lesbian/gay communities, reading books and periodicals, and discovering gay life on the Internet.

The third stage is *Acceptance*, which is the liberating time when lesbians and gay men come to accept their sexual orientation. However, they have not yet revealed their sexual orientation to most other people. Revealing their sexual orientation occurs in the final stage, *Action*, when lesbians and gay men tell friends, family, and coworkers about their sexual orientation, become politically or socially involved in the lesbian/gay community, and consider their sexual orientation to be a positive attribute.

Herdt and Boxer (1993) consider coming out as a ritual or, more specifically, a "healing rite." Although they refer to this time as a rite of passage for youth, we feel that this idea applies to people irrespective of age. Herdt and Boxer note that although some lesbian and gay youth happily and confidently come out, many are fraught with guilt due to their own shame and others' homophobia and harassment. In some cases, the harmful effects of broken family bonds and discrimination at school and work come into play. So, for many lesbians and gay men, coming out is a long, challenging, and arduous process of healing these wounds. Coming out is also an attempt to find one's place in the lesbian/gay community. As Darsey (2000) explains, coming out is a social process of creating an ever-expanding circle where people live openly as lesbian or gay.

To summarize, coming out is a complex, nonlinear, and never-ending process. People who are coming out first acknowledge that they have an attraction to members of the same gender. Individuals ascribe meaning to their feelings as "lesbian" or "gay" as they become more comfortable with their feelings. Over time, revealing sexual orientation to friends, family members, and coworkers is another feature of the coming out process. The final aspect of coming out is finding lesbian and gay friends, getting involved in romantic relationships, and becoming part of the gay community.

Gender Role, Gender Identity, and Transgender

Gender role, gender identity, transgender, and *sexual orientation* refer to distinct but overlapping concepts. *Gender role* refers to the conventional assignments of social status and social behavior by what society proscribes as *male* and *female* (Herdt, 1997). Although gender role nonconformity is not an indication of being lesbian or gay, some studies suggest that lesbians and gay men differ from heterosexuals during childhood. In research by Bell, Weinberg, and Hammersmith (1981), for example, many lesbians and gay men reported feeling "different" as children because of interests and traits commonly assigned to the other gender. Gender role conformity was noted in less than half of the gay males, whereas three quarters of the heterosexual men reported conformity.

Pillard (1991), however, challenges the notion that lesbians and gay men do not conform to traditional gender roles. He asserts that many

---

Case Study 1.5 (Patti)

Patti, a 26-year-old Latina, considers herself female, in spite of the fact that she was born with male genitalia. She has yet to start living her life full time as a female, and she comes to her first appointment after work, wearing a suit and tie. Further, Patti considers herself lesbian because she is attracted to women. This is your first encounter with a MTF (male-to-female) lesbian, and you become confused when Patti enters therapy because, although Patti refers to herself as a lesbian, she outwardly appears to be a heterosexual male.

Patti's case illustrates that even if the notion of *transgender* is conceptually clear, it can be confusing on an emotional level. We would expect that emotions would take longer than intellect to fully grasp that a biological male is a woman, and vice versa, and that it takes some time to feel comfortable with their self-labeling. If you work with transgender lesbians and gay men, you will encounter myriad issues, many of which are beyond the scope of this book. However, Patti must still come to terms with being a lesbian. Will you treat her lesbian issues differently because she is transgender? You have been taught to be authentic; would you express doubts that she is a lesbian? How would you take cultural issues related to her ethnicity into account?

---

assessment tools that measure masculinity and femininity are based on a bipolar scale, so respondents are forced into scoring as either more masculine or more feminine. Pillard examined research that uses the Bem Sex Role Inventory, which has scales that independently measure culturally masculine traits and culturally feminine traits. As a result, individuals could score higher in masculine traits, feminine traits, both (androgynous), or neither (undifferentiated). In studies that use the Bem, researchers found that many lesbians and gay men have traits that conform to their gender role and have traits that are characteristic of the other gender. Pillard calls this phenomenon *gender-role flexibility*, noting that lesbians and gay men tend to have a greater variety of temperaments and behaviors than do heterosexuals.

As with gender role, *gender identity* exists independently of sexual orientation (Lips, 2000). Gender identity refers to one's own sense of being male or female, and it does not necessarily correspond to anatomical (reproductive organs) or chromosomal gender (Clausen, 1995), as illustrated by Case Study 1.5.

Heterosexism and Homophobia

Heterosexism is an ideology that includes the cultural assumption that all people are or would want to be heterosexual. Heterosexism involves the belief that heterosexuality is the only normal model for romantic-sexual relationships, which is often used to justify ignorance or devaluation of the experience of gay, lesbian, and bisexual people in society (Iasenza, 1989). It is important to be aware of the pervasive, unconscious nature of heterosexism. It infiltrates every aspect of the culture, and it enters psychotherapy sessions. For example, when therapy begins, if you ask incoming clients the seemingly innocuous question, "Are you married?" lesbian and gay clients will perceive a lack of sensitivity to lesbian/gay issues and a devaluation of same-gender relationships.

Whereas heterosexism rests on neglect and omission, *homophobia* is as an irrational fear and hatred toward lesbian and gay men (Fassinger, 1991; Weinberg, 1972). Because we are all conditioned by traditional views of sex, homophobia is not easily detected (Gramick, 1983). Gramick asserts that homophobia has three aspects. The first aspect is fear of homosexual tendencies in oneself. Individuals develop an unconscious fear and hatred of lesbians and gay men as a coping strategy and as a mechanism for guarding against their feelings, because acknowledging same-gender attraction produces anxiety. The second characteristic of homophobia is the fear that heterosexuals will be "converted" to homosexuality. Homophobia includes the belief that gay men seduce unsuspecting boys into becoming homosexual. The third aspect of homophobia is the fear that homosexuality will become socially acceptable, resulting in the extinction of the human race.

Lesbians and gay men sometimes internalize homophobia by introjecting societal beliefs. Lesbians and gay men who are uncomfortable with their sexual orientation cling to stereotypical beliefs (Herdt, 1997) and, as a result, shame about same-gender attraction and behavior develops.

When you work with lesbian and gay male clients, keep the notion of internalized homophobia in mind. High levels of internalized homophobia lead to self-loathing, low self-esteem, and feelings of inferiority (Logan, 1996; Martin, 1982; Weinberg, 1972). Two signs of internalized homophobia are living a secret life and withholding information about being lesbian or gay from friends and family. Moving back and forth between the gay world and nongay world without disclosing sexual orientation causes people to feel fraudulent, perpetuating emotional and physical distance from family and friends. It also leads to unfulfilling, superficial relationships due to the need to hide activities, thoughts, and feelings.

Slang Terms

It is important to recognize that when lesbians and gay men use slang words to describe other lesbians and gay men, it does not necessarily devalue themselves or others. Clausen (1995) states that lesbians and gay men adopted the words *fag, dyke,* and *fairy* as a positive way to reclaim language that has been used against them.

Lesbians and gay men have also reclaimed the term *queer,* and it is used to encompass all sexual identities, including heterosexual individuals whose sexual activities deviate from society's norms. According to Humphrey (1999), queers denote "people who suffer from a combination of material disadvantages and cultural devaluations on account of their sexual orientation (lesbians, gay men, bisexuals), sexual practices (sex workers and sadomasochists), gender performances (transvestites), and gendered identities (transgendered people)" (p. 226).

❖ IDENTITY DEVELOPMENT

Life-span development models by Freud, Erikson, and Piaget, among others, include the assumption that people develop heterosexual identities (see, for example, Corsini & Wedding, 2000). The assumption of heterosexuality makes application of these theories to lesbians and gay men difficult and, at worst, inaccurate and incomplete. As a result, several researchers set out to develop lesbian and gay identity development models. In this section, we provide an

---

Case Study 1.6 (Angela, continued from Preface Case Study)

Angela reports that she has started to feel better since starting therapy. Angela continues to refer to her female partner of 2 years as her "roommate." Even though you surmise otherwise, Angela does not believe she is a lesbian. Rather, she believes that she is with a woman now, but someday she will fall in love with and marry a man.

One way Angela can reduce or resolve incongruence is by changing her self-perception. To do so, Angela will feel at some point that she "may be" a lesbian, and someday she may resolve herself to "being" a lesbian. Resolution does not happen in a straight line, however, and Angela will vacillate several times before adjusting to her lesbian identity. Resolving these differences of perception between self and others and determining the meaning of a behavior in social context is the crux of sexual identity development (Morris, 1997).

---

overview of three identity development models that pertain to lesbians and gay men.

Before we delve into a discussion of identity models, however, we would like to comment on life-span identity development. Weinberg (1983) contends that identity formation is a dynamic social process and that people pass through a variety of stages in any number of sequences while seeking to construct an acceptable self-definition. In contrast, Kaufman and Raphael (1996) assert that identity is the result of an evolving inner process, where identity unfolds as part discovery and part conscious creation. In an attempt to reconcile the two theories, Cox and Gallois (1996) note that the underlying process of identity development is motivated by a desire for congruence among our perception of a characteristic (including sexual orientation), the behavior that results from this trait, and other people's views concerning the characteristic.

To have a complete picture of lesbian/gay identity development, gender differences must be taken into account. In their review of sexual identity issues among men and women, Garnets and Kimmel (1993) came to two conclusions:

❖ Men tend to label their identity by their erotic and genital experiences. Therefore, men are apt to identify themselves as gay based on having exclusive or predominantly same-gender sexual experiences, or by experiencing more sexual gratification with men than with women.

❖ Women are more likely than men to define their identity in terms of affectional preferences, political choices, and the idea that people can choose their sexual orientation. So, women are more prone to develop a lesbian identity in the context of a relationship, as opposed to men, who develop a gay identity based on sexual experiences with other men. This notion is illustrated in Case Study 1.6 (for an in-depth discussion, see Garnets & Kimmel, 1993).

The Cass Model

Cass (1979) offers a six-stage model of identity development. She writes that the process of reciprocal interaction leads to identity formation through a complex interaction among individual factors such as needs, desires, and learned behaviors; biological factors; and environmental factors, including class, ethnicity, and social environment. Further, her model has several pathways in each stage that lead to the next stage. If movement to the next stage does not occur, it leads to what she terms *foreclosure*.

The first stage of her model, *Identity Confusion,* includes experiencing disturbing feelings that could be labeled homosexual, and these feelings cause confusion because of society's expectation that people be heterosexual. The primary focus for individuals in this stage is to cope with confusion and to resolve the inconsistency brought about by linking their behavior to the possibility of being lesbian or gay. People make a choice at this point to either foreclose development by rejecting the possibility of being lesbian/gay or to explore the possibility, which leads to the next stage.

In the *Identity Comparison* stage, people compare their same-gender behavior to what it means to be lesbian or gay, but they do so in isolation. Individuals focus on coping with the loss of a previously perceived heterosexual identity, complete with expectations of what it means to be heterosexual. In addition, individuals deal with feeling alienated and different.

If this self-examination leads to contact with other lesbians or gay men, the next stage, *Identity Tolerance*, begins. This stage is character-ized by individuals tentatively wearing a lesbian or gay identity and making contact with others who are lesbian or gay. This limited contact with others reduces isolation, but disclosure of sexual identity tends to be extremely limited. Individuals become more focused on social, sexual, and emotional needs that arise when they acknowledge that they are probably lesbian or gay.

Identity Acceptance occurs when contact with others is positive. At this point, people make selective disclosure to family and friends. At the beginning of this stage, individuals tentatively accept the gay or lesbian label but not on an emotional level. Throughout this stage, individuals develop peace of mind and fulfillment so that, toward the end of the stage, they achieve acceptance of the label on a deeper emotional level.

In the fifth stage, *Identity Pride*, individuals split the world into gay and nongay. Many lesbians and gay men develop a sense of pride about their identity, and some individuals reject the heterosexual world in an angry manner. They may devalue heterosexuals, and they see being lesbian/gay as the preferred identity. Successful resolution of this stage gives way to *Identity Synthesis*, in which people fully accept their lesbian/gay identity and consider it as merely one aspect of their total identity. Lesbians and gay men reevaluate heterosexuals and make a distinction between supportive and unsupportive nongay people. As a result, the we-versus-them mentality diminishes and the anger, alienation, and devaluation toward heterosexuals abate.

Cass's model is very useful, and it is one of the most widely studied lesbian/gay identity development models. Morris (1997), however, notes that the model has two limitations:

❖ The model assumes a neat and orderly progression through the stages. This does not allow people to return to a stage that has already been visited or to address identity issues out of the designated order.

❖ The model implies that lesbian and gay activists have not fully progressed to the final stage, Identity Synthesis.

The Troiden Model

Troiden (1988) proposes a four-stage identity development model, noting that he synthesized and elaborated on Plummer's identity development model (for more information, see Plummer, 1975). Troiden defines a homosexual identity as a perception of the self as homosexual in romantic and sexual situations. Furthermore, he indicates that identity exists on three levels:

- ❖ *Self-concept level:* Self-perception of identities, which includes sexual orientation and gender, among others.
- ❖ *Perceived level:* How people perceive others as seeing them.
- ❖ *Presented level:* Ways people present themselves in social settings.

Troiden theorizes that a lesbian/gay identity is most fully realized when the three levels are congruent.

Rather than proposing a linear stage theory, his model is based on a spiral progression of stages, where people can revisit them. Furthermore, Troiden sees identity development as akin to Maslow's (Maslow, 1998) self-actualization theory in that lesbian/gay identity development spans the lifetime.

The first stage, *Sensitization*, occurs before puberty and includes atypical gender role experiences that lead to feeling marginalized from same-gender peers or simply feeling "different." As children, individuals do not associate these feelings as either homosexual or heterosexual. As adults, however, people think back on these experiences and feelings and interpret them, in retrospect, as indicative of being lesbian or gay.

During the second stage, *Identity Confusion*, people start to connect their behavior with homosexuality and to consider the possibility that they are lesbian or gay. By this time, generally in the teen years, individuals may or may not have had a sexual experience. Whether or not they have had same-gender sexual experiences, people may feel shame, along with feeling isolated and abnormal, about the possibility of being lesbian or gay. Strategies these individuals use to reduce confusion include avoiding same-gender impulses and feelings or denying they exist, assuming an antigay stance in public settings, immersing themselves in heterosexual behavior, abusing alcohol and drugs, and considering their attractions and behavior to be a phase.

After individuals discard these strategies, *Identity Assumption* begins. In this stage, one's self-identity and presented identity are gay or lesbian. This process includes telling others about their identity, involvement in the gay community, exploration of friendships, and feeling better about being gay or lesbian. The final stage, *Commitment*, includes being comfortable with a lesbian or gay identity. In this stage, integration of sexuality and emotionality occurs. Concomitant with this integration is a greater likelihood of same-gender dating and relationships. During this stage, identity management becomes the primary challenge.

Like the Cass model, the Troiden model is quite useful. One limitation of the Troiden model, however, is that even though a large number of individuals follow a similar path, gender, ethnicity and social class give rise to other possible developmental pathways. Another shortcoming, according to Eliason (1996), is that both models lack sociopolitical and historical contexts. Eliason further notes that including these contexts, coupled with a more fluid identity model, would be an important step in developing a more inclusive and representative identity model.

The Social Identity Model

Cox and Gallois's (1996) attempt to provide an inclusive model using a social identity perspective that consists of considering the relationship of identity to a social context. Specifically, they note that identity development for lesbians and gay men, as for all individuals, is an issue of group identity as much as individual identity. The authors contend that there are two parallel, yet overlapping, processes: self-categorization as lesbian or gay and an ability to incorporate this categorization into social identity, personal identity, or both identities. They also argue that assimilating into society and considering sexual orientation as merely one aspect of identity is not necessarily the most evolved form of identity development. Rather, assimilation is one form of an evolved identity, and individuals, such as activists, can regard their sexual orientation to be their foremost identity and decline to assimilate, yet still be evolved.

Social identity theory is concerned with social influences in the development of self-concept and derivation of self-esteem. Among

Case Study 1.7 (Roberto, continued from Case Study 1.3)

Roberto grew up participating in his family's church. At age 22, he began to accept his gay sexual orientation. As he started to accept himself, he questioned his religious life beliefs because of the conflict between his religion's teachings and his gay identity. At age 24, right before Roberto started therapy, he decided to opt out of religious life altogether, feeling that his religion's condemnation of homosexuality is wrong.

Comparing one's social groups with other groups leads to social self-esteem, whereas comparing oneself with other individuals leads to personal self-esteem (Luhtanen & Crocker, 1992). This process adds an evaluative component to we/they dichotomies, leading to better than/less than comparisons, with sexual orientation as one basis of categorization and comparison. Roberto may perceive himself as gay within a social identity context, a personal identity context, or both. In other words, Roberto could simply view homosexuality as a behavior and not identify as a gay male. However, Roberto is beginning not only to enact the behavior but also to categorize himself in the gay social group.

lesbians and gay men, social identity comparisons include the relationship between lesbians/gay men and heterosexuals, the relationship of different lesbian/gay subgroups, and the interaction of a lesbian or gay identity with other social identities, such as ethnicity, gender, occupation, and class.

Cox and Gallois's model emphasizes the process of developing an identity rather than the stages or content. Their model is not devoted to a single type of identity development; by looking at multiple identities and their interrelationships, it takes other social group memberships into account. The result is a model of development that focuses on the interaction among an individual, that individual's social groups, and society.

Developing a social identity includes adopting the behaviors, characteristics, and values of the identified groups, thereby forming a we/they dichotomy. Examples of such groups include those based on sexual orientation, religion, ethnicity, gender, and activities or attributes such as sports, education level, and occupation. At times, an individual's various social identities clash, and the norms and values of one social identity are sublimated into another identity or a new, independent identity emerges. Identity sublimation is illustrated in Case Study 1.7.

When people belong to other minority groups in addition to a sexual orientation minority group, internal conflict may result. This situation requires lesbians and gay men to employ strategies to deal with these conflicts and to enhance and maintain a positive identity. Two such strategies are *social mobility* and *social change*.

There are four social mobility strategies (see Kaufman & Raphael, 1996):

- ❖ *Remaining closeted:* Moving back and forth between the gay world and nongay world without disclosing sexual orientation.
- ❖ *Capitulating:* An attempt to avoid all same-gender activity.
- ❖ *Covering:* Revealing sexual orientation only if asked.
- ❖ *Blending:* Viewing sexual orientation as irrelevant and attempting to avoid questions from others.

Social mobility strategies generally allow an individual to be perceived as part of the general culture rather than as gay or lesbian. These strategies, however, lose their effectiveness as a person adopts being lesbian or gay as part of her or his social identity, rather than just as part of one's personal identity.

Social change strategies include social creativity (which refers to altering the basis of comparison between groups) and social competition. The three types of social creativity strategies are as follows:

- ❖ Finding new dimensions to compare groups
- ❖ Redefining the value attached to existing comparative dimensions
- ❖ Selecting new comparison groups with which to evaluate. An example of this strategy is for lesbians and gay men to devalue other lesbian and gay subcultures when compared with their own lesbian and gay culture, such as when "drag queens" are ridiculed and scorned (Cox & Gallois, 1996).

Although none of the social creativity strategies works to change the status quo, social competition does work to change it. Social competition refers to working for social change. Those lesbians and gay men who adopt social change strategies are more likely to have higher self-regard than those lesbians and gay men who use social mobility strategies.

We reference the social identity model throughout the book, particularly when we discuss social identities. To help you gain a deeper understanding of the model, attempt to apply the model to your own life. When have you had to manage your personal and social identities? When have you sublimated one identity in favor of another? When have you used the other strategies? What was it like to compare one of your social identities to another? As you answer these questions, you can begin to see how your clients view their identities and attempt to deal with them. For those of you who are not lesbian or gay, you can begin to understand what it means to be lesbian or gay in contemporary society.

❖ SUMMARY

In this chapter, we defined various terms and distinguished between sexual orientation, gender role, and gender identity. We also described the coming out process and three lesbian/gay identity development models. The first two models, developed by Cass and Troiden, are widely noted and researched. The third model differs from the other two in that stages are disregarded and the emphasis is placed on social and personal identities.

In this chapter's case studies, we introduced you to Tom, a gay, married man. Brian, a young Chinese American gay male, is struggling with being gay, and Roberto, a Hispanic male who came out 2 years ago, has accepted his sexual orientation identity while rejecting his religious identity. We introduced you to Patti, a Latina, MTF transgender lesbian. Patti has just begun psychotherapy. Regarding Angela, even though her depressive symptoms have diminished since we introduced her in the Preface, she is troubled about her relationship because she is in the process of moving from the Identity Comparison stage to the Identity Tolerance stage (Cass, 1979).

We now turn our attention to an overview of issues related to lesbian/gay youth, the elderly, ethnic minorities, and various sub-cultures, trends, and phenomena within the gay community. We provide you with a discussion of social identities, including such disparate groups as lesbian feminists, bears, and Radical Faeries.

2

Youth, Elderly, Ethnic Minority, and Lesbian/Gay Subcultures

❖ ❖ ❖

L et's suppose that a client is talking to you in session and matter-of-factly states, "I was at this bar and I saw this bear—well, he was more like a cub. He looked like he was just coming off of a roll—y'know, crystal or something—but then I thought maybe he was tired. He smiled, and I smiled back, but then he just walked away. Like that! Maybe he's looking for a daddy. . . ."

If you're having trouble understanding this client, it's because the lesbian and gay culture is composed of various subcultures, each with its own words and meanings. To provide affirmative psychotherapy, it is helpful for you to have a sense of these subcultures and their unique issues and identities. When we refer to "you" in this chapter, we make the assumption that you are not in the particular group or of the ethnicity that is being discussed or, if you are, that you might be unfamiliar with the concepts being discussed.

An often unstated assumption is that lesbian/gay identity formation is the most important aspect of development when, in fact, forming one's ethnic, spiritual, and other social identities are just as important. And throughout the course of the lives of lesbians and gay men, the various identities interact with and influence one another. The influence of a particular social identity will wax and wane, and clients will enter therapy with one or more of their social identities affecting their presenting issues. Exploring the impact of your clients' multiple social identities will help you to determine the direction of therapy and the overall treatment arc.

We begin this chapter with a discussion of youth, the elderly, and ethnic minority identities. In the second half of the chapter, we examine other types of social identities.

❖ LESBIAN AND GAY YOUTH

Young men and women who come out today are doing so in a changing, more tolerant culture than that of several decades ago. Even so, the period of the teenage years is still a time when conformity is at a premium and emotional turbulence is common. It is also a time when, if lesbian and gay youth reveal their sexual orientation, they do so at risk of emotional and physical peril.

Herdt and Boxer (1993) describe three overlapping learning processes that lesbian and gay youth must go through to gain a lesbian or gay identity:

1. They unlearn the heterosexist assumptions of developing a heterosexual identity and someday getting married.

2. They unlearn stereotypes about homosexuality while struggling with the issues of social taboo, contaminated identity, and loss of status.

3. They reconstruct peer and family relationships based upon their emerging lesbian/gay identity.

Today, educational institutions are moving, albeit slowly, toward developing programs geared for young lesbians and gay men. With growing tolerance brings increased resources for lesbian and gay youth. Just a decade ago, with the notable exception of Project 10, which provides on-site educational support services to LGBT youth, there were virtually no support groups and programs in schools for lesbians and gay youth. Today, several organizations support lesbian and gay students. The Gay, Lesbian, and Straight Education Network (GLSEN) attempts to influence public policy to ensure that basic protections are in place for students and personnel, develops training materials and curricular resources for administrators and teachers, and creates learning environments that embrace people irrespective of their sexual orientation. The Gay-Straight Alliance (GSA) has student-run support groups that offer a safe and welcoming environment for LGBT students and children of lesbian/gay parents. It is also a forum for communication among LGBT and straight students.

Besides these special programs, alternative schools for LGBT youth are operating in three cities. In New York, the Harvey Milk School has been educating LGBT high school students since 1984. In Los Angeles, the Eagles Center opened in 1992. In Dallas, the Walt Whitman Community School opened in 1997.

In addition to having more resources than previous generations, today's LGBT youth are coming out at a much earlier age. In a 1988 study, Troiden found that, on average, subjects self-identified as lesbian or gay between the ages of 19 and 23. In a 1993 study by Herdt and Boxer, however, subjects self-identified as lesbian or gay at just under 17 years of age.

And today there is a large gay youth community. The community includes teen clubs and coffeehouses. Alternative proms are held in many cities, giving youth who feel uncomfortable going to "straight" proms a place to feel safe. Bulletin boards and chat rooms on the Internet provide forums where LGBT youth can express themselves. And the gay youth community also has its own vernacular. Many younger people are growing up with the term *queer* being used instead of the terms *gay* and *lesbian*. Some older lesbians and gay men consider the term *queer* to be demeaning because, when they grew up, the term was used as a form of ridicule. Today, however, the word *gay* can be used in a demeaning way (for example, the epithet "That's so gay!"), and the word gay did not exist as an epithet when older lesbians and gay men grew up. But *queer* also has a different social and political meaning than *gay*, with many young people feeling that *queer* is a more encompassing term.

Another difference between generations is that an increasing number of lesbian and gay public figures are role models for lesbian and gay youth. A growing number of famous people, from the political to the rock music worlds, are out, and young lesbian/gay people have role models to emulate and admire. Also, having lesbians and gay men in the public spotlight makes lesbian and gay youth realize that they are not "the only one," a belief that was common among their older counterparts when they were growing up.

Today, out lesbian and gay youth may be thinking about college and career choices. It is now possible to encourage younger clients to explore the world of work that is accessible to open lesbians and gay men; several books and Internet resources help them identify gay-friendly academic and business environments. We provide an in-depth discussion of career issues in Chapter 4.

Identity Development

Adolescence is when many, if not most, lesbians and gay men begin the process of coming to terms with their sexual orientation. In fact, coming out is becoming more of an adolescent process. Adolescence is the time of experimenting with new identities, which is part of the Eriksonian stage of Identity vs. Role Confusion (Erikson, 1963). Despite increased visibility, many lesbian and gay youth hide their sexual orientation. And, many young people find themselves lost, confused, and frightened by having to deal with sexual issues.

Many studies point to adolescents feeling pressure to conform to their gender roles, with boys feeling more pressure than girls to conform (see Katz & Ksansnak, 1994). There is often a shame-inducing admonishment to conform, as in Case Studies 2.1 and 2.2.

When young people associate being lesbian or gay with stigma and shame, difficulties arise with respect to lesbian/gay identity development. D'Augelli (1996) notes that critical mental health issues for lesbian/gay adolescents include the stress associated with managing sexual identity, disruptions in peer relationships, conflicts about informing the family, and negative consequences of disclosure. Other risks include isolation from affirming contexts, anxiety related to sex, and the fear of contracting HIV.

Thus, while they attempt to manage their burgeoning identity, many lesbian and gay youth are secretive about their sexual activities and try to pass as heterosexual at home and school. Those who do, however, have a harder time developing a positive identity than those who come out during adolescence.

Case Study 2.1 (Brian, continued from Case Study 1.2)

Brian recalls that his mother admonished him not to "act sissy" any time he attempted to step outside the boundaries of socially proscribed "boyhood." He also feels resentful at the public humiliation he endured from his mother's admonishments, and he didn't dare talk back to his mother due to social norms of family harmony and respect for elders. "I think now she (mother) was just trying to help me, because when I got to junior high, the kids were relentless. They called me names and threatened me all the time."

Coming out in the teen years can lead to greater self-esteem and quality of friendships (D'Augelli, 1996). Herdt and Boxer (1993) conducted a study at Horizons Center in Chicago. They found that close to two thirds of their subjects made the first revelation of their sexual identity to a same-aged peer or friend, and 75% of the subjects experienced what they called a "supportive" response.

Herdt and Boxer (1993) also found that more than half of their gay and lesbian subjects had heteroerotic experiences, which is akin to heterosexual youth sexually experimenting with the same gender. Although there are some differences in terms of same-gender experiences between males and females, in that males had an easier time exploring their sexuality, both males and females have heteroerotic experiences to help them discover their sexual orientation.

Therapy with lesbian and gay youth should include education about identity development, heterosexism, and homophobia. Providing them with a handout on lesbian/gay identity development can help normalize their feelings. Another forum to help youth discover their sexual orientation is a sexual orientation growth group. Information on how to facilitate this type of group is offered in Chapter 6.

Challenges Facing Lesbian and Gay Youth

D'Augelli (1998) reviewed research concerning the psychological impact of victimization on lesbian, gay, and bisexual youth, and he found that developmental difficulties arise in three ways:

❖ Direct verbal or physical attacks.

❖ Developmental opportunity loss, which is the lack of age-appropriate expression and exploration of social and sexual bonding. Self-doubt can result from living in a society of presumed and preferred heterosexuality (cultural heterosexism).

❖ Institutional victimization, which includes having to cope with socially sanctioned homophobia in schools, the military, and other institutions.

In explaining development challenges of lesbian/gay youth, D'Augelli states that three common experiences for lesbian and gay youth—marginalization, coping with family responses to disclosure, and issues related to HIV/AIDS—interfere with development by causing psychological distress. In particular, revealing sexual orientation to parents can be exceedingly difficult for lesbian and gay youth. At a time when parental support and understanding are vital, many parents are unable to provide it. D'Augelli and Hershberger (1993) report that only 11% of the adolescents they surveyed said their parents responded in an accepting manner to their disclosure that they are lesbian or gay. In fact, 20% of the mothers and 28% of the fathers were perceived as intolerant and rejecting.

As Strommen (1989) notes, many parents who initially disapprove become more accepting over time, but some lesbian and gay adolescents are not so fortunate. Of the gay men, lesbians, and bisexuals that Pilkington and D'Augelli (1995) surveyed, a family member verbally assaulted more than 33%, and 10% were physically abused. Hersch (1991) states that lesbian and gay youth are at a much higher risk than heterosexual youth of being kicked out of their homes.

In addition to the risks of revealing sexual orientation to their families, lesbian and gay youth face the possibility of both physical and verbal abuse in school. Although tolerance is increasing, lesbian and gay youth have become increasingly visible targets of harassment and violence. Just 10 or 20 years ago, lesbians and gay men grew up fearing discovery. Today, more lesbian and gay youth who are out fear their classmates.

"Hatred in the Hallways" (Human Rights Watch, 2001) outlines the types of harassment LGBT youth (or those perceived to be LGBT) face, and offers recommendations for school officials and government entities to protect students. The researchers conclude that high schools and junior

Case Study 2.2 (Brian, continued from Case Study 2.1)

Brian's parents were raised in fundamentalist church. In one session, Brian brings a Bible and reads aloud verses condemning homosexuality. How would you react to Brian using the Bible as a form of self-condemnation? Would you recommend that he read gay-affirming books, attend a gay adolescent group, and come out to his parents? If so, what could happen?

In this case, it is better to try to see the world from Brian's point of view and to empathize with his struggle. By the end of any particular therapy session, Brian should be able to say, "At least there's someone in the world who understands me." The most useful treatment includes providing an atmosphere where you encourage Brian and clients like him to explore self-condemnation and self-hatred, rather than a place where their beliefs are challenged and where they are reassured that everything will be okay.

high schools do not do nearly enough to create a safe environment for LGBT youth, and they lament that students are left to choose between struggling in isolation to survive the harassment as they seek an education or escaping the hostile climate by dropping out of school (p. 4).

Indeed, when you work with lesbian and gay youth, one major issue that you will encounter is the theme of isolation as a result of actual or anticipated hostility and rejection from peers. Being different and feeling different, coupled with being targeted for harassment, give rise to intense feelings of loneliness. Because of the stigma associated with being lesbian or gay, many lesbian and gay youth experience anxiety due to the fear of being outed, and they often risk disclosure to a select few friends. With the stress they experience by hiding same-gender attraction, the risk of developing depression is substantial (Savin-Williams, 1994).

Dating between members of the same sex in this context is challenging. And, as there are no "rules" for dating people of the same sex, lesbian and gay youth have new challenges to consider when it comes to dating and forging relationships. Consider Case Study 2.3.

Case Study 2.3 (Ken)

Ken, a 16-year old Caucasian, revealed that he is gay in the last session (his third). In his fourth session, he tells you about Rick, a student at his school. He explains, "Rick and I saw each other at Gay Pride. I wanted to run the other way but it was too late. It turned out okay because when I said 'hey' he said 'hey' back, and he smiled at me. At school for a few weeks, when we'd see each other in the hall, we'd smile at each other. It was cool, so one day I walked up to him and asked if he'd want to have coffee sometime. He was with some of his friends, and I think they heard me, so he yelled, 'Fuck you, faggot.' I know it was a cover-up, but it still hurt. And now he glares at me when we see each other."

Ken and other lesbian and gay youth take a risk when they tell their friends they are lesbian or gay and when they ask someone on a date. They are not only at risk of being rejected, but they are at risk of verbal and physical assault. What would you say to Ken at this point? Would you encourage emotional expression, or would you talk about his safety?

Risk of Suicide

Challenges facing lesbian and gay youth can lead them to feel tormented. When lesbian and gay youth feel fearful and develop depression, they feel they are running out of options. This places lesbian and gay youth at risk for alcohol and other drugs of abuse, in addition to sexual risk taking. It could also lead to considering the ultimate escape: suicide.

Most research shows that lesbian and gay youth are at risk for attempting suicide, but the results vary. Research by Russell and Joyner (1998) found that youth reporting same-gender attraction or same-gender behavior are twice as likely to attempt suicide than heterosexual youth. Savin-Williams (2001) found that gay and lesbian teenagers are only slightly more likely to attempt suicide than nongay teenagers. In his findings, Savin-Williams maintains that prior research

Case Study 2.4 (Ken, continued from Case Study 2.3)

In your fifth session with Ken, he starts dropping hints that he's feeling suicidal. He tells you, "Sometimes, it's just too much," and "I don't know if I can face going back to school another day." Later in the session, you assess for suicidal ideation by asking him, "Do you ever think about ending your life?" He says, emphatically, "Yes! All the time!" His response indicates that he feels relieved at finally saying it and knowing that he has a safe place to do so.

Your client's safety is paramount. How do you ensure his safety in light of the fact that you are his only outlet in an overwhelming situation? If you come to the conclusion that you must breach confidentiality, what options will Ken feel he has then?

has overstated lesbian and gay suicide rates due to the reliance on support groups and shelters as research settings.

Nonetheless, gay and lesbian youth often wait until a time of extreme emotional crisis before entering therapy—a time when they have exhausted their supply of available support. Issues that contribute to reaching the crisis point include breaking up with partners (especially when no one else knows they are dating), having negative feelings about being lesbian/gay, fearing coming out to family members and friends, and experiencing disastrous results when they do come out.

When lesbian and gay youth are confronted with crisis situations, you should first consider safety and provide crisis-intervention. Crisis intervention refers to giving clients time to vent problems, mentally noting each problem as the client airs it, asking them to rank the problems from most to least serious, and taking a solution-oriented approach to the most serious problem(s). Further, you should perform a thorough assessment of their support system.

Also, after you have assessed for the client's level of potential self-harm by asking if there are means and a plan, any threats should be taken seriously, and increasing the frequency of sessions may be warranted. Providing emergency numbers, gay hotlines, and crisis lines helps lesbian/gay adolescent clients feel safe between sessions. We provide hotline phone numbers in the appendix.

If the client is in imminent danger, you should maintain as high a level of confidentiality as is legally and ethically feasible. For example, if a client's suicidal gestures force you to break confidentiality, and if this client has not yet come out, there would be no reason for you to disclose the fact that your client is lesbian or gay to others.

❖ ELDERLY LESBIANS AND GAY MEN

In spite of the high and growing numbers of elderly lesbians and gay men, this population historically has had little to no support services. Elderly lesbians and gay men experience many of the same challenges as elderly nongay people. However, some issues relate specifically to this population. For example, stereotypes about elderly lesbians and gay men may be internalized, which influence their mood and behavior, in turn affecting the coping strategies that they could employ.

McDougall (1993) reviewed six of the most commonly held but unsupported stereotypes about elderly lesbians and gay men: (a) gay men perceive their loss of youth faster than heterosexual men and consequently desire much younger partners; (b) gay men become desperately lonely and socially isolated in their final years; (c) gay men become depressed and chronically unhappy with a nonexistent sex life; (d) aging for lesbians is easier than for gay men because lesbians do not function at the same level of physical competitiveness; (e) older lesbians live out the negative image of the spinster or crone, with feelings of loneliness, isolation, and rejection; and (f) being lesbian or gay is, in and of itself, a problem in old age.

Research conducted on aging lesbians and gay men does not support these notions, and only a minority of the population has excessive difficulty with issues related to aging (Berger & Kelly, 1996). Older gay men were less concerned than younger gay men about disclosing their sexual orientation and had more solid and stable self-concepts. Berger (1996) found that few of the men in his survey were desperately lonely or isolated. Rather, these men preferred the company of men their own age, nearly half lived with a partner, and almost 75% viewed themselves as well liked among gay men. Further, these men reported satisfaction and happiness in their lives, with few men reporting being gay as worrisome.

Although data for lesbians are not as abundant, older lesbians tend to build networks of friendships that act as substitutes for biological family relationships (Raphael & Robinson, 1980; Wolf, 1980). As with studies of elderly gay men, these researchers found that many participants reported joy and satisfaction, and more than half of the women sampled lived with a partner. Older lesbians preferred similarly aged partners, and those who began relationships when older stated that potential partners were relatively easy to find.

Because of their life struggles, many elderly lesbians and gay men have coping mechanisms not acquired by their heterosexual counterparts. In interviews with 100 elderly lesbians and gay men, Wolf (1982) documented the strengths they reported. The strengths, which respondents said were culled in their youth, include independence, hobbies, a social network of friends and acquaintances, and increased personal autonomy. Wolf (1982) suggests that these coping mechanisms prepare elderly lesbian and gay lesbians and gay men to adjust to old age. Friend (1988) states that gender role flexibility earlier in life translates into better self-care for elderly lesbian and gay adults. For example, gay men may already know how to cook and sew, and lesbians may already be familiar with chores related to financial management and household maintenance.

These data should not minimize the challenges facing older lesbians and gay men. This population historically has had little to no support services. In a study of 13 Midwestern nursing homes, researchers found that there were no services programming specifically targeted for elderly lesbians and gay men (Berger & Kelly, 1996). Also, institutional policies create problems for this population in many ways. For example, sexual and romantic intimacy for same-gender couples in retirement facilities and nursing homes is problematic. Many hospitals limit visitation to blood relatives or husbands and wives, so same-gender partners are often excluded. Insurance benefits and homestead survivorship rights of surviving same-gender partners are generally not available.

One issue for some elderly lesbians and gay men is reticence to disclose sexual orientation in hospitals and residential centers. Although many elderly lesbians and gay men are comfortable revealing sexual orientation to friends and family, they may prefer not to come out to

---

Case Study 2.5 (Theresa)

Theresa, a 72 year-old African American woman, calls you for an appointment. She is agitated and talks about having insomnia and anxiety. Her partner of 22 years, Susan, broke her hip and was admitted to a nearby hospital. Susan's children do not want Theresa to be at the hospital at the same time that they are visiting. In addition, the last time she was at the hospital, Theresa overheard Susan's children talking about contesting Susan's will, which leaves everything to Theresa. Theresa is afraid that they might take her to court, which would drain much of her savings.

Theresa is facing the devastation of having a partner with failing health, in addition to having to cope with stress related to the way Susan's family has reacted. What kinds of diagnoses would you consider? What would you do if she refused a psychiatric referral or if she seemed scattered and disoriented? How would you help empower her or advocate for her?

---

staff because it could affect their level of care. Other elderly lesbians and gay men are afraid that revealing their sexual orientation will negatively effect their retirement plans and social network.

Another problem is that some families of origin re-enter the family member's life and attempt to exclude their relative's partner at a critical time. This situation includes barring the partner from participation in funeral and burial decisions or contesting contracts and wills, as in Case Study 2.5.

Laws in many cities and states are changing to protect same-gender partners. Also, corporations and organizations are providing same-gender partner benefits. This advancement has allowed some elderly lesbians and gay men more rights and choices in healthcare. Moreover, retirement housing and assisted living facilities for lesbians and gay men are growing. Currently, Rainbow Adult Community Housing in San Francisco; Gay Family Compound in Cuerneville, California; Palms of Manasota in Palmetto, Florida; and Rainbow Manor in Ottowa, Ontario, Canada serve elderly lesbians and gay men.

Finally, due to the AIDS crisis, elderly lesbians and gay men have had to deal with the great difficulty of coping with repeated loss. However, that also means that they have had much more opportunity to confront death and dying, so the now-aging generation of lesbians and gay men is in some ways better prepared to deal with death than if they hadn't dealt with untimely AIDS-related deaths.

Many issues press upon elderly lesbians and gay men who are entering therapy. Some elderly lesbians and gay men will be experiencing depression. Elderly lesbians and gay men experience isolation when they are separated from their spouses and friends due to institutional barriers or through death. You may have to ask direct questions to elicit the information you need rather than be able to rely on volunteered information. Some elderly lesbians and gay men turn to alcohol and other drugs, along with the purposeful or inadvertent abuse of prescription drugs, as a form of coping. Quality of life should continue to be a consideration with respect to elderly clients. Therefore, you should consider making referrals to treatment programs and 12-step groups. If transportation is a problem, many cities offer transportation discounts and special accommodations for elderly individuals.

Other appropriate interventions for lesbian and gay elderly clients include supportive counseling and evaluation and adjustments in their social networks. A cognitive-behavioral approach could help elderly lesbians and gay men deal with day-to-day issues by examining distressing thoughts, finding diverting activities, and restricting emotional distress to journals or to specific times and places, such as counseling sessions. Financial counseling and medical referrals may also be necessary (Berger & Kelly, 1996).

If you include lesbian and gay reading materials in your waiting room and therapy office, you may build trust with elderly lesbian and gay clients prior to the initial session. Clients are more apt to disclose their sexual orientation when they perceive you as "safe." We provide information and suggestions about the physical office environment in Chapter 3.

The late stages of life include the developmental challenge of Integrity vs. Despair (Erikson, 1963), and therapy involves assisting clients in navigating end-stage decisions and developing pride and a sense of integrity connected with their life's accomplishments. This sense of pride and integrity can be strengthened by the therapeutic relationship. When you help clients to see their accomplishments, you can assist them in achieving self-acceptance in their later stages of life.

❖ ETHNIC MINORITIES

The many consequences of discrimination act as barriers to identity formation for both lesbians/gay men and ethnic minorities. Thus, treatment for ethnic minority lesbians and gay men often revolves around identity issues such as, Who am I? With which groups do I identify most clearly? What role does sexual orientation play in my life? How open am I willing to be? These and other questions should be explored by raising provocative issues with respect to merging a lesbian/gay identity with an ethnic minority identity.

Many forces help to shape the identities, mental health, and well-being of ethnic minority lesbians and gay men. Diaz, Ayala, Bein, Henne, and Marin (2001) studied how the oppressive forces of homophobia, poverty, and racism affect the mental health of gay and bisexual Latino men. We include their research at the beginning of this section because these forces impact all ethnic minority lesbians and gay men.

Diaz et al. (2001) collected data in Miami, New York, and Los Angeles from 293 Latino MSM. They found that negative mental health outcomes, such as low self-esteem and social isolation, are related to a history and current experience of social discrimination due to sexual orientation and ethnicity, as well as financial hardship related to unemployment and poverty. These mental health outcomes, in turn, are related to symptoms of psychological distress, including anxiety, sad or depressed mood, and suicidal ideation.

Not only do social forces have an impact on ethnic minority lesbians and gay men, but mores from their native countries also influence the identities and mental health of this population. As Cox and Gallois's (1996) notion of social identity theory suggests, ethnic minority lesbians and gay men find themselves in a double bind: They don't want to risk disclosure because they want to be accepted within their ethnic cultures but, at the same time, they wish to live openly as lesbians and gay men.

Many ethnic minority lesbians and gay men fear lack of support from their families and the community, which influences decisions about coming out (Jones & Hill, 1996). Decisions that ethnic minority lesbians and gay men need to make include the number of people to tell, whether or not to ask these people to keep it a secret, and the timing of disclosure. At the same time, prejudice in the general lesbian and gay community often marginalizes people of color by placing them on the fringe of the gay community. Coming out by entering the lesbian/gay community leads to frustration and disappointment when individuals do not gain the acceptance they had hoped for.

Moreover, according to Gutierrez (1997), differences in culture affect the way clients pursue mental health services. Making a decision to seek out psychotherapy is difficult for many people, but it can be particularly difficult for individuals in various ethnic minorities. In many cultural groups, the norm is to seek advice from pastors, parents, or friends of the family when problems arise, which only serves to increase the double bind mentioned earlier. In some cultures, engaging a stranger to discuss personal problems is considered taboo. Ethnic minority lesbians and gay men who seek counseling are therefore acting counter to another cultural norm. For ethnic minority lesbians and gay men who are seeking therapy, finding professionals well versed in the issues of both cultures is difficult. As a result, many individuals choose therapists who belong to one minority, but not both, and the most pressing issues tend to dictate the choice (Jones & Hill, 1996).

Although internal conflicts occur, developing a dual identity as an ethnic minority and a lesbian or gay man need not ultimately clash. Many ethnic minority lesbian and gay clients integrate their social identities and are comfortable with occupation, spirituality, and relationships with others. As is the case with all lesbians and gay men, it is often an arduous journey, and culturally sensitive treatment is a way to enable clients to merge their identities.

In the following sections on ethnic minorities, we do not intend to present an exhaustive description of ethnic minority values and beliefs. Rather, we focus on those cultural beliefs, taboos, and traditions that tend to influence the way lesbians and gay men are treated and the effects on their lesbian/gay identity development. This information is presented so that you can maintain sensitivity to these differences, while being aware of additional challenges that clients face if they come out while attempting to maintain cultural and family ties.

It is important to keep in mind that considerable diversity exists among ethnic groups on the basis of ancestral heritage, national origin, generation, language, and socioeconomic status (Garnets & Kimmel, 1993). Therefore, generalizations regarding social norms do not hold for every person in the particular minority under discussion. In addition, the view of much of the world toward homosexuality is becoming more tolerant, so some clients will be influenced by cultures with an enlightened view. Other clients will be influenced by cultures that are still extremely oppressive.

Finally, although Loiacano (1993) proposed that clinicians use the following questions when working with African American clients, we feel that they apply to work with all ethnic minority lesbian/gay clients:

1. Does the client perceive support for his or her dual identity in the community?

2. Are there groups organized specifically for the needs of Black American gay men and lesbian women in the area, or are there groups in which racial and sexual minorities find both acceptance and validation?

3. What personal issues might the client have to confront in developing a gay identity while still affirming his or her Black identity? What messages has the client received from his or her social environment regarding the compatibility of being Black American and gay or lesbian?

4. What assumptions does the counselor (or client) have about ways of expressing one's homosexuality (e.g., the level at which one is "out") that might not be realistic for a Black American in his or her particular community?

5. Given a predominantly White community, what other Black American gay men and lesbian women can be identified as supportive, and how have these individuals been received in the local gay community?

6. What are the client's preferences about seeing a counselor who is gay or lesbian, Black American, or both? As these questions imply, development never takes place in a social vacuum, and thus it is beneficial to consider the social, political, and interpersonal climate of the client. (pp. 372-373)

African American Lesbians and Gay Men

African American lesbians and gay men feel a significant pull from their two cultures. Biases in both communities leave many African American lesbians and gay men feeling estranged from both cultures. As a result, lesbian/gay identity development, as well as attempts to reconcile the two social identities, can be challenging.

Loiacano (1993) examined dual identity issues in a qualitative study by interviewing six African American lesbians and gay men. Analysis of the interviews resulted in three emerging themes: finding validation in the lesbian and gay community, finding validation in the African American community, and integrating both identities.

Participants in the study consistently noted the importance of acceptance within the African American community, so much so that the need for acceptance could foretell the level of openness about their sexual orientation. Some respondents indicated that it was easier to stay hidden than to be disenfranchised by the African American community. Albeit of limited application due to the sample size, the results of the study support previous findings that discrimination within the community can diminish positive affiliation, which reduces available support from peers.

A study conducted by Ernst, Francis, Nevels, and Lemeh (1991) reported a lack of social tolerance for lesbians and gay men in the African American community. Upon exploration, they found that their African American nongay subjects held several beliefs that furthered social intolerance toward African American gay men. For example, some of the subjects said that gay men further reduced the population of available African American males already decimated by high incarceration rates, interracial relationships, and increased incidence of premature death.

Sexism adds another dimension; African American lesbians experience discrimination in both the gay male and African American communities (Loiacano, 1993; Mays, Cochran, & Peplau, 1986). The majority of women in Ernst et al.'s study experienced more discrimination as a result of gender and ethnicity than because of sexual orientation. However, the younger, poorer, and more masculine-looking subjects reported more discrimination as a result of sexual orientation than because of gender and ethnicity.

Many African American families use churches as a source of community. Some church teachings have contributed to the views held by many African Americans toward lesbians and gay men. Many African American churches hold literal biblical interpretations that reflect condemnation of same-gender sexual behavior and the belief that lesbian or gay sex is inherently sinful. Therefore, open lesbian and gay male individuals risk losing a major source of comfort and connection within the community. It has also been suggested that this position contributes to internalized homophobic feelings and attitudes among lesbian and gay African Americans, and it leads to feelings of inadequacy and diminished self-worth (Jones & Hill, 1996).

Beliefs that impede the development of a positive identity also stem from the African American community's views on gender roles. Gender-specific behaviors tend to be well defined, and when people vary from these norms, it could result in ridicule or ostracism. Because African American lesbians and gay men deviate from proscribed sex roles, their ability to form close relationships and to develop a support system may be adversely affected.

Mays, Cochran, and Rhue (1993) explored the impact of cultural biases and beliefs by examining the relationships of eight African American lesbians. The researchers discovered that discrimination plays a significant role in impeding relationships with non-African American lesbians and gay men. Furthermore, many of the respondents reported that they had been involved in interracial relationships but found that cultural differences were a barrier and, in some instances, these differences led to the demise of their relationships.

The participants minimized the potential for unpleasant experiences by not divulging their sexual orientation to coworkers and family members. The women primarily socialized with other African American lesbians and indicated that this was the easiest route for reducing potentially stressful encounters. Consequently, at the time of the interviews, all eight women were romantically involved exclusively with other African American women.

Discrimination that African American lesbians and gay men experience in the lesbian and gay community can create feelings of inferiority in a culture that is already perceived as second class. When questioned, many Caucasian lesbians identified the term *lesbian* to be representative of Caucasians, acknowledging the term *lesbians from ethnic minorities* to connote lesbians of color (Karina, 1998). This conceptualization contributes to African American lesbians feeling marginalized in the community.

Case Study 2.6 (Angela, continued from Case Study 1.6)

After 3 years in her relationship, Angela has started to come to terms with being a lesbian. Now, she says, "I want to spread my wings, to have a life outside of my relationship. I am so upset because I realize I was so afraid of losing the support of my church. I couldn't be me. So, here I am, happy to start going to a lesbian support group at the community center, thinking I'd be welcome, but some of the women were clearly uncomfortable with my presence." As she finishes this sentence, Angela starts to cry.

How would you validate Angela's experiences? What would you say about discrimination? Would you ask Angela to consider going back to the group and ask the other women for the reasons for her perceived discomfort, and would you suggest to her that the other members might have been uncomfortable with *any* new group member? Or would you ask her to consider going to another group? If you offered the latter suggestion, what if Angela found the same situation in the new group?

In our experience, we have found support for these findings. Several African American clients have told us about experiences ranging from subtle acts of discrimination to hostile attacks from others in the lesbian and gay community. Examples of subtle actions include being closely watched by Caucasian lesbian/gay shop owners and having to show two or three ID cards, instead of only one ID card (as required of Caucasians), when they enter gay nightclubs. Case Study 2.6 illustrates the uncomfortable feelings that arise as a result.

In spite of culturally oppressive forces, or perhaps in part because of it, a vibrant African American lesbian and gay male culture has emerged. Often considered part of the "Harlem Renaissance," the first area of gay black expression was in literature, followed by art and filmmaking (Rowden, 2000). Even the church, which has often been part of the oppressive forces toward African American lesbians and gay men, can be a haven where "many gay men could lead relatively open lives and express their personalities despite the church's putative rejection of homosexuality as a sin" (p. 19).

Paying attention to the results of social discrimination toward African American lesbian and gay clients will help you to tease out the multifarious issues. As a result, you should assess for social isolation, lowered self-esteem, and despondency. Moreover, much time in therapy is spent with clients' quests for self-acceptance and to develop coping strategies. Thus, therapy often involves a dual aspect of an exploration of esteem issues, while at times focusing on day-to-day aspects of living. Furthermore, anger at societal discrimination is often an issue for African American lesbian and gay clients, and an important part of the therapeutic process is promoting expression of anger and loss.

Bibliotherapy related to African American lesbian and gay experiences helps clients clarify presenting issues. Referring clients to organizations that are composed of and welcome ethnic minorities is helpful. One example of a welcoming organization is the national organization Men of All Colors Together (MACT), a social and educational organization whose major purpose is for men of different ethnicities to meet one another.

Latina Lesbians and Latino Gay Men

Cultural backgrounds of Latinas and Latinos range from Mexican to Puerto Rican to South American to Cuban, with varying levels of acculturation and adherence to cultural values. Certain aspects of Latina/o culture affect Latina/o lesbian and gay men more directly than others.

One influence is the cultural characteristic of *machismo*, which encourages Latinos to be sexually aggressive in an attempt to validate virility and manhood. Gonzalez and Espin (1996) report that married, highly sexually active Latino men, or *hombres*, who consistently take the insertive role in same-gender encounters, view these acts as extramarital sex and do not perceive themselves as gay or bisexual. Being the dominant partner is not poorly perceived, whereas there is great stigma associated with being the feminine *maricon*. Abhorrence and ridicule are directed at men who are the anally receptive partners. The insertive and receptive roles that are derived from the attitude of *machismo* create consistent expectations in same-gender encounters, and men who are in the sexually receptive role have often been encouraged to play the role since their youth.

For Latina lesbians, their role has been defined in part by *marianismo*, which sets the standard for women to be self-sacrificing and subservient. Although closeness among Latina women is encouraged, overt acknowledgment of lesbianism is more restrictive than in the general culture. These restrictive attitudes add further stress to Latina lesbians who would like to participate in their ethnic community (Espin, 1993).

Consequently, Latina lesbians are rendered invisible. For example, if a closeted lesbian Latina decides not to marry, she will not be questioned about her decision, and excuses involving career aspirations and asexuality are accepted. This phenomenon leads to what Espin (1993) refers to as "silent tolerance." And this lack of acknowledgment of Latina lesbians' experience helps explain why many Latina lesbians choose to live in communities that know little about their ethnic culture, because leading a double life could become too difficult to endure (Gonzalez & Espin, 1996).

This silent tolerance may also lead Latina lesbians to feel angry, frustrated, and hurt because taking part in behavior that violates cultural norms has a high personal cost (Espin, 1993). But Espin cautions that understanding the unique challenges of identity development among Latina lesbians should be tempered by recognizing that certain experiences are similar to those encountered by lesbians from every cultural background. Therefore, it is important to be sensitive to specific cultural and class issues and to distinguish them from issues facing all lesbians. It is equally important to understand how your own cultural background influences your responses to Latina lesbian clients and your worldview. Espin notes:

> As with all clients, it must be remembered that each woman's choices express something about who she is as an individual, as well as what her cultural values are. . . . Any encouragement of their coming out as lesbians should be done with sensitivity to the other components of identity. (p. 362)

Other cultural norms that influence lesbian and gay Latinas/os include *familismo*, or sense of family, and *respeto*, or respect of elders and authority figures (Páres-Avila & Montano-López, 1994). As one

---

Case Study 2.7 (Roberto, continued from Case Study 1.7)

Roberto has left individual therapy to enter group therapy. In today's session, Roberto mentions that he lives at home with his mother and two brothers. He says, "It is really stressful for me sometimes. My brother does nothing around the house and, when I say something, my mother defends him." Don, one of the non-Latina/o group members, says, "You really need to move out. You wouldn't have all these problems." Other group members nod in agreement.

Roberto replies, "You don't understand me or my culture. I'm not going to move out of my house. My family is part of my support."

What can you do to help the non-Hispanic group members develop sensitivity to this cultural norm? How can they come to understand that ties between family members provide a buffer to the outside world? How can you, at the same time, help Roberto to understand the frustration of the other clients in the group?

---

example of *familismo,* many lesbians and gay men (as is the case with many Latina/o unmarried adult children) continue to live with their families into adulthood. See Case Study 2.7 for an illustration.

Sex and sexuality are rarely discussed in many Latina/o families. In general, parents do not discuss sexual matters with their children, and it is common for partners to not discuss sex with each other (Gonzalez & Espin, 1996). The focus on procreation and the condemnation of same-gender relationships by the Catholic Church supports this norm, and it is a source of anxiety and alienation for Latina/o lesbians and gay men. As a result, less acculturated, more traditional Latina/o families are less likely to accept lesbian and gay male family members.

Rodriguez (1996) notes that given the barriers to positive identity development—discrimination, heterosexism, antigay sentiment, religious condemnation, and lack of communication about HIV/

AIDS—Latina/o lesbians and gay men tend to develop support systems through compassionate family members or in the lesbian and gay community. This support is essential in developing a Latina/o gay male or lesbian identity. However, as with African American lesbians and gay men, Latina/o sexual minorities are discriminated against by the lesbian and gay community. The general gay community's ethnic and class bias can lead to similar barriers to developing a lesbian/gay identity. As a response to the need for safe places for Latina/o lesbians and gay men, organizations and bars catering exclusively to Latina/o lesbians and gay men have emerged.

The degree to which Latina/o individuals self-identify as lesbian or gay also affects their identity development. Furthermore, approaching lesbian and gay Latina/o clients based upon level of acculturation will affect intervention decisions. Interventions for this population take place at the family level and even at the community level so that the difficult process of self-acceptance can begin (Gonzalez & Espin, 1996). For example, you may wish to include a minister or trusted family members in treatment in specific ways. If desired by the client, you might offer referrals, consult with them, or ask others to attend a counseling session.

Gutierrez (1997) notes that many Latina/o clients tend to prefer solution-focused and directive approaches to therapy. Thus, with some clients, you may wish to concentrate on solution-focused interventions, such as uncovering choices by finding out what has worked for your client in the past, focusing on strengths and prior successes, and offering suggestions.

Asian/Pacific Islander American Lesbians and Gay Men

Asian/Pacific Islander Americans (API) encompass more than 25 different ethnic groups, with distinct languages and various religions (Chan, 1995). According to Nakajima, Chan, and Lee (1996), people's country of origin and religion influence their attitudes toward homosexuality. Although Eastern Asia tends to be particularly intolerant, countries such as the Philippines and Thailand are more accepting of homosexuality. Moreover, the rise of Christianity in previously tolerant countries such as Korea and Taiwan, and the rise of a mental illness model of homosexuality, has increased discriminatory practices in these countries (Whitman & Mathy, 1986).

Influences on Asian American lesbians and gay men have their origins in religious and cultural traditions such as Confucianism, Hinduism, and Buddhism. Confucianism has a profound impact in Eastern Asian countries, such as Japan, China, and Korea, in dictating interpersonal interaction (Hong, Yamamoto, & Chang, 1993). Confucianism is geared toward men and traditional families. Family roles are well defined, and sons, particularly first-born sons, are held in high esteem. East Asian marriages may be prearranged and serve the purpose of providing good lineage for future generations. Women are expected to remain monogamous within a marriage. Men, however, may have male or female lovers, as long as they are married and produce sons (Nakajima et al., 1996).

Social harmony is very important in Asian tradition, and "saving face" is an act of sacrifice, when an individual forgoes her or his needs for the sake of the family. Thus, many lesbian and gay male Asian Americans marry to save face. If a son did disclose his homosexuality, Asian American families would perceive him as selfish and disrespectful, partly because his disclosure is an indicator of autonomous and independent thinking (Han, 2000).

Because of the combination of the belief in saving face and a tendency toward prohibitions around sex (and a predisposition toward indirect communication in general), it is very difficult for gay children to come out to their families (Han, 2000). This pressure from the Asian American culture drives many Asian American lesbians and gay men to separate from their families and to assimilate into the lesbian and gay community (Nakajima et al., 1996). Wat (1996) explains the predicament that many lesbian and gay Asians encounter when they consider coming out:

> The implication that homosexuality is a Western phenomenon reaches deeper into the lives of many queer Asians. To occupy an identity that tradition has not allowed room for is, for many Asian parents, to reject the validity of that tradition, and by extension, of the family whose foundation rests on that very tradition itself. If a language barrier has made coming out difficult, possible charges of betrayal and of disgraces to the family have kept many of us, as well as our parents, in the closet. (p. 76)

Fung (1998) notes that although many risks are associated with coming out, it can be accomplished:

In coming out, we risk losing this support [families and ethnic communities]. . . . In my own experience, the existence of a gay Asian community broke down the cultural schizophrenia in which I related, on one hand, to a heterosexual family that affirmed my ethnic culture and, on the other hand, to a gay community that was predominantly white. Knowing that there was support also helped me come out to my family and further bridge the gap. (p. 118)

Some Asian cultures have a tradition of tolerance or acceptance of cross-dressing. For example, *hijras,* a religious sect in India, are men who have their genitalia surgically removed and live as women. These individuals are considered lower in the social hierarchy than males with intact genitalia but maintain a certain level of respect in some communities (Weinrich & Williams, 1991). Other examples include *katoey* in Thailand, *acault* in Burma, and *banci* in Indonesia, all of whom are men who act in the female role and cross-dress (Nakajima et al., 1996).

Because these cross-dressing cultural traditions are in opposition to current Asian gay male roles in the United States, many immigrant cross-dressing men tend to be alienated. As an example of the clash of cultures, Manalansan (1996) discusses conflict between two factions of gay Filipinos in the United States. When emigrating from the Philippines, many cross-dressing men, *bakla,* reject assimilated Filipino American men. *Bakla* claim these assimilated men are internally homophobic and are attempting to mimic Caucasian men. Conversely, the more masculine, assimilated Filipino American men see the cross-dressing practices of *bakla* to be low class or archaic.

Regardless, as Mangaoang (1996) states, young Filipinos in the United States who come out have an easier time than those who came out in the 1970s. Organizations for Asians and Pacific Islanders have emerged in larger cities, and many API lesbians and gay men do not have to face the isolation that they would have had to endure 20 or 30 years ago.

Barriers to positive identity formation, however, are still plentiful. For the most part, the general culture treats as exotic and stereotypes East Asian Americans. The dominant culture expects that Asian American gay men will be passive and sexually submissive, which causes difficulties for Asian American gay men in developing new relationships with non-Asians. In addition, an examination of gay male pornography conducted by Fung (1998) found that the few images of Asian Americans showed them in mostly in subservient and sexually receptive roles.

This oppression found in the dominant culture and in the gay and lesbian community causes resentment. For example, Wat (1996) describes his feelings when a Caucasian man attempted to ingratiate himself by using Mandarin and flirting with Wat as the Caucasian man's Asian American lover stood next to them:

> I hated his gaze; I hated his grin; I hated his assumptions. When he asked me where I was from, a question often asked of Asians, he was less concerned with my roots than with his own fascination about my (racial) difference. . . . The fact that he and others like him can openly and publicly approach Asian men in such an offensive manner is a testimony to the imbalanced power dynamics existing in gay communities. (p. 73)

Cultural factors, assimilation tendencies, shifting traditions, and religious beliefs influence the identity development of Asian American lesbians and gay men. Moreover, identifying with the lesbian and gay community creates challenges for Asian Americans who are attempting to integrate their social identities. Assimilation could increase their internalization of Asian stereotypes as they merge into gay culture.

Many assimilated Asian Americans have little self-awareness of their culture and may even deny membership. Accounts exist of Asian American lesbians and gay men who avoid other Asian Americans because they do not want to be associated with them (Hom, 1996; Mangaoang, 1996). Thus, developing a positive lesbian/gay identity among Asian American lesbians and gay men may be problematic.

Some lesbian and gay Asian Americans do not find that they are able to integrate their two social identities. Takagi (1996) notes,

> Many of us experience the worlds of Asian American and gay American as separate places—emotionally, physically, intellectually. We sustain the separation of these worlds with our folk knowledge about the family-centeredness and supra-homophobic beliefs of ethnic communities. Moreover, it is not just that these

communities know so little of one another, but we frequently take care to keep those worlds different from each other. (p. 25)

In times of distress, such as illness or relationship dissolution, Asian American lesbians and gay men may feel compelled to address personal identity issues. Likewise, HIV-infected Asian American gay men often seek out other Asian Americans when issues related to death and dying occur, so that they can have support from individuals who understand cultural and family issues (Nakajima et al., 1996). Most large cities have support and social groups for Asian American lesbians and gay men.

When treating Asian American lesbians and gay men, you should be aware that coming out to one's family may be extremely slow or nonexistent. Many Asian Americans are reluctant to come out to their families less due to fear of ostracism than out of respect for the cultural norm of saving face. Understanding that well-adjusted Asian American clients may never divulge their sexual orientation to family members will assist you in reorienting yourself away from the expectation (per lesbian/gay identity stage models) that coming out is essential for mental health. Further, encouraging clients to come out to their families could be seen as ignorant or a lack of respect for Asian cultural values. For Asian American clients who do attend family therapy, the cultural norm of sacrificing self in favor of the family may still surface.

Native American Two-Spirits

To Native Americans, the terms *gay*, *lesbian*, and *bisexual* are considered culturally biased (Tafoya, 1996), whereas the term *two-spirit* more accurately reflects certain individuals in Native American cultures. To be *two-spirited* is to bridge the physical and spiritual realms. In many tribes, two-spirits are associated with power, vision, and spirituality, often possessing an esteemed ceremonial or healing role. Historically, two-spirit individuals were considered sacred, and they held high places in the social hierarchy. The term often used to describe people with two spirits is *berdache* (Tafoya, 1996).

If two-spirits participate in same-gender sex, it does not mean that they self-identify as gay, lesbian, or bisexual, so to place labels precludes developing an understanding of Native American two-spirit clients. For example, a sexual relationship between a female-bodied "male" and a heterosexual female (or a male-bodied "female" and a heterosexual male) is considered to be a heterosexual relationship (Thomas & Medicine, 2000), and to consider it to be a same-gender relationship would be inaccurate.

As with other ethnic minorities, degree of acculturation influences the level of adherence to cultural norms. Many Native Americans have an accepting attitude toward sexual diversity and view sex as a vehicle for relaxation and entertainment (Williams, 1996), whereas others have adopted a condemning attitude toward people who live outside the norm.

Two-spirits tend to be androgynous and see the world from both male and female perspectives. They may cross-dress or in some other way violate gender norms. Tafoya (1996) states that many tribal languages contain terms for individuals who do not fit the concept of completely male or completely female. In the Navajo nation, *nàdleehé* refers to a male in the role of a female, and *dilbaai* refers to a female in the role of a male; among the Lakota, there are *winktes*; in the Crow nation, *botes*; and in the Tewa, *kwid'o*.

To point to the subtleties within the Native American culture and how the nuances of the culture are lost on non-Native American observers, Tafoya (1996) gives the example of a famous Crow *bote* (two-spirit). An individual is shown in a photograph wearing clothing with abalone disks sewn across the bodice. Crow women decorated their clothing with a variety of animal teeth, shells, and beads but not abalone disks. To a non-Native American observer, it appeared that the *bote* was dressed as a woman when, in actuality, the person was dressed as a two-spirit *bote*. Another distinction among two-spirits is that stage theories of identity development are inadequate in explaining two-spirit development (Tafoya, 1996). In families with strong cultural traditions, a two-spirit adult would be two-spirit from early childhood, and internal stages are irrelevant from a Native American perspective.

In fact, some Native Americans shift from a gay identity to a *berdache* identity. Some *berdaches* reside on, or have returned to, their reservations, and some have assimilated into the lesbian and gay culture. On the other hand, as Williams (1996) notes, many *berdaches* move from a *berdache* identity while on a reservation to a gay identity in an urban culture, with only a partial adjustment to urban life, as they retain elements of their former lives from tribal culture.

Due to cultural shifting and development, there has been a renewed interested in two-spirit life and culture. Williams (1996) states that the gay movement and *berdache* tradition have had a mutual impact on one another and, as a result, Native American lesbians and gay men are retaining some of their lesbian/gay identity while exploring their two-spirit status. Kallimachos (2000) observes,

> Native two-spirit peoples are experiencing a re-awakening to their validity, and to the cultural and spiritual roots, of their inner calling. Many who . . . had sought escape from the isolation and rejection by accepting modern "gay" identities, are now reconnecting with their heritage by way of groups like the Native Gay and Lesbian Gathering. They are re-interpreting their identity in terms dictated neither by white culture nor by ancient customs, or perhaps by both. The result is a mix peculiarly their own, which by breaking with both traditional as well as modern forms remains true to the essence of two-spirit life.

You should consider several other issues when treating two-spirit people (Tafoya, 1996). Reducing power differences between you and your Native American clients increases respect for therapy because an egalitarian environment reflects a cultural norm. You can create this atmosphere by seeking opinions of clients and showing respect for cultural beliefs.

Behavior of Native Americans may seem unusual or even pathological until you understand the cultural significance of the behavior. Thus, commenting on seemingly unusual behavior will be detrimental to the therapeutic relationship, and consulting with references and colleagues is preferred over providing interventions that could hinder the therapeutic alliance. As previously noted, the idea of a same-gender orientation is confining or not applicable to Native American individuals who live as two-spirit people. Therefore, when Native American clients tell you something related to two-spirit concepts you do not comprehend, asking for help in understanding those concepts serves the dual role of equalizing the relationship and enabling you to have greater awareness.

Another potential difficulty during therapy is that English language words to describe emotions are not part of some Native American languages. Asking clients to clarify their emotions may evoke responses in the form of metaphor, stories, and pictures, when words cannot convey meaning; these avenues should be encouraged. In many Native American cultures, an indirect way of asking questions allows the client to be spared from embarrassment and to not be rejected directly. Although it may not be a significant mistake to be direct, it does violate a cultural norm and may be met with perceived resistance or noncompliance.

Tafoya (1996) states that the sense of isolation experienced by two-spirit individuals is probably not much different than the isolation experienced by the larger lesbian and gay community. However, there are many two-spirit American tribes and families who embrace their two-spirit family members. Therefore, some Native American clients may present with issues unrelated to being two-spirit.

❖ LESBIAN/GAY CULTURE

In today's urban gay community, there are so many subcultures that it would be difficult, if not impossible, to describe all of them. Therefore, the following section is an introduction to several social subcultures.

Before we turn to discussing the specific subcultures within the lesbian and gay community, we provide you with a description of the context of the myriad subcultures and organizations. In large cities and in many smaller and medium-sized cities, openly gay neighborhoods and areas have emerged. These areas have retail establishments, organizations, and community centers that cater to the needs of lesbians and gay men.

However, as Markus (2000) notes, lesbians and gay men have membership in a "perceived" community rather than a physical community. So the gay community is more than a conglomeration of establishments and organizations. Rather, it is a feeling of belonging and sense of common struggles, interests, and shared history. To illustrate, we received a letter from a person who read one of Jeff's newspaper columns (Chernin, 2001) on Gay Pride:

This is the first year I have ever attended a Pride celebration. Although in my 40s, I have never lived a gay life—closeted or otherwise—primarily because of religious involvement and tons of guilt. I am not totally out now, but have finally admitted it to myself and have told several friends this past April, which was the first time I ever admitted it out loud to anyone. Although having an established career and "straight" life makes it scary to think in terms of totally coming out, that is my goal. I have come further already than ever in my life and it feels wonderful. . . . The main point I am trying to make is that I feel a real sense of pride in being gay and realize it is only possible because of the sacrifices so many people have made in the past. The Pride parade in Minneapolis brought that sense of pride and recognition of who we are and "we are here" home to me. (anonymous, personal communication, July 12, 2001)

Lesbian/gay organizations are arranged around common interests, such as square dancing, gardening, and book reading clubs. There are political organizations that cross the political spectrum, including lesbian and gay coalitions, gay rights lobbies, minority coalitions, and human rights organizations. Sports enthusiasts can choose from among several organizations. Religious organizations cover the spectrum of denominations. A predominantly lesbian and gay denomination, the fellowship of Metropolitan Community Churches, provides an affirming environment for lesbians and gay men. Most larger cities offer support groups for lesbians and gay men, including groups for gay and lesbian parents; gay and lesbian teens; children of gay/lesbian parents; 12-step recovery groups for alcohol, drug, and sex addicts; and coming out support groups.

There are restaurants and coffeehouses that cater to the local gay community in most major cities. The gay press has become an integral part of the community, and local and regional newspapers provide news items, in addition to advertising and community resources. Many of these newspapers are online, and in the appendix we offer a Web site with links to many of these resources.

Larger cities have community centers, which serve as a central location for group meetings and support services. For smaller to mid-size cities, there are still several options for lesbians and gay men, including support groups and religious organizations. When community centers are not available, lesbians and gay men find alternative meeting spaces, including public buildings and people's homes. There are organizations that serve lesbians and gay men living in rural areas.

Lesbian/Gay Subculture, Trends, and Phenomena

In this section, we present various subcultures, trends, and phenomena to give you an idea of the diversity that you will encounter in your practice. Many of the following groups are part of clients' social identities.

AIDS Memorial Quilt

The AIDS Quilt is intended to memorialize all of the people who have died of AIDS. Many of the 44,000 panels offer homage to gay men. Friends, lovers, and family members sew panels of the Quilt in honor of loved ones. For panel makers and viewers alike, a common response is intense grief; it is not uncommon to see people sobbing at the panel of loved ones lost to AIDS.

Barebacking

Barebacking is a phenomenon that took root in the 1980s among a small group of gay men; this practice became known as *barebacking* in the 1990s. These men intentionally participate in unsafe sexual practices, whether they are HIV-positive or HIV-negative. Some stories have circulated about "Russian roulette" sex parties, in which one unidentified guest is HIV positive. There is a subgroup of HIV-negative men, known as "bug chasers," who actively seek out HIV-infected sexual partners.

Bear Culture

As is the case with the general culture, the gay male community has proscribed socially constructed standards regarding what is considered beautiful and sexually attractive. As the masculine, bearded or mustached "gay clone" disappeared, the gay ideal of youthful, extremely well-built, smooth-skinned, "masculine" men arose.

The bear subculture came about in silent opposition. "For some it is an attitude (or better, a lack of 'attitude'), and for some it is an image, a gay sexual icon of desirability" (Wright, 1997, p. 2). A bear is generally someone with "a large or husky body, heavy body hair . . . [with] a social and sexual inclusiveness—men in their thirties, forties, and fifties, ranging from slender to stocky to chubby (though generally on the heavier side), usually with beards and perhaps body hair, and from a range of social classes" (p. 21).

Butch-femme

There is a subculture of lesbians who identify as butch or femme. Butch women, who tend to be culturally masculine, and femme women, who tend to be culturally feminine, have certain characteristics. It is not exclusively an outward projection because being butch or femme can be an attitude or "an energy." There are many kinds of butches and femmes. Butches include soft butch, hard butch, and stonebutch. Femmes include high femme, stonefemme, and powerfemme. Some femmes desire butches, others desire femmes, and still others desire both, and the same is true for butches. Many femmes and butches prefer not to call themselves lesbian. Some prefer to be called queer, others prefer to be associated with transgender, and some prefer no label at all.

Choruses and Marching Bands

Larger cities have lesbian and gay choruses and marching bands, which perform as part of Pride celebrations and at performing arts halls. A national organization was formed to support the lesbian and gay choruses and marching bands in the United States.

Circuit Parties

Circuit parties are weekend-long dance parties and events that are held around the world, and gay men often travel from city to city to attend them. Started rather loosely, these events have evolved into more formalized, corporate-sponsored events. A new term has spawned from circuit parties: the term *circuit queen* is used to denote someone who routinely attends circuit parties. Many of the men who attend these events use drugs and engage in sexual activities through-out the weekend.

Drag Culture

In the lesbian/gay culture, drag queens are men who dress in women's clothes, and drag kings are women who dress as men. Many lesbians and gay men view drag as entertainment and dress in drag professionally. For others, cross dressing is a lifestyle, whether they are entertainers or not. Drag should be distinguished from transvestism, which is a form of fetishism—i.e., dressing in opposite-sex clothing for sexual stimulation.

Case Study 2.8 (Brian, continued from Case Study 2.2)

Brian tells you about going to a gay bar for the first time. "I went with a friend, y'know? And this guy was cruising me and I cruised him back. He was really cute, but he was with a group of, y'know, friends. Anyway, I hope I see him again."

In this context, Brian and the stranger cruised each other, but it didn't mean that they were looking for casual sex. To Brian, it means that they looked at each other and found one another attractive. In regard to going to his first gay bar, what does this experience tell you about Brian's identity development? Would you start using different interventions? If so, how would you start to treat Brian differently?

Gay Bar

For cities that have gay bars, the *gay bar* plays an integral part in lesbian and gay community life. In spite of the proliferation of other resources and organizations, the gay bar is still the institution at the center of gay life for many people. Some bars have music in the background, and men and women come to drink and talk. Other bars are known for their music, with intricate light shows and professional deejays that play energetic dance music. Specialized dance bars, from country to disco, serve diverse clientele in many cities.

The gay bar is a major meeting spot for many lesbians and gay men, and some bars have the reputation of being primarily for meeting sexual partners. These bars are known for *cruising*, which means going out to look for casual sex. Other bars have a reputation for being primarily social, and people go to such bars to see friends, have drinks before going to dinner, and so on. Cruising can have different meanings in different settings, which is illustrated in Case Study 2.8.

Gay Male Sexual Meeting Places

Gay men (more generally, MSM) meet in various places to have sex, such as parks, bars, restrooms (tearooms), bookstores, bathhouses, and sex clubs. Some bathhouses are primarily sexual but have a social component, with workout rooms and even Sunday brunch, and sexually oriented bookstores can be social meeting spots for "regulars," in addition to being places for anonymous sex. Sex clubs, however, tend to be straightforward sexual spaces, with large open rooms for sex to take place.

Gay and Lesbian Press

The gay and lesbian press caters to the needs of lesbian and gay individuals by providing alternative local, national, and international news, information on the arts, and local community activities. Many local papers are now available online, and the appendix includes local and national press Web sites.

Gay and Lesbian-Specific 12-Step Groups

Although Alcoholics Anonymous (AA) and other 12-step groups have a philosophy of "live and let live," many lesbians and gay men feel more comfortable attending gay-specific 12-step programs. From AA and NA (Narcotics Anonymous) to CoDA (Codependents Anonymous), most large cities have groups that are specifically for lesbians and gay men.

HIV/AIDS Community

Over time, a community concerned with HIV/AIDS has developed, which includes treatment and policy activist organizations, healthcare agencies, social groups, and support groups. Gay newspapers carry "positive personals," and some nightclubs have special nights or events for people who are HIV-positive.

Leather and S/M

For some lesbians and gay men, both leather fetishism and S/M (sadomasochism) have gone beyond sexual practice and have become separate subcultures. However, some people see leather and S/M as one subculture. The Leather community has its own code, cultural practices, and even its own Pride symbol: a blue, black, and white flag with a red heart that has also been adopted by other fetish and S/M groups. Organizations such as the Gay Men's S/M Association and the Lesbian Sex Mafia are dedicated to support and education for S/M.

Lesbian Feminists

A subculture for lesbian feminists arose out of the feminist movement. This subculture created a visible lesbian culture and community, including women's centers, feminist books and bookstores, music festivals, coffee houses, media, literature, clinics, and religious alternatives (Esterberg, 1996).

Lesbian Nation

Starting in the 1980s, a more openly lesbian sexual scene emerged, with its own woman-made pornography and sexually oriented bars (Esterberg, 1996). Often in conflict with lesbian-feminists, Lesbian Nation quickly broadened its boundaries to include butches and femmes, working class and ethnic minority lesbians.

LGBT Pride (Gay Pride)

Every year, many cities celebrate the heralding of the modern LGBT movement, usually with parades, festivals, and marches. In 2001, there were more than 100 LGBT Pride events in the United States (see the appendix for a Web site listing of cities that have LGBT Pride celebrations).

National Coming Out Day

Since it was first observed on October 11, 1987, National Coming Out Day (NCOD) has been an annual event when people are encouraged to come out to friends and loved ones. It has evolved into an educational campaign, with public events around the country.

Outing

Outing is publicly announcing a person's homosexual orientation against his or her wishes, and it generally happens to closeted lesbians and gay men who have endorsed antigay policies and initiatives. Over time, many of the outed individuals embrace the lesbian/gay community and vice versa, and news of their outing fades from public view. Others, however, deny the label "gay" or "lesbian" and attempt to squelch speculation.

Political Activism

Political activism is a long-held tradition in the gay community. Groups focus on issues such as fighting for equal rights for lesbians and gay men, developing antidiscrimination laws that include lesbians and gay men, and legalizing same-gender marriage. Political activism is often intertwined with other aspects of the gay community, so fundraising at gay bars and other organizations is not uncommon. Political action committees, Stonewall Democrats, Log Cabin Republicans, watchdog groups, and HIV/AIDS political groups exist, with both grassroots and national organizations being part of the political fabric.

Radical Faerie Fellowship

Radical Faeries are unorganized groups, or circles, of gay men who center their spiritual lives on pagan doctrines. Influenced by Native American traditions, Radical Faeries' spiritual beliefs include traditions and tenets from the druid culture, Wicca, Tao, shamanism, and Hinduism. They utilize pagan rituals to validate and celebrate their lives as gay men. *RFD*, a forum for Radical Faerie beliefs, is a reader-written magazine that includes poetry and art.

Sports and Athletics

Athletic and sporting groups have become a fixture in most lesbian and gay communities. It is important to note that, as is the case with other organizations, people in sports organizations are drawn by a common interest, such as archery, soccer, softball, or baseball. As important, however, is that these organizations form a social outlet that serves purposes beyond their stated goals. Sporting events have become part of Gay Pride, as evidenced by the Gay Games (quadrennial events akin to the Olympics but for LGBT people), and AIDS rides and marathons (annual events that test the mettle of long-distance bike riders to raise money for AIDS organizations).

❖ SUMMARY

Many issues confront lesbian and gay youth, elderly, and ethnic minority lesbians and gay men. Lesbians and gay men must find their way in the gay community. Being adolescent, elderly, and/or an ethnic minority often makes the journey to self-acceptance more challenging.

As a result, several lesbian and gay subcultures exist. The number of choices that lesbians and gay men have in finding social support may make finding one's place in the community easier. However, the process can be problematic when lesbians and gay men find barriers to acceptance in the gay community and when they feel a pull from having multiple social identities.

In the case studies, Angela is moving from Identity Tolerance to Identity Acceptance (Cass, 1979). She is using her anger as fuel for coming out. Desiring to be accepted by other lesbians, she is surprised at the level of racism she finds in Caucasian lesbians, which triggers sadness and disillusionment. Brian is starting to get angry at having to live with constricting social proscriptions. He goes to a gay bar for the first time and has a positive experience. Roberto, who has made a transition from individual therapy to group therapy, has made non-Hispanic group members aware of a part of his culture. Ken is a Caucasian teenage adolescent who is experiencing harassment from his peers to the point where he is feeling suicidal. Theresa, an elderly lesbian, wants to focus on tending to her ailing partner. Instead, she finds that her partner's family has pulled the rug out from under her.

In the next chapter, we discuss the foundations for affirmative psychotherapy for lesbian and gay men. These foundations, both physical and psychological, provide a framework from which to provide affirmative therapy.

Part II

Affirmative Psychotherapy and Counseling in Individual, Couple, and Group Modalities

❖ ❖ ❖

3

Creating the Foundation for Affirmative Psychotherapy

Environment, Language, Assessment
Instruments, and Training and Education

❖   ❖   ❖

To provide affirmative psychotherapy, a physically and psychologically inclusive environment is vital to making lesbian and gay male clients feel comfortable and secure. The physical environment, which clients experience upon entering your place of work, starts in the lobby and continues in your office. The psychological environment includes values, attitudes, beliefs, and behaviors that you convey to your clients by your verbal and nonverbal communication and by assessment instruments you administer and interpret with them.

❖ PHYSICAL ENVIRONMENT

From the first moment lesbian and gay clients enter your office, they evaluate their surroundings for comfort and security. You can create an environment that feels comfortable for lesbian/gay clients in overt and in subtle ways. For example, if you place lesbian/gay magazines on a table along with other periodicals, it will minimize speculation as to whether or not you are lesbian/gay friendly. Not only will lesbian and gay clients' comfort increase, but lesbian and gay clients may have their first therapeutic experience by seeing magazines that acknowledge their presence. It will also begin to challenge heterosexist assumptions of clients who are newly out or uncomfortable about their sexual orientation.

As for other ways to provide an affirming foundation in the office environment, Perry and Barry (1998) note that bulletin board items, such as flyers for gay 12-step group meetings or upcoming same-sex workshops, help lesbian and gay male clients feel visible. The feeling of acceptance this engenders in these clients will help set the tone for their therapy sessions. Providing lesbian/gay resources has many possible therapeutic benefits, including modeling inclusivity, displaying respect and positive regard, and challenging clients' internalized homophobia. Having self-help books for lesbian and gay clients on your bookshelves can facilitate making specific recommendations because you can easily show clients various books. You can refer clients to the Internet or to major bookstores, which generally have a selection of related offerings. Public libraries, especially branches located in gay communities, usually have a selection of lesbian and gay books. Because self-help books are being written at a breakneck pace, however, it is impossible to keep up. Therefore, in addition to providing clients with book titles, you could recommend that they go to bookstores or libraries to find books that they feel pertain to them. We include a list of self-help books in the appendix.

Another way to create an affirmative physical environment is to have other available written materials on hand. With newly out lesbian/gay clients in particular, handouts and articles (preferably copies that they can take home with them) can educate clients about coming out challenges, family issues, and relationships. Moreover, lesbian and gay magazines are available in most metropolitan areas. The themes of these magazines include HIV/AIDS, youth, couples, and families. Many cities have a "gay yellow pages," which is a directory of organizations, retail establishments, and professionals who serve the gay community. Lesbian/gay newspapers and gay yellow pages available in your office enable clients to easily learn about community resources.

❖ LANGUAGE

Because heterosexist bias is an inescapable aspect of living in the culture, it is nearly impossible to avoid the use of heterosexist language. To provide an affirmative foundation, however, it is important to be aware of language that you use so you can minimize heterosexist language. Obvious heterosexist language has a potentially deleterious impact on clients. Reactions can range from mild irritation to extreme hurt. Heterosexist language also reduces trust, so it becomes especially important to be sensitive to the language you employ.

Language Used During Therapy Sessions

Heterosexist bias includes using language that assumes clients are heterosexual. If you use the opposite sex pronoun for clients' partners, they may become hesitant to reveal personal information, feel annoyed at your assumption, or have questions as to your competence. Presuming heterosexuality can also contribute to clients' internalized homophobia. In general, using inclusive language helps clients feel more at ease and reduces the possibility that detrimental consequences will develop.

One way to increase client comfort is by mirroring the clients' language concerning relationships. For instance, many lesbian and gay male individuals use the term *partner* or *spouse*, whereas others use *significant other, lover, boyfriend, girlfriend, roommate, husband*, or *wife*. Furthermore, terminology chosen by clients can be a clue as to how they view their relationships, giving you insight into the client's level of commitment and feelings about having same-sex partners, as in Case Study 3.1.

As noted earlier, some clients, including those who are younger, use alternative terms for themselves and other lesbians and gay men, such as *faggot, dyke, queer*, and *fairy*. Because many of these terms have been added to the lesbian and gay vernacular, you will need to clarify the context to determine if they are derogatory. It is important to understand that these terms are common usage for some clients, and mentioning these terms does not in itself imply internalized homophobia. On the other hand, using these terms disparagingly may indicate internalized homophobia or a way to feel superior over other social groups, as is illustrated in Case Study 3.2.

Case Study 3.1 (Angela, continued from Case Study 2.6)

Angela continues her growth toward integrating a positive lesbian identity into her overall identity. From the first time she came to see you, Angela has used the term *roommate* to refer to her partner. In this session, however, Angela refers to her partner, Jodi, as her girlfriend. Recognizing the shift in language, you say to her, "I noticed you used the term *girlfriend* to talk about Jodi." Angela smiles and says, "I was wondering if you'd notice. Yeah, she's my girlfriend. It's time to stop talking around that. Yeah, I care about her. She is."

Acknowledging Angela's new term for Jodi is significant for Angela because it signifies a shift in the way she not only views her relationship but also herself. Angela has moved from thinking "I could be lesbian" to "I am (or most probably am) lesbian" and is more comfortable with her sexual orientation.

Case Study 3.2 (Brian, continued from Case Study 2.8)

During session, Brian mentions that he went to the Pride celebration last Sunday. As he's talking about the event, he complains, "Did you see the news about Gay Pride? All you saw were those drag queens. I hate them." You ask, "Why do you hate them?" Brian replies, "It's because that's what middle-America will think about us. If all they show are drag queens on the news, that's what people think we are, y'know? And I'm not one . . . one of those . . . I never, *never* dress up in women's clothes. That's for femmy faggots, and I'm not. . . . It sucks that people think that way about us." You reply, "You are very angry at them." Brian replies, fuming, "Those queens are ruining it for us."

Would you confront Brian, telling him that he is displaying internalized homophobia, or would you continue to empathize with his anger? If you decided to confront him, when would you do so? Do you feel that Brian is a good candidate for a coming out group or perhaps group therapy sometime in the future?

Language Used on Intake Forms

Another place to be aware of language's impact on lesbian and gay clients is on intake forms. Omitting information that pertains to lesbians and gay men reflects heterosexist bias. For example, intake forms that include terms such as *married*, *divorced*, and *widowed* leave out same-gendered relationships. *Married/significant other*, *divorced/relationship dissolved*, and *widowed/death of partner*, however, acknowledge them. See the Admission Form on p. 68 for an example of an inclusive intake form.

❖ PSYCHOLOGICAL ASSESSMENTS

Instruments Containing Heterosexist Bias

Many psychological assessment instruments contain heterosexist bias. Awareness of this bias can lead to discussing the particular limitations and biases in psychological assessments, which helps to create a more affirmative environment for lesbian and gay male clients. Sometimes, results from assessment instruments used for the general population do not accurately predict the results for lesbian and gay male respondents. This situation occurs because of heterosexist bias in research techniques. One example of this bias is when researchers norm their instruments using presumed heterosexual subjects and write questions using biased language. When this occurs, some items, scales, and inventories cannot be accurately interpreted for lesbians and gay men.

In the extreme, bias in psychological assessments can have major consequences. One of the most famous examples using the results of an assessment instrument to determine peoples' fates involved the research of Goddard (1917). Goddard assessed the intellectual capabilities of 178 passengers immigrating to the United States from Eastern European countries. According to his newly developed IQ test, he found that several groups of immigrants were intellectually inferior. A few years later, immigration was restricted for these groups. However, after these immigrants resided in the United States for several years and had a better command of the English language, their IQ scores "rose" dramatically. Because IQ yields a number that is relatively stable over a lifetime, it is likely that his erroneous conclusion affected public policy.

ADMISSION FORM

Name: _____ Date: _____

Address: _____

City: _____ State:_____ Zip: _____

Phone #: _____ E-mail address: _____

Ethnicity: _____ Age: _____ Birthdate: ___/___/___

Highest grade completed: _____ Social Security #:___ /___ /____

Employer :_____

Address: _____

City: _____ State:_____ Zip: _____ Phone #: _____

May I contact you at work? Yes _____ No _____

Relationship status: Single _____ Married/significant other _____

Divorced/relationship dissolved (date) _____

Widowed/death of partner (date) _____

Spouse/partner name: _____

Spouse/partner employer: _____

Address: _____

City: _____ State:_____ Zip: _____ Phone #:_____

Emergency contact: _____ Phone #: _____

Source of referral: _____

Likewise, earlier studies examining psychological adjustment of gay males used samples that were often drawn from unrepresentative groups. For example, Exner (1969) and Raychaudhuri and Mukerji (1971) found that gay males and gay male sociopaths, respectively, scored significantly higher on Reflection responses on the Rorschach test than a comparison group of college students and depressed subjects. However, Exner recruited gay male subjects from a mental hospital, and Raychaudhuri and Mukerji recruited self-identified gay male prisoners. So, results from these studies were never generalizable, although attempts were made to do so.

Little information is available regarding the difference between lesbian/gay male and heterosexual test results on commonly used psychological assessment instruments. Gonsiorek (1995) suggests that most commonly used personality assessment instruments were not performed with open, well-adjusted lesbian and gay male subjects.

Three types of heterosexist bias occur in commonly utilized psychological assessments (Morin & Charles, 1983). The first type of heterosexist bias is *omission bias,* which refers to ignoring the possibility of a respondent being lesbian or gay. It applies to items, scales, and instruments that omit concepts and circumstances associated with the lives of lesbians and gay men. The second type, *connotation bias,* occurs when words with negative connotations are associated with references to minority groups. Words such as *homosexual* or *gay* appearing alongside words such as *child molester* or *alcoholic* imply psychopathology among lesbians and gay men. In many textbooks, information on lesbians and gay men appears in chapters alongside sexual deviations, including fetishes, sadomasochism, zoophilia (sex with animals), and sexual dysfunction.

Contiguity bias, the third type of bias, occurs when scales used for diagnosing mental illness are placed alongside scales which are intended to measure characteristics of lesbians and gay men (Morin & Charles, 1983). One example of this type of bias exists in the Minnesota Multiphasic Personality Inventory (MMPI-2). The primary scales indicate psychopathology, and for Scale 5, the Masculinity-Femininity scale, a high score indicates, among other traits, homoeroticism. Referencing homosexuality amid diagnoses of paranoia, depression, and other forms of mental illness is contiguity bias.

To mitigate the effects of heterosexist bias in psychological assessment instruments, you should familiarize yourself with them to determine which questions pertain (or not) to the lives of lesbians and gay men. When you are aware of heterosexist bias in assessment instruments, you can alert clients ahead of time and interpret results properly for clients.

In general, determine if the researchers normed the instruments for lesbian and gay male subjects, and consider the levels of reliability and validity. Reliable, internally consistent scales are necessary for generalization of the results, and documentation in the form of a written report with the instrument or from subsequent studies should be available. If the assessment claims to be multidimensional, there should be empirical data relating to the separate interpretations of the subscales. If you require additional information to evaluate assessment instruments, consult with colleagues, textbooks on psychological research, and professional journals. Consider contacting the creator(s) of the instrument if little published psychometric evaluation data is available. The developers of various instruments are often privy to unpublished information. Keep in mind, however, that you should not make any conclusions based on psychological assessments alone. Rather, you should use psychological tests as part of an overall assessment.

Two other instruments that contain heterosexist bias include the Social Readjustment Rating Scale (SRRS) and the Sexual Addiction Screening Test (SAST). Both instruments assume that respondent relationships are heterosexual and that all children have a mother and a father. For these instruments, you will want to prepare your clients for the limitations, and you will need to work together to determine how to make the questions applicable to them. In contrast, instances of exemplary practice of inclusive language include the Strong Interest Inventory (SII) and the Beck Depression Inventory (BDI) (Chernin, Holden, & Chandler, 1997). You may wish to review these instruments to see how they differ from the others.

Useful Assessment Tools for the Practitioner

Using the assessment instruments discussed in this section to assess sexual orientation, degree of internalized homophobia, or attitudes toward lesbians and gay men can be helpful in your work with clients.

Sexual Orientation Scales

Assessing sexual orientation is desirable in many instances, in particular to help clients clarify their sexual orientation (Holden & Holden, 1995). If the instruments are based on the assumption that homosexuality is a normal variation of human sexuality, then the instruments are being used in an affirmative way.

Klein, Sepekoff, & Wolf (1985) developed the Klein Sexual Orientation Grid. The grid measures sexual orientation, which ranges from homosexuality to bisexuality to heterosexuality. Respondents complete questions using a seven-point Likert-type scale. It examines emotional and social preferences, lifestyle, and self-identification, in addition to sexual attraction, fantasies, and sexual behavior. Coleman (1987) developed the Assessment of Sexual Orientation. Coleman's assessment and Klein et al.'s grid may be used in conjunction with clinical interviews when clients are questioning their sexual orientation.

Scales Measuring Internalized Homophobia

Several instruments have been designed to measure internalized homophobia among lesbians and gay men, and others assess heterosexuals' attitudes toward lesbians and gay men. In regard to internalized homophobia, Shidlo (1994) suggests that if people were to clarify the term *homophobia* and incorporate religious and cultural influences of prejudice, the concept would be more elegant for empirical research. She designated the term *homonegativity* to reflect these clarifications because the defensive nature of the term *phobia* clouds accurate assessment.

Shidlo (1994) states that homonegativity serves four functions in developing a structure for affirmative psychotherapy:

❖ It appears that most lesbians and gay men experience some degree of internalized homophobia as a consequence of acculturation.

❖ Introjecting negative thoughts and feelings leads to psychological distress.

❖ Reduction of perceived internalization is useful as a measure in therapeutic settings.

❖ The construct is used to organize and explain the variables unique to lesbians and gay men.

Two instruments provide good measures of homonegativity (Shidlo, 1994): the Nungesser Homosexuality Attitudes Inventory (NHAI) and the Index of Homophobia (IHP). Hudson and Ricketts (1980), who created the IHP, observed a low inverse correlation between homophobia and education, which suggests that the more formal education individuals have, the less likely they are to have higher amounts of homophobia. Pagtolun-An and Clair (1986) revised the IHP and performed a factor analysis and concluded that the scale was indeed unidimensional.

Scales Measuring Attitudes Toward Lesbians/Gay Men

Several researchers developed assessment instruments to determine the attitudes of heterosexuals toward lesbians and gay men. Larsen, Reed, and Hoffman (1980) created the Heterosexual Attitudes Toward Homosexuality Scale (HATH), which contains 20 positive and negative statements regarding the rights of lesbians and gay men and any perceived threat that they represent.

MacDonald, Huggins, Young, and Swanson (1973) developed a similar instrument, the Attitude Toward Homosexuality Scale (ATHS), but they did not provide reliability or validity information. Herek (1984) revised this scale's questionnaire and provided validity and reliability information. Several researchers have used this version and other revisions of this scale, with reports of sufficient internal consistency, construct validity, and content validity (Schwanberg, 1993).

Millham, San Miguel, and Kellogg (1976) created the Homosexuality Attitude Scale (HAS) to assess attitudes toward lesbians and gay men over a series of dimensions. The researchers found attitudes toward both lesbian and gay males that included beliefs about the dangerousness of lesbians and gay men, a preference for lesbians over gay males, aversion to cross-sexed mannerisms (mannerisms traditionally proscribed to the opposite sex), moral reprobation, a preference for gay males over lesbians, and personal anxiety. The personal anxiety factor contained items related to anxiety in the presence of known lesbian or gay men, disgust with lesbians or gay men, and a desire to have no contact with lesbians or gay men.

Scales Measuring the Fear of AIDS and Homophobia

Researchers have also developed instruments to assess the level of fear that individuals possess toward AIDS itself, as well as how that fear affects individuals' level of generalized fear of lesbians and gay men. Interestingly, the Fear of AIDS Scale and the Homophobia Scale (Bouton et al., 1987) were subjected to factor analyses to determine if they both measured homophobic fear. There was only a small correlation between these attitude scales, indicating that they were indeed measuring different constructs.

❖ EDUCATION AND TRAINING CONSIDERATIONS

Education and training play a vital role in developing an affirmative therapeutic foundation for lesbians and gay men. The recent increase in diversity training has brought more educational and training programs that include information on providing affirming treatment. Nonetheless, the need for affirmative training is still great. Rudolph (1990) conducted a survey of 52 counselors and trainees on their attitudes toward homosexuality using the Attitudes Toward Homosexuality Scale and the Homosexuality Attitude Scale. Rudolph found that many counselors and trainees were comfortable with the notions of equality for lesbians and gay men, and they accepted lesbians and gay men based on their own moral standards and belief that homosexuality is not an illness. The students did, however, have a strong negative reaction to the idea of eroticized interactions between lesbians and between gay men. So, when the discussions stayed on an intellectual level as to the rights of lesbians and gay men, there was little difficulty. But when same-gender sexual behavior became specific, therapists and trainees experienced discomfort. Also, as we discussed in the Preface, recent studies in 2000 and 2001 still point to discomfort and lack of knowledge among many mental health practitioners.

To help reduce this discomfort, many colleges are teaching lesbian- and gay-affirmative therapy. In some schools, lesbian and gay issues are addressed primarily in multicultural counseling courses, whereas in others they are incorporated throughout the curriculum.

Betz (1991) states that schools should consider two factors when including educational material about lesbians and gay men. First, a core curriculum approach includes discussing lesbian and gay issues in each course, including counseling theory and techniques, research methods, appraisal and assessment, human development, and career development. Professors should have a working knowledge of this material. Professors who have limited experience in this area, however, could include a variety of readings for discussion or invite guest lecturers to present material. Second, professors' attitudes influence the way they present the material on lesbian and gay issues. The depth of coverage and the tone of the discussion are functions of professors' attitudes and beliefs with respect to the subject matter.

Iasenza (1989) maintains that a model could be implemented to aid clinicians, but it also applies to educators. Siegel's (1985) model in working with lesbians includes reading lesbian and gay literature, exploring sexual orientation issues in therapy, working with lesbian and gay male clients, and pursuing relationships with lesbian and gay male colleagues. Using Siegel's suggestions, nongay educators can develop new understanding and empathy for lesbians and gay men and facilitate their professional growth by setting aside judgmental thoughts and reactions (Iasenza, 1989). Iasenza also notes that by placing a gay-friendly supervisor in charge of practica, trainees will be able to receive effective feedback in a supportive teaching environment. If no professor on the faculty feels comfortable assuming this role, the department could offer in-service training by educator/clinicians who specialize in lesbian and gay issues.

The last suggestion Iasenza makes is that educators should foster an environment where lesbian and gay male students feel comfortable to disclose their sexual orientation and discuss challenges related to being lesbian or gay. However, nongay students who are struggling with accepting lesbians and gay men should be given the opportunity to disclose their discomfort and their prejudices, fears, and beliefs. These concerns should be safely explored in dialogues among students and their professors in the classroom.

Another way to develop an affirmative environment is to attend workshops and seminars offering information on lesbian and gay male treatment. It is important for interns and trainees, as well as clinicians, to attend such seminars and workshops. Local lesbian and gay organizations and local chapters of national professional organizations often provide workshops that cover lesbian and gay issues. Staying current in lesbian and gay literature is another strategy. The *Journal of Homosexuality* and *Journal of Gay and Lesbian Psychotherapy* are devoted to publishing articles concerning lesbians and gay men.

A final consideration in staying current on issues of treatment with lesbians and gay men is through communication with colleagues.

Through collegial support, you can more readily develop innovative approaches to counseling lesbians and gay men. Discussing lesbian and gay male clients leads to acquiring new insights, which further builds the foundation for an affirming and safe therapeutic environment.

❖ SUMMARY

The office environment provides the starting point for affirmative therapy. Language that you employ, both spoken and written, has an impact on your lesbian and gay clients. Two places to check for hete-rosexist bias include intake forms and assessment instruments. Although you have control over intake forms, you must at times use assessment instruments that contain heterosexist bias. In instances where that is the case, alerting clients ahead of time is helpful in mini-mizing the negative impact of heterosexist bias and in interpreting the results.

At times, you may need to assess clients' sexual orientation, atti-tudes toward lesbians and gay men, level of internalized homophobia, and impact of HIV on attitudes toward lesbians and gay men. Ethical use of these instruments in practice and research is part of providing an affirmative environment.

Another important factor in providing an affirmative environment is education and information for treating lesbians and gay men. In uni-versities, incorporating diversity in the core course curricula is ideal, but having a separate course on sexual minorities is valuable. Having gay-friendly supervisors, inviting lesbian and gay clinicians to talk to students, and employing other creative strategies help students over-come homophobia. Once they graduate, practitioners continue to grow by attending workshops, reading lesbian and gay journals, and dis-cussing issues with colleagues. Overall, these elements provide a solid foundation for affirmative psychotherapy.

Regarding the case studies, we continue to follow Angela's growth as she learns to accept a lesbian identity and integrate it with her African American identity. Brian, who is not as far along in his identity development, experiences conflict about being gay. Instead of dealing with it directly, he takes advantage of social change strategy, an often-used defense that we discussed in Chapter 1. In essence, Brian is experiencing major discomfort, but this is a common stop on the road to self-acceptance.

In the next three chapters, we focus on assessing and treating lesbians and gay men in individual, couple, and group settings.

4

Affirmative Individual Psychotherapy

Themes and Issues

❖   ❖   ❖

In Part I of this book, we discussed how lesbian/gay culture differs from the general culture, but do these differences translate into requiring different treatment for lesbian and gay male clients? We hope that, after the first three chapters, the answer to the question is becoming conceptually clear, that yes, differences within this population require specific treatment considerations.

So, what are some of the differences in treatment? Although many similarities exist with respect to experiences faced by all clients, lesbian and gay clients perceive and process these experiences differently. Furthermore, lesbians and gay men encounter unique challenges, including the coming out process, lesbian/gay identity formation, and discrimination based on heterosexism and homophobia.

These considerations will influence your treatment plan and course of treatment. To present these issues, we have organized the next three chapters as follows: This chapter discusses treatment for psychotherapy with individual clients; in Chapter 5, we present topics relating to couples and family psychotherapy; and in Chapter 6, we discuss support groups and group psychotherapy. In each chapter, we include interventions and techniques that you can employ.

We describe the topics in these chapters using the Adlerian life tasks, or challenges, as a framework. Alfred Adler, a pioneer in humanistic psychology, developed individual (holistic) psychology (Adler, 1964). He felt that individuals have to meet the challenges of (a) social relationships, (b) occupation, (c) spirituality, (d) relationship to self, and (e) romantic relationships. We discuss the first four challenges in this chapter, as well as issues involving HIV/AIDS; as noted previously, we take up same-gender relationship issues in Chapter 5.

Before we discuss the specific life tasks, we would like to note that in treating lesbian and gay male clients, several themes are present. These themes generate areas of exploration in therapy that are relevant to clients' lives. Stein and Cabaj (1996) note overarching themes in treating lesbians and gay men:

1. In developing a sexual identity, lesbians and gay men notice how their experiences differ from the general culture.

2. Coming out is a lengthy process, and individuals vary in their rate of disclosure.

3. As individuals develop a lesbian or gay identity, a variety of feelings experienced in the process emerge.

4. Issues such as intimacy, dependency, and aggression are all complicated by the interaction with internalized homophobia.

5. Sexuality issues of lesbians and gay men may be difficult to discuss and explore for both therapists and clients.

When you treat lesbian and gay clients, it is important to keep these themes in mind from the outset of therapy. In the first session(s), you can assess clients' expressiveness and communication style; acknowledgment needs, ability for introspection, and ability to set and maintain boundaries; quality and status of relationships; coping strategies (helpful and counterproductive); value system and its origination; and sense of self (Falco, 1996). Making mental notes of perceived levels of internalized homophobia and areas of conflict and confusion will help you tailor a treatment plan targeting the presenting problems.

❖ SOCIAL RELATIONSHIPS

A major area of concern for lesbians and gay men is social relationships. Many lesbians and gay men develop a *family of choice*—a group of friends that they can celebrate with and call upon in times of need and duress. When lesbians and gay men face outright rejection from their families of origin, their families of choice become critical.

Family of Origin

The family of origin is an area of great concern for many lesbians and gay male clients. When lesbians and gay men come out, they have to deal with wide-ranging reactions from different family members. You will frequently hear about concerns regarding family of origin with your clients, particularly when family members reject, distance themselves, or treat clients differently when they come out. Likewise, many lesbians and gay men detach from their families, particularly prior to coming out, and attempt to reestablish relationships with family members after they come to terms with being lesbian/gay.

For individuals who come out during adolescence, initial reactions by family members have a more direct impact on their daily lives than for lesbians and gay men who come out as independent adults. Initial reactions also influence their ability to tell others outside the family and how they view themselves in the future (Stein, 1996).

When families learn of the same-sex orientation of a family member, they undergo a process that parallels coming out. Many times, families initially react unsupportively because discovery of their family member's sexual orientation gives rise to homophobia, shame, and guilt. As a result, many family members urge lesbians and gay men to get help to change their sexual orientation. Many are admonished not to tell other family members, such as aunts, uncles, or grandparents. Although some families do not change their views after their initial reactions, most do make progress, with at least some members of their families learning to accept their lesbian or gay family member.

Case Study 4.1 (Ken, continued from Case Study 2.3)

After 10 sessions, Ken's mother Donna called you to tell you that her husband wants to remove Ken from therapy. You asked Donna if they would consider a family session. She informed you that they would accompany him to his next session. During this session, Ken's father, Peter, complains about his son's attitude. Peter dislikes the fact that Ken has become more open about his sexuality and is more defiant toward his parents, and he blames therapy for the change.

In the session, how would you balance the need to support Ken while validating his parents' concerns? Would you question Ken about why he's being more disobedient and find out what Ken really needs from his parents? Further, how would you explain to Peter and Donna that Ken's behavior is necessary for him to develop an independent identity? Could you also ask Peter to be more understanding while still setting limits on Ken's behavior? Would you also consider helping Peter and Donna with parenting techniques, such as delineating the consequences for Ken if he violates their rules? If so, what would your timing be regarding these interventions?

You can align with different family members, modeling respect by actively listening and empathizing with the family members. In regard to Peter's discomfort about Ken being vocal about his sexual orientation, you can educate Ken about his parents' "coming out" process. Ken could learn to respect their feelings if you remind him that his own difficulty to accept his sexual orientation is not very different than his parents' struggle.

Ken's family could benefit from several family therapy sessions. The goal for the family of origin is to learn to adjust to Ken's sexual orientation, as you walk the line between supporting Ken and helping other family members adjust to the knowledge of Ken's orientation. Furthermore, as with many families, Ken's parents feel responsible for his sexual orientation. In fact, the idea that mothers are to blame for raising "sissy boys" is still part of the culture. Fathers also experience guilt and may react by withdrawing or rejecting their children, either temporarily or permanently (Stein, 1996).

When you work with adolescents, lesbian and gay, you may experience subtle (or not so subtle) pressure from families to view the lesbian or gay client as the identified patient (the person in need of treatment). Therefore, when you provide family therapy with members of a lesbian or gay client's family of origin, it is important to address the system and not the symptom, as we discuss in Case Study 4.1.

A common reaction to disclosure is for family members to grieve. Grieving should be encouraged among family members, including the lesbian and gay family members, for the loss of their expectations regarding their future. When parents wish to see their children get married and have children, they must first grieve this loss before they can come to accept their lesbian or gay children.

Eventually, most families learn to bridge gaps in their relationships and develop acceptance toward one another. One way to facilitate progress toward acceptance, in addition to promoting communication and modeling a nonjudgmental attitude, is to refer family members to organizations for families of origin, self-help groups for families of lesbian and gay men, and reading materials. Resources are available for clients' families at lesbian and gay community centers, in books, lesbian/gay newspapers, the Internet, and telephone hotlines. In the appendix, we list several avenues of support for families of origin. One organization that is particularly valuable to families with a lesbian or gay family member is Parents, Families and Friends of Lesbians and Gays (PFLAG). Members of PFLAG help families adjust to their family member's sexual orientation, and the organization provides a forum for small-group discussions about issues that arise due to having a lesbian or gay relative.

Friendships

For lesbians and gay men, friends become an essential part of their lives partly because development includes cultivating intimate and long-lasting groups of support. Nardi (1999) notes that, for gay men who have been rejected by their families of origin, friends become their only family. Thus, friendships give lesbians and gay men a sense of belonging. Because many lesbian and gay individuals have a history of feeling different, of not being a part of a group, it becomes critical to feel accepted by others. Having friends increases feelings of self-worth, which lays the groundwork for developing a positive identity. In fact, it is often through daily encounters with friends that lesbians and gay men define themselves.

One major difference with same-gender friendships between lesbians or between gay men, compared with same-gender relationships between heterosexuals, is that it is possible for friendships to take on a sexual component. As Nardi (1999) suggests, the process of forming close friendships is similar in many ways to forming romantic relationships. Thus, although it is uncommon for lesbians and gay men to have an ongoing sexual component to their friendships, sexual attraction may exist. And many gay men start out with a sexual experience with someone and later become friends, or they start out as friends and let any sexual attraction lie dormant until it dissipates. Many lesbians, on the other hand, start out as friends and later become romantically involved, becoming partners, as they decide to add a sexual component to their friendships.

For both lesbians and gay men, identity is strengthened and maintained through friendships within lesbian and gay organizations and neighborhoods. Friendships also link personal identity with membership in the community, where personal tastes, politics, religious views, and sexual styles are shared with like-minded individuals (Nardi, 1999). Friendships are also inextricably woven into the narrative histories and coming out stories of lesbians and gay men. So, when gay and lesbian clients tell you about who they are, who they hope to be, and who they are becoming, they are relating their sense of place in the larger community. Networks of friends are also at the root of efforts to develop a collective identity, build communities, organize a political presence, and create residential, commercial, and sexual spaces. As a result, participation in the gay community, its neighborhoods, and organizations nurtures lesbian/gay identity and strengthens friendship networks. For example, attending a gay film festival or going to a Pride event enhances a feeling of community and provides places to make new friends.

Thus, friends become the mechanism for not only learning about and maintaining a lesbian/gay identity, but also for entering the gay community; for organizing into social, religious, and political groups; and for providing a sense of history and collective identity. Friendships are the route for clients to understand themselves as individuals and as citizens of a larger community. Case Study 4.2 illustrates the importance of having lesbian and gay friendships.

As this case study illustrates, social support is essential as a buffer to the stress related to stigmatization. DiPlacido (1998) discusses "stress-buffering factors" that help lesbians and gay men deal with

---

Case Study 4.2 (Ken, continued from Case Study 4.1)

Ken comes to his session looking upbeat for the first time in many weeks. You open the session in the usual manner, asking him how things are going. Ken cheerfully tells you that he met a girl in his class who came out to him earlier in the week. "I'm so excited to meet someone, y'know, like me. She's really cool, and I never thought Claire was a dyke. She's so . . . normal! We like the same bands and the same movies. We're going to a movie this weekend. I can totally be myself with her. I told her about that thing with Rick, and she just laughed. She laughed! Claire said it was his loss and that she always suspected he was queer. And she said we're going to get him so bad, she's going to make him apologize for what he did to me, or else she's going to out him."

Now that Ken has opened the door to developing a social support system, where could you refer him for additional support? Would you consider referring him to a social group or a coming out group? Going to a coming out group could be very helpful for Ken, especially in light of the fact that he feels that he doesn't fit in to a larger peer group, but when do you think is the proper timing for the referral?

---

discrimination, counting friendships and the gay community as two main sources of social support. For lesbians and gay men without a social support system, participation in a social group or coming out group becomes critical for their emotional health, and these groups become training grounds for future social relationships. In Chapter 6, we provide an in-depth discussion of the therapeutic factors related to support groups and group therapy, and we offer models for various types of support and psychotherapy groups.

❖ OCCUPATION

Lesbian and gay clients may have difficulty making decisions about careers and jobs, and challenges related to being lesbian or gay can influence clients' choices. In a hostile or unwelcoming work environment, lesbians and gay men may not be able to manage their identity satisfactorily. If they decide not to come out, they may develop strategies to lead coworkers to believe they are heterosexual.

Two such coping mechanisms related to remaining closeted in the workplace may be derived from the social mobility strategy (Kaufman & Raphael, 1996). The first coping mechanism is *blending*, which includes dodging questions and redirecting conversations. The second strategy is *covering*, which typically involves limiting time with others. The difficulty with these approaches is the resulting increase in feelings of isolation and phoniness. For example, one employee of a large company described his feelings of isolation and lack of social support when HIV-related symptoms forced him to stop working. He indicated that although he seemed well liked, his guarded, surface relationships resulted in few people from the organization staying in contact with him after he left (Woods & Lucas, 1993).

In general, practicing deception becomes increasingly difficult. The need to remember to withhold or modify stories can be very stressful. When deceiving others becomes unsatisfying or too pressure-filled, individuals may decide that it is time to explore other options. This phenomenon in its broadest form is known as *entrepreneurial flight*, which refers to the experience of lesbian and gay employees leaving hostile or unwelcoming workplaces, moving to lower paying jobs, or opening their own businesses (Woods & Lucas, 1993). Individuals might choose to leave more conservative organizations for opportunities in gay-friendly environments. Purcell and Hicks (1996) note that the predicament of disclosing their sexual orientation can be so disturbing that many lesbians and gay men leave their careers altogether in favor of ones they consider more accepting of them.

However, in a positive trend, an increasing number of corporations have instituted nondiscrimination policies and benefits for same-gender partners. Some companies that are unwilling to provide same-gender couples with full benefits have nonetheless added items such as bereavement and family leave for employees with same-gender partners, as well as relocation expense reimbursement for both partners.

The level of gay-friendliness of an organization is a very important consideration for many lesbians and gay men. Examples of gay-friendliness, in addition to offering benefits for same-gender partners, include an environment conducive to bringing same-gender partners to company events, having company sponsored lesbian and gay support groups, and encouraging displays of photos on desks that include same-gender partners.

Gay-friendliness leads to positive workplace consequences. Ellis and Riggle (1995), who surveyed 167 lesbians and gay men, found that openness about sexual orientation correlates with job satisfaction. In fact, feeling comfortable with self-disclosure of activities, people, and relationships influenced the respondents' intention to stay in their jobs, and it was related to a higher level of productivity. Furthermore, the researchers found that individuals reported higher levels of overall life satisfaction when they reported greater comfort in the workplace.

These themes of occupational choice, options for clients who want to come out, and costs of deception often surface in therapy. Sometimes, lesbians and gay men use deceptive strategies because of a high level of fear or a high level of internalized homophobia rather than as a result of being in a hostile atmosphere. Unfounded fears about what other employees think about them may keep lesbian and gay employees from coming out, which in turn could lead to a lower level of job satisfaction. Therefore, it is useful to explore whether their companies or organizations are unwelcoming or whether lesbian and gay clients are afraid because of their beliefs about what other people think about them. Indeed, fear of coming out could signify clients' projecting their own homophobia onto others.

Another source of difficulty is a change in clients' belief system or attitude. For example, clients' dissatisfaction with their jobs may reflect a shift in values. Consequently, they may feel vaguely uncomfortable with their jobs or occupations because of this shift but may try to pin their feelings on issues related to sexual orientation. In contrast, situational stressors related to clients' sexual orientation also cause work-related problems. These stressors lead to a diminished ability to cope with job-related stress. If the difficulties are situational, devising healthy coping strategies with clients could alleviate immediate stress, and they could apply these new strategies in the future. Coping strategies include coming out to one or more select persons at work, updating their resumes to start preparing for a possible job change, and talking about their lives and their challenges with a trusted coworker.

For clients who want to come out at work, you may offer them the option of testing the waters. This option includes making a casual mention of current events or issues related to lesbians or gay men to coworkers and, perhaps, supervisors. Clients who fear being exposed to the entire company or their division could reveal their sexual orientation to their immediate supervisors, ensuring that if word gets out, clients' supervisors are already informed. Still another option is to have clients consider an "ask/tell" policy, whereby clients tell other employees about their personal lives only if asked. In conjunction, you can ask clients to consider the option of acting "as if" their sexual orientation is not an issue at work. They could act naturally by bringing their partners to company functions, letting other employees come to their own conclusions about the nature of their relationships.

When clients are dissatisfied at work and choose to explore options, career counseling and values clarification assists clients with determining which kinds of jobs or careers would better fit their needs. Career development instruments for career development planning, such as the Strong Interest Inventory (Strong, 1927), are useful in evaluating the skills, interests, values, and needs of lesbian and gay clients. Assessing work environments through traditional means (for example, by using a dictionary of occupational titles) can help clients to understand specific job tasks, career options, requisite training, and job opportunities.

However, Gelberg and Chojnacki (1996) point out that these resources do not assess workplace heterosexism. Therefore, they recommend the use of the person-environment fit (P-E) approach, which examines the qualities of the person (e.g., interests, values, experience, stage in the coming out process, and skills), the work environment (e.g., eligibility requirements, work opportunities, interpersonal climate of the workplace), and the interaction between persons and their environment. In addition, you can refer clients to the several books and Web sites that rate the level of gay-friendliness of corporate environments.

❖ SPIRITUALITY

Because most lesbians and gay men grew up with religious injunctions that state that engaging in homosexual acts is sinful, it is not uncommon for lesbians and gay men to view religion through the lens of pain, contempt, and distrust. As a result, many lesbians and gay men go through a period of distancing themselves from organized religion. Glaser (1994)

Case Study 4.3 (Angela, continued from Case Study 3.1)

Angela has been seeing you for several months, and she recently turned to the issue of religion. She spent much of her life thinking that she would go to hell, but she recently started to believe that God must have made her "this way" and won't condemn her. In this session, she reveals that she is angry at God for making her a lesbian, and she is angry with her church and her family. At the same time, she is afraid that God will punish her for her anger. She's also upset that no one, including you, can give her answers.

What interventions do you feel would be useful at this point? Would you reflect back to her the feelings of betrayal and hurt that have run through this scenario, or is it more important to first help her sort out her conflicting feelings? To sort out her feelings, you could use the empty chair technique or recommend journaling as homework. Do you think she might be resistant at this point to these interventions? If so, why?

It could take Angela several months or years to be ready to consider a referral to support groups or an affirming religious group. So, when would you be likely to find an opening to discuss these kinds of referrals?

---

states that interpretation of the Bible has been used as a means to propagate prejudice against lesbians and gay men, and he points out that certain religions revise or ignore views on biblical issues such as polygamy and dietary restrictions, yet passages that condemn homosexuality are frequently cited. Lesbian and gay clients often cite such inconsistencies as reasons to distance themselves from the religion in which they were raised, as we illustrate in Case Study 4.3.

Despite such feelings of anger and betrayal at their religious upbringing, many lesbians and gay men turn to the spiritual realm to help define and understand a being greater than themselves, to seek moral guidance, and to develop a sense of community (Perlstein, 1996). Because of their spiritual needs, many lesbians and gay men attempt to reconcile their religious upbringing and beliefs with their sexual orientation.

Fortunately, in nearly every religious denomination, lesbians and gay men have a place to turn for spiritual guidance. Many places of worship embrace their lesbian and gay parishioners and acknowledge relationships between same-gender couples by performing union cere-monies, whereas others tolerate but do not approve of lesbians and gay men. Support groups exist for each major denomination. Examples of religious lesbian and gay support groups include Dignity/USA (for Catholics), Honesty (for Baptists), and Evangelicals Concerned (for Evangelicals).

Many lesbians and gay men return to the religion of their upbring-ing and ignore or tolerate discriminatory beliefs. Others raised in a particular denomination find an affirming denomination when they return to the spiritual realm. In contrast, some lesbians and gay men never leave their family of origin's religion. Of those, many agree with religious proscriptions against homosexuality, which fuels internalized homophobia. The resulting confusion, torment, and shame become recurring themes in their spiritual journeys.

In response to mainstream religious views toward lesbians and gay men, Reverend Troy Perry founded The Universal Fellowship of Metropolitan Community Churches (UFMCC) in 1968, which today has more than 300 congregations. UFMCC was created for lesbian and gay male Christians, and part of UFMCC's mission is to serve people who seek to integrate their spirituality with their sexual orientation. The following is an excerpt from an introduction to UFMCC found on its Web site:

> Metropolitan Community Churches (MCC) were founded by Rev. Troy D. Perry in 1968. This Fellowship of Churches plays a vital role in addressing the spiritual needs of the lesbian, gay, bisexual, and transgendered community around the world. For those of us who were raised in a religious atmosphere, homosexuality was usually associated with shame and guilt. As a result, many of us were cut off from the spiritual dimension of our lives. Metropolitan Community Churches provide an opportunity to explore a spiritual experience that affirms who we are.

> Today, as self-aware and self-affirming gay men and lesbians, we reclaim the fullness of our humanity, including our spirituality. We

find great truths in the religious tradition, and we find that our encounter with God is transformational and healing. . . .

Thousands of individuals have experienced emotional healing and reconciliation from abuse and oppression, and countless members and friends credit their involvement in the Fellowship and its congregants with saving their lives. We experience our communities of faith as places of healing and hope, places of reconciliation with family, with self-esteem, and with individual spirituality. (UFMCC, 2002)

Alternatively, some lesbians and gay men shed organized religion altogether and consider themselves to be spiritual, with some following more esoteric paths. The search for spiritual growth may lead clients to explore eastern religions, Wicca, paganism, metaphysics, theosophy, goddess worship, and humanism, among others. Nonetheless, a discussion about attitudes and beliefs with respect to religion could lead to talking about unresolved feelings stemming from their religious upbringing, which can lead to an opportunity for exploration and closure.

Therapy is often a place where lesbians and gay men explore issues related to spirituality. Overall, when you encourage an exploration of spirituality, along with informing clients about religious and spiritual community resources, you are providing an atmosphere where clients can deepen their spiritual lives. You will also be assisting them in reconciling their spiritual identity with their lesbian/gay identity.

❖ RELATIONSHIP TO SELF

There are many complexities related to the relationship to oneself, which is fluid and often confusing. New forces are at work to influence the relationship to self when a lesbian or gay identity is added to one's self-concept. And just as the social forces of discrimination and stigmatization influence social relationships, occupation, and spirituality, internalized homophobia is an inescapable part of one's relationship to self. While you read this section, keep in mind that, as Meyer and Dean (1998) suggest, a high level of internalized homophobia is related to demoralization, depression, anxiety, and post-traumatic stress. The category *relationship to self* encompasses issues involved in coming out,

---

Case Study 4.4 (Brian, continued from Case Study 3.2)

Brian has been out to his friends for a year, but up until today's session, he has not expressed a desire to come out to his parents. As is the case with many first generation Chinese Americans, Brian does not want them to feel the shame that would be brought to his family. In today's session, however, Brian tells you, "I want to come out to my mother. She has been asking questions about dating and relationships, and I can't lie anymore. Besides, I think she knows already. My father never asks questions, and I think he would be very upset, so I do not want to tell him."

Should you dissuade Brian from coming out to his mother or ask him to really think about the consequences? Would you encourage Brian to tell his father at the same time he tells his mother, or would you wonder aloud if his mother would tell his father anyway? How would you approach cultural considerations? Although Brian has many reasons to reveal his sexual orientation to his father, he has legitimate reasons for not telling him. For example, Brian's father might kick him out of the house or put Brian's mother in the position of choosing between them. He could also cut Brian off from family and financial ties.

Would you offer Brian the option of bringing his mother so he could come out to her in session? If you role-played with what Brian would say to his mother, how could you help Brian prepare for possible reactions? How could you coach Brian about what to do if his mother says she would tell his father?

---

bereavement related to the coming out process, substance abuse, and eating disorders, which are presented in this section.

Coming Out

Initially, lesbians and gay men find overwhelming the thought of telling other people about their sexual orientation. As a result, clinicians may become impatient with a slow pace, which can lead to overt or subtle ways to persuade clients to come out. Persuasive tactics, however, can lead clients to believe that you are minimizing their feelings. If you are successful at persuading clients to come out, coming out prematurely can lead to maladaptive ways of coping and a greater negative impact on relationships with friends and family than if they came out at their own pace.

Recall that coming out is an interwoven process of becoming more comfortable with being lesbian or gay and revealing sexual orientation to others. You should encourage clients to express their discomfort about being lesbian or gay and to explore their reluctance to tell others. This kind of examination can lead to insights about the origins of introjections, which can lead to eventually disowning them. You are helping clients in the coming out process by providing a place where clients feel safe to explore shame, discomfort, and challenges about being lesbian or gay.

Conversely, if you express concerns or doubts about coming out after clients have decided to do so, it will possibly confuse them and make them question their decision to come out. Or, it may make clients less trusting of you. Therefore, as much as it is desirable to have clients consider potential losses, drawbacks, and negative reactions, once clients have decided to come out, keeping the focus on *when* and *how* to come out, as opposed to *whether* to come out, is the most beneficial direction. One way to learn about client pacing is to refer to the developmental models described in Chapter 1. These models can help you to sort out appropriate referrals and interventions. We illustrate proper pacing in Case Study 4.4.

In general, you should encourage clients to consider various options about how to come out. One possibility is face-to-face contact with others, but some clients prefer to write "coming out letters." This is a way to communicate what needs to be stated without fear of immediate negative feedback, worry about leaving out important points, or dread at the thought of outright rejection at the time of disclosure. When you suggest coming out letters as an option, you could encourage clients to read them to trusted friends or read their letters in session before sending them.

One way to help prepare clients for potential reactions, as stated in the questions in Case Study 4.4, is to role-play. Role rehearsing is useful in individual therapy, but a group setting is especially effective because it affords a greater range of feedback and provides the opportunity to receive suggestions from peers. You could ask clients to play themselves when they come out to others. Two advantages of this option are that clients can rehearse what they are going to say and will respond to reactions that they were not expecting. Another option is to have yourself or another group member play your client's role, and ask your client to play the person to whom he or she will be coming out. One benefit of this option is that clients have the chance to develop greater empathy for how others will feel and react.

Loss of Life Image

Issues of loss occur throughout the life span for all individuals, but certain kinds of losses apply particularly to lesbians and gay men. Although devastating losses for lesbians and gay men occur as a result of losing friends and loved ones due to AIDS (see a discussion of this topic later in the chapter), losses with respect to coming out also have a significant impact upon clients' lives. Initially, lesbians and gay men must deal with intangible losses in childhood as they begin to realize that they are different from others. As adolescents or adults, when they start to come to terms with being lesbian or gay, they must deal with losses related to a preconceived life image based on societal expectations and reinforced by the family.

Herdt and Boxer (1993) observe that lesbian/gay youth must suffer the death of who they once were, with only a promise of what they will become. They call this process "grief for the lost self," and losses for lesbians and gay men, irrespective of age, include the loss of heterosexual status and privilege. They must come to terms with the fact that there is no opportunity for legally sanctioned marriage, no legally sanctioned same-sex parental rights, little chance for joint or inheritable retirement benefits, and risk of insult or injury when being affectionate in public places. Lesbians and gay men must find ways to acknowledge and work through these losses. Worden (1991) defines grieving to include thoughts, feelings, and behavioral changes that occur following a loss. Lesbian and gay male clients may not recognize all aspects of loss when acknowledging their sexual orientation, and grief work often continues for years as clients identify additional losses.

Substance Abuse

Although researchers have found differing rates of addiction (Beatty, 1983; Cabaj, 1992; Finnegan & McNally, 1987; McKirnan & Peterson, 1989), it appears that both licit and illicit substance abuse rates are higher among lesbians and gay men than among hetero-sexuals. Researchers have made several conjectures as to the higher rate of substance abuse in the lesbian and gay population. According to Ratner's (1993) review of the literature, contributing factors for sub-stance abuse include internalized homophobia, rejection by the family, low social support, stress related to leading a double life, coming out, and fear of AIDS.

Another historical factor, and an important factor in today's lesbian/gay culture as well, is the bar scene. In some bars, drinking, smok-ing, and other drug use may be encouraged. Because bars have been the major meeting places for many lesbians and gay men, it becomes easier to abuse alcohol and other drugs. The very ordinariness of it can cause people to feel obligated to drink. As an added pressure, abstaining could result in being ostracized or belittled. Bars are commonplace in most cities and are often very popular. In smaller cities and towns, gay bars may be the only places for lesbians and gay men to socialize.

As noted in Chapter 1, it is not uncommon for people to go through a period where they feel discomfort or hatred about their sexual orien-tation. This results in a higher risk of escaping by abusing alcohol and other drugs. To cope with discomfort about sex, many lesbians and gay men consume alcohol and other drugs as a way to reduce their discomfort and inhibitions.

In urban gay cultures, "club drugs" have become popular, espe-cially among lesbians and gay men who go to raves, circuit parties, and dance clubs. Some drugs that are particularly popular in the gay male community are described here; the first is related to body building, and the others are considered club drugs.

Steroids

Anabolic steroids are synthetic substances related to the male sex hormones (androgens) that promote skeletal muscle growth and development of male sexual characteristics. Steroids are taken orally or by injection, and its street names include andro, anabols, arnies, gym candy, balls, bulls, and juice.

Although some steroid use is related to combating weight loss due to HIV/AIDS, many gay men use steroids to develop the "perfect body," developing an obsession with looking big. According to Bergeron (2000), body image and size are often connected to whether or not gay men feel attractive and desirable. Therefore, steroid use can be tied to body image and overcoming feelings of insecurity. Long-term use of steroids can cause several types of medical problems, including diabetes and liver damage, among others. Potential emotional complications include agitation and anger (known as "roid rage"), anxiety, and psychosis.

GHB (Gamma-Hydroxybutyrate)

GHB is a colorless, odorless, powerful, and fast-acting central nervous system depressant. Users report that GHB has euphoric and sedative qualities in a party environment. Common names for GHB are liquid ecstasy, G, Georgia Home Boy, and Grievous Bodily Harm. GHB's analogs (substances that produce GHB in the body) include Blue Nitro, Revivarant, Thunder Nectar, Weight Belt Cleaner, SomatoPro, and G3.

GHB is often synthesized in household laboratories and its ingredients include floor cleaning products, nail polish removers, and super glue removers. GHB comes in liquid, powder, and capsule forms. The liquid form of GHB is most commonly mixed with water and sipped. In powder form, dose strength is fairly uniform but, in liquid form, GHB concentration varies widely. Potential dangers include overdosing, especially when mixed with alcohol or other drugs, particularly depressants. Addiction can develop from regular use.

Ketamine (Ketamine Hydrochloride)

Ketamine is a dissociative anesthetic with the power to separate the mind from the body and diminish pain. Ketamine produces dreamy effects similar to those produced by picncyclidine (PCP) and is hallucinogenic in higher doses. Street names include Special K, Vitamin K, and K.

Depending on the amount, ketamine can induce a range of reactions, from feelings of pleasant weightlessness to out-of-body or near-death experiences. Ketamine is prized for its dissociative high, and it is often used in combination with other drugs. Some users say it has an aphrodisiac effect and lowers sexual inhibitions. Although the high wears off after 2 hours, mental acuity and muscle coordination are impaired for up to 24 hours. Other dangers include "k-holes," in which users become immobilized. Severe k-holes stop respiration. Other risks include psychological or physical dependence.

Ecstasy (3, 4-Methylenedioxymethamphetimine)

Ecstasy is a widely abused synthetic drug and, although it is an amphetamine derivative, its effects resemble mescaline. Nicknames include X, E, XTC, and MDMA. Generally, ecstasy comes in pill or capsule form, and the high lasts from 4 to 8 hours. People who use ecstasy report a feeling of euphoria, lowered inhibitions, an increase of mood sensitivity, empathy, and energy. Users say they are friendlier, happier, and more connected to other people when high.

As with any drug, ecstasy contains impurities or is diluted with other drugs, such as para-methoxy amphetamine (PMA), PCP, and methamphetamine. Complications include dehydration, heat strokes, and heart attacks, which can occur while dancing. Long-term use can lead to brain damage. Ecstasy can render antidepressants ineffective.

Crystal Methamphetamine

Crystal methamphetamine is a form of amphetamine (speed), and it releases very large amounts of dopamine. Common names for crystal methamphetamine include crystal, crystal meth, Crissy, Tina, crank, and speed. Crystal in powder form is snorted. It is also smoked, injected, and booty bumped (inserted in the anus).

The effects of crystal methamphetamine can last up to 12 hours. People who use crystal report a feeling of being sharp, talkative, in control, and better able to concentrate. Users also report that crystal heightens sexual arousal and increases stamina by delaying orgasm, and they report highly intense orgasms. However, after long-term use, the urge to ejaculate becomes all-consuming. Impotence is a long-term consequence, and users develop "crystal dick," which is the inability to have an erection.

Because crystal is very powerful, the post-high crash leads to depression, anger, and irritability. Long-term use can cause paranoia and delusions, and it can lead to permanent brain damage, especially in areas related to memory and mood. Because users report caring less

Case Study 4.5 (Roberto, continued from Case Study 2.6)

Even though Roberto describes crystal meth as a "white man's drug," he started using it four years ago. In a recent group session, one of the other group members, David, talked about his boyfriend giving him crystal for the first time, and that he had a good time. Roberto angrily says, "Of course it's fun. Can you name a drug that isn't? Stay away from that one. It'll kick you to the curb faster than anything."

Roberto talks about his addiction to crystal for the first time, adding, "It was fun for me at first, too. The sex was incredible. When I wasn't having sex, I could keep my mind focused on one project at a time. Then, the projects got out of control. One time I brushed the bathroom wall for three hours with a toothbrush, and I did only one tile. After a few months, sex wasn't fun anymore. I became a bottom because I got crystal dick. Nothing else mattered except having sex. One time I masturbated for hours and noticed my sheets were wet. When I looked down, there was blood on the sheets. As if that wasn't bad enough, I started thinking people were following me and looking in my window. That's when I went for treatment. But 2 months before that, I went to the doctor. He didn't notice the scabs on my face, from digging. I was hoping he would say something to me. I would have gotten off of it then."

A client telling his story has a much greater impact on other group clients than anything you, as a therapist, can tell them about drug abuse. How could you acknowledge Roberto's courage for talking about his addiction for the first time without shaming David, who admitted to using crystal? Would you educate the group about crystal, or would you trust in the group process to help an admitted crystal user? What referrals might you give to David, if any, and would you do it in a group session or would you ask him to have an individual session?

about safer sex when high on crystal, using this drug often leads to high-risk sexual activities. Moreover, when crystal is booty bumped, it is usually mixed with butter, causing latex to erode. So, even when condoms are used, booty bumping carries risk of HIV transmission.

We discuss Roberto's reaction to another group member using crystal in Case Study 4.5.

Substance Abuse Treatment

Although an in-depth discussion of substance abuse treatment is beyond the scope of this book, here we offer an overview of treatment of addiction, and we focus on interventions that can be made in conjunction with substance abuse treatment and for people in recovery.

Recently, an increasing number of substance abuse treatment options have been extended to lesbians and gay men. Further, most cities have self-help groups for various types of addiction specifically for lesbians and gay men, and the Internet offers virtual self-help groups. This array of choices makes it easier for you to offer referrals to lesbian and gay male clients.

For substance abuse treatment programs, the biggest challenge often involves the staff's limited knowledge about sexual orientation issues. In fact, clients have mentioned that they have had to educate staff about lesbian/gay issues. It is therefore helpful to empower clients. When clients seek treatment, encourage them to ask if the program has lesbian/gay staff, current lesbian/gay clients, and programs specifically for lesbians and gay men. Many lesbians and gay men choose not to disclose their sexual orientation in treatment, but nondisclosure is a factor in relapse. Interestingly, Cabaj (1996) indicates that some characteristics of addiction resemble internalized homophobia. These attributes include denial, fear, anger, anxiety, depression, guilt, shame, isolation, and hopelessness. When lesbian/gay clients are willing to address issues related to sexual orientation, they are more likely to stay sober.

Although including one's family of origin is generally helpful in treating addiction, encouraging clients to include family members is not necessarily indicated for lesbian and gay clients. Moreover, pressuring clients to come out during family sessions during early recovery can be harmful because they may not be ready to come out, and others are not ready to handle rejection or hostility. Therefore, treatment related to family of origin should be paced slowly, and exploring reticence to include the clients' families of origin in family sessions can uncover other issues.

Although there are more public role models for adolescent clients today, the relative lack of community role models may increase their sense of isolation, which can lead to alcohol and drug use. Lesbian and gay youth may also use alcohol and drugs to escape from bad situations at home and at school, and they may be experiencing depression. These lesbian and gay youth are at particular risk because of the possibility of acting impulsively when high, which could lead to, among other consequences, intentional or accidental overdose.

As with adolescents, elderly lesbians and gay clients experience increased risk for substance abuse. Alcohol- and drug-related issues may be difficult to assess and treat, but you should take a history and assess current use of substances so that you can determine if clients are abusing alcohol or drugs. Greater social isolation and decreased mobility due to aging can significantly diminish contact with a social support system, which can lead to alcohol or other drug abuse. Elderly lesbians and gay men are also at risk for prescription drug abuse.

If you have lesbian/gay clients who are struggling with addiction, several behavioral interventions are effective for relapse prevention. For instance, internal and external triggers should be assessed because general triggers and triggers unique to lesbians and gay men can lead to relapse. Internal triggers unique to lesbians and gay men include distress about self-disclosure of sexual orientation or fear of discovery. External triggers include societal discrimination; going to parks, bars, and bathhouses/sex clubs; attending social gatherings; taking part in gay community activities such as Gay Pride; and surfing the Internet. For some clients, even going to the gym can be a trigger.

For lesbian and gay alcoholics, one of the more challenging aspects is learning how to live well without drinking in a society saturated with alcohol. You should encourage clients to avoid situations and people who promote alcohol use. Because this means giving up people and places associated with drinking, you should prepare clients for the possibility that it could result in the loss of their current social group. It is important to note that leaving the bar scene can lead to an increased sense of isolation. Therefore, you should periodically assess for socialization and involvement with others as a form of relapse prevention. It is also helpful to intervene in ways to help boost clients' confidence, so they can learn to be around others in a social setting without the use of substances. Because clients may be uncomfortable meeting new people without alcohol or drugs, role playing is a useful tool.

Substance abuse treatment tends to be most effective when the focus is on clients' present circumstances—including situations that lead to relapse—rather than on issues related to the past. This approach helps ensure that clients learn new, healthier coping strategies (Cabaj, 1996). Learning to socialize without alcohol or other drugs, however, can be a long and difficult process. One intervention is to give clients incrementally more challenging homework. The first task may simply be to go to an alcohol-free social event or to say hello to a stranger at a coffeehouse, progressing to the point where clients can ask others on a date. In addition, you can help clients find alternative places to social-ize, which means you need to be aware of organizations and referrals in your area.

You may wish to refer lesbian and gay clients to 12-step programs that are general or primarily lesbian/gay. General 12-step groups usually welcome lesbians and gay men, but some lesbian and gay clients do not feel comfortable attending nongay meetings. Therefore, many clients prefer referrals to gay/lesbian 12-step groups. You should encourage clients to go where they feel comfortable. Over time, many clients find that they are just as comfortable in primarily heterosexual groups. Moving to a nongay group could result from a higher degree of comfort with heterosexuals, but it could also reflect other moti-vations, such as anxiety about being in a gay environment. Thus, reasons for moving from one group to another should be explored.

Finally, Alcoholics Anonymous and Narcotics Anonymous have "roundups," which are annual conferences and celebrations for sober lesbians and gay men. The conferences include keynote speakers and break-out sessions on various topics related to addiction, recovery, and being lesbian/gay, as well as a social component.

Eating Disorders

An in-depth discussion of treatment for eating disorders is beyond the scope of this book. In this section, however, we provide you with an overview of issues related to eating disorders among lesbians and gay men.

It has been suggested that lesbians might be less prone to eating disorders than heterosexual women because of less emphasis on body image among lesbians. Researchers offered that less focus on body image and lower levels of body dissatisfaction and dieting among lesbians support this conjecture. Heffernan (1996), however, did not find support for this notion in her research. She found that the level of bulimia nervosa in her lesbian sample was close to the rate for heterosexual women. For the lesbian subjects sampled by Heffernan (1996), there appeared to be a stronger relationship in using food as a way to subdue negative emotions, rather than using food as a way to deal with body dissatisfaction. Moreover, binge eating could be a maladaptive coping strategy for lesbians to manage stress. Finally, Heffernan reported that rates of dieting among the lesbians in her sample were not significantly different than rates among heterosexual women.

Eating disorders have traditionally been thought of as women's diseases. Several studies, however, have found an incidence of eating disorders among men. Two studies found that the majority of men with eating disorders were either gay or had some conflict about their sexual orientation (Herzog, Norman, Gordon, & Pepose, 1984; Schneider & Agras, 1987). Herzog, Newman, and Warshaw (1991) found that physical attractiveness and physical appearance are highly valued among gay men, and any resulting body dissatisfaction places these men at greater risk than heterosexual men for eating disorders. One possible explanation is that both gay men and heterosexual women are seeking to attract men, and men have been shown to be more concerned with the physical attractiveness of partners than women (Hatfield & Sprecher, 1986).

Siever's (1996) research supports previous studies in comparing rates of eating disorders among heterosexual men and gay men, but he notes that internalized homophobia has not been researched as a factor in contributing to eating disorders among gay men. Some lesbians reported less stress with respect to body dissatisfaction and less difficulty with aberrant eating behaviors after they came to terms with their sexual orientation. The interactions of these phenomena are not clear, and more research is necessary.

When working with lesbian and gay clients who have eating disorders, it is important to identify identity issues related to being lesbian/gay that fuel the problem. Although cognitive-behavioral treatment works well for clients with eating disorders, you should assess and explore sexual history, feelings about being lesbian or gay, and level of social support.

❖ HIV/AIDS

In working with lesbian and gay male clients, it is important for you to be familiar with the impact of HIV (Human Immunodeficiency Virus) and AIDS (Acquired Immune Deficiency Syndrome) on individuals and the community. This section covers topics related to risk for sero-conversion, psychological factors relating to disease progression, adjustment to HIV/AIDS, depression, euthanasia, and the social consequences of AIDS on the gay community.

In her article on the social consequences of AIDS, Cassens (1985) asked readers to consider several notions about the disease. Although her article was written in the early phase of the epidemic, her ideas still apply:

> Consider the fears and uncertainty of the gay man diagnosed with AIDS. For some men, the major decision will be with whom and when to share the news of diagnosis. . . . The time has finally come when disclosure of sexual orientation is no longer an option, and the reactions of family and friends must be confronted.
>
> Add then to these grim cloaks of certain death and possible rejection by family yet another mantle, that of guilt. . . . Fear and guilt combine to produce inordinate levels of anxiety in both those with and those who believe they have AIDS, often preventing them from effectively coping with their illness.
>
> Guilt further magnifies the sense of isolation and estrangement many gay men have experienced throughout their lives. . . . He may, in fact, feel he is unworthy to receive care. The limited knowledge of the social life of the gay community . . . impairs the practitioner's ability to comprehend and address the social ramifications of the disease. (p. 768)

Clients entering your office may be confronted by these issues and, although progress has been made to extend the lives and quality of life for people with AIDS, there is still no cure. Highly active antiretroviral therapy (HAART) fails to work for many people, and the arduous task of adhering to a strict medication regimen is not always easily followed.

Discussing HIV/AIDS in therapy has become especially important because, despite of many years of education and outreach, rates of HIV infection are on the rise. According to the Centers for Disease Control (2001), HIV infection rates have increased in several U.S. cities. The incidence rate among African American gay men is reported to be 15%, so 15 out of 100 African American gay men are infected with HIV each year.

Risk Factors for HIV-Negative Gay Men

The high rate of infection means that therapists need to understand and educate clients about HIV-prevention and other HIV-related issues. Weiss (1997) notes,

> Among gay men, the relationship to HIV/AIDS is undoubtedly present and takes on varying forms—being positive, being negative, not having been tested, fearful of having been infected, fearful of becoming infected, guilt-ridden for being infected, guilt-ridden for not being infected, caring for those who are infected, and mourning those who have died. HIV/AIDS play a role in many of the decisions made by gay men . . . where to live, whom to become intimate with, and whom to tell they are gay. (p. 32)

Although younger men are affected by HIV, it has had a particularly harsh impact on middle-aged and elderly gay men. Gay men in age groups that have survived the epidemic must contend with simultaneous, often conflicting emotions. Survivor's guilt includes a combination of relief, guilt, and confusion. Many of these gay men have lost a major part of their support system, resulting in isolation. Unfortunately, loneliness is a risk factor associated with having unprotected sex, which can lead to infection (Martin & Knox, 1997).

In addition, clients can develop post-traumatic stress, which has several symptoms that could increase sexual risk. Many people with posttraumatic stress disorder (PTSD) experience numbing, feelings of detachment, and difficulty concentrating, along with anxiety. These symptoms can lead to clients making poor decisions regarding safer sex. Thus, it is important to assess for PTSD when working with clients who have lost loved ones to AIDS. Two other factors related to sexual risk taking are a bleak outlook toward the future and lack of current life satisfaction (Kalichman, Kelly, Morgan, & Rompa, 1997). These factors lead to a reduced motivation to initiate and maintain safer sex practices. Consider the following quote by a young man who wrote to an advice column in the AIDS magazine *A & U*:

> It scares me to see how many people in the gay community promote barebacking and other forms of unprotected sex. . . . I've always used condoms when having sex with others but I am guilty of having multiple partners. I'm like the rest of the world, often giving in to the sense of emptiness I sometimes feel, which I use as an excuse to compromise my well being. So I have practiced "unsafe" safe sex. I'm still HIV-negative. However, in light of (this) current trend I'm seriously reconsidering my sex life. . . . It scares me . . . because these people have taken away my ability to delude myself into being okay with my own unsafe sex practices. But I should be grateful to them, since their calls have given me a chance to change; they have served as a wakeup call. (Gale, 2001, p. 20)

One implication for counseling is to be aware that clients might slip into despair. Some clients talk about missing dead friends and wishing to join them. They may be overwhelmed with grief, and you will need to address safety as well as grief and loss. Another factor associated with sexual risk taking is the loss of a primary partner. Mayne, Acree, Chesney, and Folkman (1998) found that a period of increased sexual risk taking is related to the death of a partner; this period, rather than occurring at the point of bereavement, tends to happen several months later, especially among men who develop new relationships.

Treatment considerations include helping clients become aware that new relationships could lead to unsafe sexual practices. Furthermore, you should be aware that clients with high levels of social support and unchanged levels of alcohol or drug use are still at risk for unsafe sexual behavior (Mayne, Acree, Chesney, & Folkman, 1998). McKirnan, Ostrow, and Hope (1996) point out that sexuality is an area that has a nonrational, emotional core. Often, unbalanced emotional states minimize feelings of personal vulnerability and increase the chances for impulsive sexual behavior. Many gay men who are diligent about having safer sex find themselves having "slips," or occasional encounters when passion precedes rational thinking.

HIV Testing

Getting tested for HIV can be very stressful, so when clients tell you that they will be getting tested for HIV, you can offer various types of support. Prior to testing, several interventions that are beneficial include providing relaxation training, encouraging clients to express fears related to testing, and assisting with options, such as having friends accompany them to the test site. It can also be helpful to design a plan regarding who to contact if clients test positive. You can also suggest options for the timing of obtaining the test results. For example, you could suggest that they obtain their test results immediately prior to coming to a session. Having a therapy session right after they obtain test results can facilitate your assessment for suicide potential and allow you to begin appropriate crisis intervention. The days and weeks following HIV/AIDS diagnosis is one period when clients are at risk for attempting suicide.

Once diagnosed with HIV, people with HIV/AIDS feel that control has been taken away from them in many aspects of their lives, and they may develop a sense of hopelessness. Because a sense of control has an inverse relationship to depression, you should attempt to empower your lesbian and gay clients to find appropriate areas of control.

Adjustment to an HIV/AIDS Diagnosis

Weiss (1997) notes that being diagnosed with HIV is like dealing with a series of losses. Some losses are experienced immediately, whereas others are feared future losses. One loss that is both actual and feared simultaneously is the loss of life image, because people with HIV can no longer take physical health for granted. The certainty of a future becomes shakable. Long-term plans are shelved or scrapped. The dreams of being in a long-term relationship fade, and prior assumptions about what it means to have a career, a loving partner, and a long life are eclipsed.

Reactions to an HIV-positive diagnosis are similar to those of other grief reactions, and they include several stages. These stages are not linear and may be revisited. The first stage includes shock and denial, followed by a period marked by anger, guilt, self-pity, and anxiety. Bargaining, which follows the stage of depression, ultimately leads to acceptance (Ostrow, 1997).

An HIV/AIDS diagnosis often brings up feelings that are similar to those related to the stigma of being lesbian or gay. In fact, the process of adjusting to an HIV diagnosis parallels the coming out process in many ways. Newly HIV-diagnosed clients deal with revived shame and losses related to a prior life image. Your clients will also be confronting concerns similar to those when coming out, such as whom to share their diagnosis with, when to tell them, and how to convey the information. Another related similarity between coming out and revealing HIV status involves adjusting to a new identity. Weiss (1997) observes that some men intertwine a gay identity with an HIV identity. As a result, many gay men see HIV as a punishment for having sex with other men. This belief, as Weiss remarks, leads to problems related to sexuality and spirituality.

Rabkin et al. (1997) examined the role of social support to counter hopelessness and depression, and they found that social support is particularly important as a buffer to stress. They note that mental health professionals also play a role in the containment of Axis I disorders by providing direction, guidance, and counseling for clients and caregivers. Katz et al. (1996) agree, noting that people with HIV/AIDS who are not depressed could experience a preventive and overall beneficial effect on their well-being from mental health care.

After the initial diagnosis, persons with HIV eventually resume dealing with issues related to living. As they adjust to day-to-day issues, challenges resurface with respect to dating, relationships, and work. We illustrate such a challenge in Case Study 4.6.

Another issue with which people with HIV must sometimes deal is becoming too sick to work; as a result, they lose a part of their identity. When clients have to leave work, it is important to help them adjust to a nonworking life. This process would include grief work over lost jobs and loss of identity. A more recent challenge for people with AIDS is when they reenter the workforce. After adjusting to a life without work, the prospect of returning to work has been buoyed by recent advancements in medical treatment for AIDS. We identify these problems in Case Study 4.7.

Case Study 4.6 (John)

John, a 33-year-old African American client, learned he was HIV-positive 2 years ago. He hasn't dated since he learned he was positive, and he is thinking about dating again. Recently, John met someone on the Internet, and the two have been chatting online for a couple of weeks. He is thinking about asking him on a date. "I haven't dropped the bomb yet because I don't know if he's positive. A couple of guys were interested in me until I told them. I want to tell Steven before we have sex, but I'm afraid I'll scare him away. So do I tell him before the first time and possibly scare him before he gets to know me? If I don't tell him, he will be pissed. But since I always use condoms, should I wait until after our first time?"

How can you help John sort out these complex issues that involve fear of rejection and abandonment? If you react negatively to the possibility of John not telling Steven he is HIV-positive before they have sex, what do you do with those feelings in session? Do you give him answers to his questions?

Topics to explore include helping John express his fear of rejection as well as his frustration with finding a partner. You can help him to decide whether to limit dating exclusively to individuals with HIV. It is important to empathize with concerns about dating and offer referrals to social organizations and support groups that offer options for people with HIV/AIDS.

Responses to People Adjusting to an HIV/AIDS Diagnosis

Many people who have adjusted to having HIV/AIDS feel that they can influence its course. In their study on adjustment to HIV, Ross, Hunter, Condon, Collins, and Begley (1994) note that most participants in their study felt that they could influence the course of HIV through diet and exercise. Thus, clients motivated to make lifestyle changes may reduce or stop alcohol consumption, implement stress management strategies, get sufficient rest, and maintain a high level of social support.

Case Study 4.7 (Bill)

Bill is a 47-year old Caucasian client who has been in individual therapy for 1 year. He has been HIV-positive for 12 years and, when his health declined, he started receiving supplemental security income (SSI) for his disability. With his HAART medications, however, he has been feeling better, with normal T-cells and virtually no HIV virus detected in his blood.

Bill is able to go back to work, but he is afraid that his medications could stop being effective. He is also fearful that he will get neuropathy as a side effect of the medication and that the pain could render him disabled again. Bill is also worried that fatigue or an opportunistic infection will force him to take long leaves of absence, and he is concerned that he will be unable to afford rent and food if he has gaps in his income. In addition to feeling fearful, Bill is angry that he had adjusted to the thought of dying, and he had made end-stage plans and paid for his funeral. Now, he has to readjust to living, including thinking about getting a job, even though he is concerned about when his health will fail again.

It is not uncommon to feel upset when adjusting to the thought of living. Clients have spent years winding down and getting their affairs in order only to find out, as several clients have described it, that the rug has been pulled out from under them. How would you deal with Bill's fear and anger? One option is to help him frame his situation in terms of a grief reaction to the abrupt changes in his life. Would you spend more time helping him to express his anger, or would you focus on reframing his thoughts so that he can see the good in the situation? How would you educate him about grieving and help him grieve?

Researchers Hays, Magee, and Chauncey (1994) asked persons with AIDS what actions from their support system they considered to be helpful and unhelpful. One unhelpful action the respondents noted is to treat them with sympathy. The individuals with HIV/AIDS said they do not wish to be patronized or treated with pity. Rather, they favor self-empowerment. So, part of your role in working with individuals with HIV/AIDS is to act as an advocate and a source of hope, encouragement, and compassion.

Individuals with HIV/AIDS also considered therapists questioning their doctors' care to be unhelpful (Hays, Magee, & Chauncey, 1994). If you question the quality of a client's medical care, you need to walk a fine line between suggesting a second opinion and raising doubts about the care they are receiving. It is impossible for therapists to stay current on all medical issues, so it is more important to know the resources available to assist people with HIV, especially those who are newly diagnosed, than to know about particular medical treatments and clinical drug trials. Moreover, medical issues are beyond the scope of practice for mental health clinicians. It is still helpful, however, to be knowledgeable about the types of opportunistic infections and the side effects of medications so you can offer referrals when necessary.

The act considered to be most helpful among respondents was expressing love and concern through deeds or words. Because it is the most appreciated response, your kind words and deeds will foster a solid therapeutic alliance. Along with words, there are other acts that can strengthen the therapeutic relationship. When clients' health does not permit them to come to session, one accommodation is to conduct sessions in the hospital, in their homes, or by phone. Consider adjusting your 24-hour policy for canceled sessions. At times, allowances should be made for clients who do not feel well enough to come to session or who make last-minute doctor's appointments that conflict with therapy appointments. Offering a sliding scale or free therapy is a consideration for clients with HIV/AIDS. It is ethical practice to contribute to the community in some way, and offering low- or no-fee services for those with the financial hardship is one way to make a contribution.

A beneficial intervention, as noted by individuals with HIV/AIDS, includes providing encouragement through positive statements concerning the ability to cope with the disease (Hays, Magee, & Chauncey, 1994). So, part of your range of responses should include providing positive statements for effective coping skills demonstrated by persons with HIV/AIDS. For instance, you can observe improvements in mental wellness, energy level, and self-care. A helpful factor cited by persons with HIV/AIDS is providing them with an opportunity for reciprocating the help that has been given to them. Reciprocating allows clients to maintain a sense of dignity. One way to put clients in a position to reciprocate is to place them in a support or therapy group because these settings provide opportunities to help others. Another way to allow for reciprocity is to be flexible with your gift policy. You may wish to accept small handmade gifts or tokens from clients who cannot pay.

Grimes and Cole (1996) observe that people with HIV/AIDS relate quality of life to level of self-help. Implications for therapy include advocating independence with respect to daily living. A simple way to equate self-help with quality of life is to remind clients that coming in for therapy is a form of self-care, and that the decision to do so has influenced their lives. Other useful actions reported by persons with HIV/AIDS include providing a philosophical perspective, interacting naturally, and providing information and solicited advice (Hays, Magee, & Chauncey, 1994). For example, discussing existential aspects of life or clients' philosophy or spirituality in relation to HIV can be very beneficial. Regarding the wish to be treated naturally, it is possible to act naturally in counseling with few constraints.

The Impact of HIV/AIDS on Identity Development

People with HIV/AIDS are likely to be living in two life stages simultaneously. In addition to dealing with challenges involved in their chronological developmental stage, Linde (1994) notes that AIDS disrupts the natural flow of life because it forces most individuals to prematurely face death and dying. They are forced to think about issues such as retirement, social security benefits, burial, wills, and other aspects of the final stages of life. When clients approach the end stage of their lives, you should broach the subject of making choices about end-stage decisions. Termination issues should be discussed openly so that the clients' dignity, as well as the authenticity of communication, is maintained. Another subject that should be discussed is funeral arrangements. For example, clients may wish to discuss the possibility for the therapist and/or group members to attend or speak at their funerals.

You can assist clients by discussing referrals to attorneys (who can draw up living wills and designate power of attorney to friends or family members) and funeral homes, but clients may ask you whom you think they can trust. If you are aware of attorneys or agencies that provide low-cost or free services, you will be better equipped to make these types of referrals. Often, local gay and lesbian centers offer low- or no-cost legal services. If you are aware of gay-friendly funeral homes, you can also assist your clients with this referral. Providing support and encouragement for clients in end-stage planning is a difficult but necessary task.

According to Linde (1994), having HIV may lead to self-evaluation and, if the developmental crises encountered are successfully traversed, personal growth may result. In fact, many individuals who have HIV/AIDS make productive changes. Often, once these end-stage tasks are behind them, persons with HIV/AIDS are left to enjoy many facets of life and focus on living rather than dying.

HIV/AIDS and Depression

In general, it is important to distinguish between clinical depression and depression due to the illness or to side effects of medication, and you should refer clients with depression for a medical evaluation. Furthermore, a neuropsychological referral may be indicated because HIV affects the brain and central nervous system (Ostrow, 1997). Although studies suggest that people who have adjusted to an AIDS diagnosis are at no greater risk for depression, many lesbians and gay men will experience depression as a consequence of having HIV/AIDS. Further, as noted previously, HIV-related depression is often related to unemployment, developing symptoms of AIDS, and lack of social support.

Markowitz et al. (1995) compared the effectiveness of two types of therapy to treat depression. They defined the first, labeled *interpersonal psychotherapy,* as brief therapy, the aim of which is to help clients link mood to events and to subsequent changes in their social environment. Therapists ask clients to discuss events and situations that are causing depressed feelings and then to categorize them into one of four areas: grief, role dispute, role transition, or interpersonal deficits. By using specific interventions and staying in the here and now, therapists direct clients toward what clients wish to achieve and the options available for achieving them.

Markowitz et al. (1995) compared interpersonal therapy to *supportive psychotherapy.* They defined supportive psychotherapy as nondirective, Rogerian (person-centered) psychotherapy with educational elements to address depression and HIV. They found that, although both types of therapy were effective, interpersonal psychotherapy directed toward specifically treating depression was more effective than supportive psychotherapy. The researchers found that significant improvement occurred within 16 interpersonal psychotherapy sessions, with mood especially being improved.

Suicide and Euthanasia

When you work with people who have HIV/AIDS, you will likely see clients who have a strong wish to die. A distinction should be made, however, between suicidal ideation due to mental anguish and the desire for euthanasia. Ultimately, it is best to think beforehand about how you will react to clients who express a wish to die. You have an ethical obligation to report clients who are in imminent danger of killing themselves (see Chapter 7 for a discussion of ethical considerations), but some clients who are not in an imminent danger of killing themselves will express a wish to end their own lives, and you will find yourself in the position of exploring feelings and decisions with them.

In general, people who are facing a life-threatening, chronic disease feel suicidal at some point(s) during the course of the disease. Rabkin, Remien, Katoff, and Williams (1993) found that one third of people with AIDS who have lived with the disease for more than 3 years revealed thoughts about wanting to die, and one fourth of the subjects considered suicide as a future option. O'Connor (1997) notes that risk factors for suicide include isolation, substance abuse, history of psychiatric illness or suicide attempts, and major losses. It is important to consider lethality level high when any of these factors is present.

Clients may mention that they have the means to commit suicide, such as having enough drugs on hand to kill themselves when things get too painful. In these cases, because clients have the means and a plan to commit suicide, lethality level appears high. However, the thought of suicide is sometimes a form of coping, and clients may view this as having security and control over their lives. Indeed, hoarding medication or making other life-ending plans are ways in which clients exert a sense of control over when to end the battle against their disease, which can be a comfort to them. Van den Boom (1995) found a correlation between arranging for euthanasia and better adaptation to having AIDS. Clients who discussed euthanasia as an option more often utilized active coping mechanisms and social support than clients who did not discuss euthanasia as an option. And people do not always attempt euthanasia alone. It is not uncommon for clients to make pacts with friends and relatives to assist with euthanasia (Green, 1995). The decision to end their lives is rarely made in isolation, and in a study by Van den Boom (1995), the majority of people with AIDS who contemplated euthanasia felt it was a "well-considered decision" (p. S183).

AIDS-Related Bereavement

With respect to the death of clients' partners, there are continued issues of invisibility and lack of support for survivors. Due to the devaluation of same-gender relationships, friends and family are often not aware of the magnitude of the loss. This situation places additional strain on surviving partners, and it contributes to depression and anxiety amidst grief and loss.

With respect to HIV/AIDS, issues include discrimination, survivor's guilt, and complicated grief reactions. Much of the work with survivors includes facilitating expression of loss in regard to losing their spouses and outliving their partners. This involves initiating discussions about what the clients miss about them, "talking" to deceased loved ones using the empty chair technique, asking clients to bring photographs of their deceased partner to session, and eliciting stories involving the past. It is also helpful to encourage letter-writing and journaling of thoughts and feelings.

To prevent overwhelming feelings of grief over the course of a day, one option is to talk about containment. To contain their grief, clients are asked to limit periods of grief to a certain time of day and a certain length of time. When painful feelings surface, clients can mentally note that they will grieve during the designated time at their designated place, such as when they are at home, in a therapy session, or with friends.

It is important for clients to be able to express feelings of anger and grief. Many stories seem beyond belief and, as with survivors of other types of trauma, their stories may be all they have. Clients experiencing global loss have a decreasing ability to trust (Nord, 1997), and it becomes important for you to establish a stable environment for people who have lost most, if not all, of their support system. It is equally important to be sensitive to clients' fear of abandonment. Even telling clients about an upcoming vacation, for example, can create a sense of dread for them. Clients who are experiencing global loss appear calm when they may actually be emotionally overwrought or numb. Eliciting disclosure of their losses may lead to clients deeply feeling and experiencing their losses during session. Sometimes, clients mention that they do not wish to cry because they are afraid they will never stop crying. Comments such as these are actually preparation for grieving, and clients could be evaluating your response to assess their perceived level of emotional safety.

Referrals to bereavement groups are generally advantageous. In many cities, community centers offer bereavement groups specifically for people who have lost their partners to AIDS, whereas some centers offer general bereavement groups. Timing is an important factor in referring clients to a bereavement group, and clients generally need to wait several months of more after the death of their loved one before they are comfortable attending a bereavement group.

❖ SUMMARY

Psychotherapy for lesbians and gay men requires specific treatment considerations. One framework for working with lesbians and gay clients is to explore universal themes in terms of how these issues are perceived and experienced by lesbians and gay men. These themes include familial and social relationships, spirituality, occupation, and relationship to self. Included in relationship to self are many treatment issues to consider, including issues related to coming out and loss of life image, as well as substance abuse and eating disorders. Clients and the lesbian/gay community are affected by HIV/AIDS, and clinical issues include risk factors for HIV-negative gay men, HIV testing, adjusting to an HIV diagnosis, stages of HIV, regaining health due to HAART medications, end-stage decisions, and bereavement.

In the case studies, Ken faced his parent's discomfort about his sexual orientation, and his parents have taken steps toward their own "coming out" process. Ken has also found his first lesbian friend who is open about her sexual orientation. Angela has been sorting out her feelings about her religious upbringing. Her anger is a sign of moving toward reconciling a spiritual identity with her lesbian identity. Brian has taken a large step in the coming out process by thinking about coming out to his mother. In group, Roberto admitted that he has an addiction and chastised another client for trying crystal methamphetamine, a highly addictive drug that is popular among some gay men, particularly in urban areas.

John learned he was HIV-positive a year ago and is beginning to consider dating again. Bill, who has had AIDS for 12 years, is dealing with the challenges of reentering the workforce after being on disability. Bill's and John's situations are strikingly similar because their challenges include forging a new social identity, confronting occupational choices, and dealing with dating and relationships.

We considered the first four life tasks in this chapter; in the next chapter, we turn to the topic of same-gender relationships and families headed by lesbians and gay men. The main topics of Chapter 5 are relationship development, roles of the therapist, special issues facing same-gender couples, and assessment and treatment considerations with respect to couples and families.

5

Treatment Issues for Couples and Families

❖ ❖ ❖

For lesbians and gay men who are interested in dating and long-term relationships, there are few relationship role models and socialization rules. So, lesbians and gay men must openly or tacitly create rules for dating and relationships. This situation can become problematic because each person must learn nuances in the dating and relationship realms, and each couple must forge a unique set of relationship rules.

Lesbians and gay men confront the same relationship challenges as heterosexuals, but they approach these challenges differently due to gender role socialization, heterosexism, and homophobia. Furthermore, lesbians and gay men must confront issues unique to them. It becomes the therapeutic task to explore all of these issues and to help lesbian and gay male clients develop the means to improve their relationships.

Many same-gender couples enter therapy with uncertainty and conflict about how to approach relationship challenges. Challenges include how to deal with the division of labor, power differences, legal and financial issues, and possible lack of support from families of origin. Another potential difficulty is when to disclose the nature of their relationship to family, friends, and coworkers.

❖ DEBUNKING SOME CULTURAL NOTIONS ABOUT SAME-GENDER COUPLES

Although myths about same-gender relationships have declined, many misconceptions about the type and quality of their bonds remain. Peplau (1993) explored some of these beliefs about same-gender couples, and we summarize them in this section as well as offer a more realistic picture of same-gender relationships.

One unfounded cultural belief is that lesbians and gay men do not desire lengthy relationships and are unable to sustain them. As early as 1978, however, a landmark study by Bell and Weinberg (1978) found that 40% to 60% of gay male subjects were involved in a committed relationship. As for lesbians, Peplau (1993) found that the percentage of lesbians in long-term relationships was close to 75% across several studies.

Blumstein and Schwartz (1983) conducted a longitudinal study of a large group of lesbian, gay male, unmarried heterosexual, and heterosexual married couples to examine the quality and duration of their relationships. For couples partnered more than 10 years, rates for relationship dissolution were similar: 6% for lesbians, 4% for gay men, and 4% for heterosexual married couples. Thus, it appears that for couples in long-term relationships, sexual orientation is not a factor in relationship termination rates.

Peplau (1993) observes that another false impression is that lesbian and gay male couples cannot be happy because their relationships are dysfunctional and maladaptive. In a study by Peplau and Cocharn (1980), 50 gay men, 50 lesbians, 50 heterosexual men, and 50 heterosexual women were asked about overall relationship satisfaction, how well they liked their partners, and their level of intimacy. On all measures of relationship satisfaction, there were no significant differences noted among the groups.

The subjects were also asked to describe the best and worst aspects of their relationships. The results were forwarded to panels of judges who were not told the sexual orientation of the respondents. When the judges evaluated their responses, they could not correctly identify which statements came from gay men, lesbians, heterosexual men, or heterosexual women. Other studies have validated the findings related to relationship satisfaction (see Peplau, 1993), and these studies suggest that lesbians and gay men have similar rates of relationship satisfaction as heterosexual couples.

Another false assumption is that lesbian and gay relationships have two gender role types—i.e., a "husband" and a "wife." Although role-playing exists for a minority of same-gender couples, this situation is generally not the case. As an example, most household tasks are divided according to the willingness of each person to accept them and the desirability of particular chores (Peplau, 1993).

The final misconception we'd like to mention is that lesbians and gay men in relationships are isolated. To the contrary, lesbian and gay couples develop caring, supportive networks of friends and family. Aura (1985) conducted a study of 50 lesbians and 50 heterosexual women. These subjects were matched for age, education, and number of years in a relationship. Results indicate that both groups had similar levels of social support. Not surprisingly, heterosexual subjects tended to call on biological family to meet their needs, whereas lesbian participants were more likely to call upon their friends. Kurdek (1988) found that lesbian and gay male couples' rate of satisfaction with their social relationships was not significantly different from heterosexuals' rate of satisfaction. Most lesbians and gay men cited their partners and friends as their primary social network but, parting with Aura's findings, 81% of the gay men and 86% of the lesbians listed a mother or sister as a source of support.

❖ RELATIONSHIP STAGES

Understanding the stages of same-gender relationships is useful in providing a conceptual framework for working with couples. In this section, we first provide two models: one for gay male couples and one for lesbian couples. At the end of this section, we discuss the problems that can result from *stage discrepancy*—i.e., when partners do not traverse through the stages at the same rate.

Stages in Gay Male Relationships

McWhirter and Mattison (1984) delineated six stages of gay male relationships. Their model emphasizes major characteristics and challenges within each stage. They caution that not all gay male couples fit these stages, and stages can overlap.

The first stage, *Blending*, occurs during the first year. Major characteristics include *merging*, which involves a discovery of common interests and an avoidance of conflict; and *limerance*, which refers to intense longing, a high frequency of sexual activity, and persistent thinking and powerful feelings about the other person. Fears that the other person could leave emerge in this stage because there has been little time to build a relationship foundation. As a result, the end of limerance is a critical juncture for many couples. Several potential threats to the relationship arise at this time, including jealousy, learning about differences in one another, and no longer overlooking faults of the other person.

Blending gives way to the second stage, *Nesting*. In the second and third years, making a home together becomes a major task. Developing compatibility is another, more difficult, task, and it is often begun amid dawning ambivalence about the relationship. One challenge for couples is to keep their romance alive. Many couples recognize that their love has not diminished; rather, it has changed. It is at this point that the couple can build a relationship foundation in earnest, with a more realistic picture of one another emerging.

The next stage, *Maintaining*, occurs during the third through the fifth years and is characterized by establishing independence, which began in the latter part of the Nesting stage. Former interests that have been put on hold are rediscovered, and new ones are individually developed. The degree of difficulty during this transition depends upon how individuals perceive the establishment of independence. Some couples view this time as the loss of the relationship, and conflict is a way to obtain reassurance that partners still care for one another. Also, partners may drift apart if common interests are not developed. Some couples rethink sexual monogamy, either individually or as a couple. Although a certain amount of independence is being established, the other task of this stage is creating traditions. Each couple forges customs, such as celebrating special events or having weekly dinners with friends. Establishing tradition gives couples a sense of shared history and stability.

Stage four, *Building*, occurs during years 5 through 10. This stage is characterized by collaboration and dependability, along with knowing one another at a deep level. This comfort may lead to neglect of the relationship, and one challenge during this period is to stave off complacency. At the same time, the need to confer on certain matters decreases. If the couple continues to keep open lines of communication, this period becomes a time of continued relationship growth.

Stage five, *Releasing*, occurs in the 11th through the 20th year. The quality that takes center stage is trust. In addition, each partner harbors a higher degree of acceptance toward the other person, without any illusions of being able to change him or her. Friendship and companionship are the hallmarks of this stage, and there is an increasing possibility to fully merge finances. However, the propensity to take one another for granted simultaneously increases. Thus, feelings of loss and sadness about the relationship may emerge.

Neglect toward one another diminishes in *Renewing*, the stage that occurs after the 20th year. Permanence is a given, which provides security. Often, health problems related to aging develop, and these personal problems wax and wane in importance. McWhirter and Mattison note that, in general, closeness is restored during this stage, with a feeling that the relationship is a safe place. In addition to renewal, reminiscence is a hallmark of this stage, which allows the couple to relive happy times.

Stages in Lesbian Relationships

Slater (1995) offered a five-stage model for lesbian relationships. Slater states that lesbian families' sources of stress and strength are influenced by society's views toward their sexual orientation. Hence, the stages are also influenced by society's views. This situation forces couples to devote energy to developing coping strategies to deal with these conditions during the course of their relationships. Slater (1995) further notes that for lesbian couples, family life cycle and identity development are inextricably interwoven, and factors such as ages of the partners and length of time out of the closet affect the duration, tasks, and issues of each stage.

Due to the propensity for women to associate sex with emotional intimacy (Slater & Mencher, 1991), many lesbian couples have a truncated dating period. This situation leaves hastily formed couples unequipped to handle issues that may emerge (Slater, 1995). Individual identity development is enhanced as the relationship grows, however, and individuals' level of internalized homophobia is reduced with increased contact in the lesbian community.

Stage one, *Formation of the Couple*, is often reached after a short dating period. Many lesbians, depending on their age and previous experiences, develop relationships more slowly. In fact, some lesbians know each other as friends, often for many years, before coupling (Slater, 1995). The first task is to build a cohesive bond, causing personal boundaries to loosen. At the same time that they are attempting to build trust, the partners develop a shared method for handling relationship stress and managing conflict. Each partner begins to replace romantic notions of the other with a more realistic view.

Stage two, *Ongoing Couple-hood*, is characterized by the initial passion giving way to deeper intimacy. Partners tend to spend more time together, and each person learns about the other's values and personality. Daily rituals and patterns begin to take on meaning for the couple, and demonstrations of future commitment appear, such as planning for future vacations, beginning a garden, and making mutual friends. As each partner recognizes the risk she has taken, however, the intrepidity of the first stage gives way to fears of disappointment and abandonment. Intense fusion between the partners is often in conflict with the need for separateness. Traversing through the challenges of this stage leads to a more solid relationship foundation. Sexual intimacy is still prevalent, albeit not as intense as it was during the first stage. Nonsexual contact becomes more commonplace, with lesbian couples using various ways to increase their bond.

The third stage is known as *The Middle Years,* and this stage is characterized by feelings of permanency and long-term commitment. The couple forges cohesion and, within this context, partners deepen their trust. As trust increases, they are more willing to critique themselves and change ingrained patterns, with an accompanying willingness to adapt the relationship to each partner's continuing growth. However, the most rewarding aspects of a deepening commitment can give rise to newfound fears. A lifetime commitment means that the partners must accept the other person's limitations. They may feel a heightened sense of loss, with growing fears that vitality within the relationship itself could fade. In this stage, one or both partners may be reaching midlife, creating the possibility for an unstable relationship period. This dual phenomenon, reaching individual mid-life and relationship mid-life, fuels fears of stagnation. Conflict and distance could result if the partners begin to equate the relationship with a restriction on personal growth. On the other hand, one or both partners could commit themselves to avoiding the upheaval that this stage could bring. If

---

Case Study 5.1 (Tom, continued from Case Study 1.4)

Tom, who has been separated from his wife for 4 months, met Jim 2 months ago. Tom tells you that he's in love with Jim and that Jim is everything Tom's ever wanted. Tom spent the previous session extolling Jim's virtues, and he said he wants to move in with Jim. In today's session, Tom is crying about Jim's wish to see other people. He tearfully tells you, "I don't understand it. Everything was going so well. A few days ago, I told him that I loved him, but he didn't say anything. I knew something was wrong. He seemed to pull away after that, and he told me that we should see other people. He must be scared of commitment."

Rather than being afraid of commitment, Jim could have been scared off by Tom moving too quickly. Tom is dating a person that he is sexually attracted to for the first time, which is a task usually accomplished in adolescence. Tom's feelings are like a "first crush," and he is misinterpreting messages that Jim is sending him. So, Tom is rushing into the relationship stage of nesting while Jim considers their relationship to be in the dating phase.

For couples experiencing stage discrepancy, describing relationship stages is a starting point for couples to develop a framework to articulate their needs and to find agreeable solutions. How and when would you approach Tom with information about conflict that arises as a result of being in different relationship stages? Would you recommend couples therapy for Tom and Jim? If you point out to Tom that his identity development has been stunted as a result of coming out later in life, would that be helpful to him?

---

the couple works through fears and ambivalence about staying in relationship, they will find enough strength to overcome this relationship difficulty.

The couple reaches stage four, *Generativity*, after a challenging period, including possibly a relationship crisis. A growing awareness of their own mortality could lead to a search for a deeper sense of relationship purpose. Generativity can also translate into a renewed interest in their children's lives or, for many lesbian couples, a desire to have children for the first time. For others, it translates into new undertakings that will surpass their lifetimes.

A radical shift in priorities, goals, and daily life due to aging and the related task of retirement characterize the fifth stage, *Lesbian Couples Over 65*. With greater amounts of free time when both partners retire, a new negotiation process begins concerning the amount of separateness and togetherness each partner desires. At the same time, many couples have to adjust to health-related changes. Lesbian couples who have been together for many years and are over age 65 grew up during an era of severe repression and discrimination. Thus, there is a greater tendency for these couples, compared with younger couples, to hide their relationship and have a higher degree of internalized homophobia.

Stage Discrepancy

For both gay men and lesbians, traversing through the different stages is not linear. One potential problem occurs when couples are emotionally in different relationship stages (Mattison & McWhirter, 1987). Because each person travels at dissimilar emotional speeds in a relationship, one partner may assume that the other person is in the same stage, when in fact the two are in different stages. This problem arises in Case Study 5.1.

❖ ASSESSMENT AND TREATMENT FOR SAME-GENDER COUPLES

Performing an Assessment

In the initial session, you should perform an assessment to determine presenting problems and relationship history. It is also helpful to explore relationship strengths and areas for improvement based on each partner's perception. An assessment includes questions about communication, friendship and family support, level of commitment, sexual satisfaction, and agreements with respect to sex. It is important to solicit information about prior relationships, history of alcohol and other drug use, their coming out narratives, and current feelings about being lesbian or gay. You should also assess for religious upbringing and current spiritual practices. All of these areas can be sources of relationship strengths and difficulties.

During the assessment, be sure to ask the couple how they met and what initially attracted them to each other. Having couples recount what brought them together sets a positive tone for future sessions and could give them hope for a better relationship. Moreover, the way same-gender couples meet could influence how they approach relationship issues. For example, couples who meet in bathhouses or sex clubs may approach sex outside the relationship differently than couples who meet through mutual friends and who never go to public sexual spaces.

Another part of the assessment is to observe the couple's communication style. For example, noticing which person makes the initial call for an appointment, noticing who generally answers your questions first, and noting the way the couple responds to one another during the session are all valuable pieces of assessment information.

Roles of the Therapist

When providing therapy for same-gender couples, you perform three distinct roles: educator, mediator, and role model. These roles overlap and can be difficult to perform because four sets of dynamics in couples therapy exist simultaneously: the couple dyad, each client with you, and a group of three individuals.

The educator role includes exploring issues such as how internalized homophobia and outside stressors affect the relationship. You may teach the couple about relationship stages and stage discrepancy, how internalized homophobia affects the relationship, and how to resolve differences. You should also teach communication skills, such as assertiveness, to partners who are having difficulties with communication. Teaching clients to dialogue using active listening fosters better communication. You may need to demonstrate active listening in addition to teaching what it is. For deadlocked issues, a difficult but potentially enlightening intervention is to have partners switch roles using reflective listening, with one person advocating from her or his partner's perspective and the other partner acting accordingly. You may also need to teach clients about the value of "I" statements and how to assert themselves without becoming aggressive.

The mediator role emerges when you validate each side of the story, encourage each partner to share feelings with the other person,

---

Case Study 5.2 (Mark and Rick)

Mark and Rick have been together for 10 years. They are entering therapy because they have been experiencing major problems in their relationship. Mark, who has AIDS, called you for the initial appointment. In session, Mark says he found a phone number in Rick's pocket and later caught Rick and another man having sex in their apartment. He says that Rick violated two agreements: there can be no "call-backs" (that is, only anonymous sex with others is allowed), and they cannot have sex with another partner in their apartment. Rick replies that, because of his increasing fear of contracting HIV and their "boring" sex life, he will continue to see Joe, though he agrees not to have sex with Joe in their apartment again.

Is there any way to reach a compromise in this situation? What do you think is really going on in this relationship? If Mark is increasingly dependent on Rick, could this be Rick's way of asserting his independence? What does it mean that Rick is not going to honor their agreement? And what will that do to the relationship?

---

and persuade clients to search for creative and mutually agreeable solutions to problems. Clients often speak of the therapist as being a "referee" in negotiating relationship difficulties. It is critical to be impartial when you help couples to navigate through the myriad issues that surface in relationships. It is easy to relate to one partner more than the other, and using visual and verbal cues to remind yourself of the importance of being impartial can help you be objective. For example, placing your chair in front of the clients so that it is positioned in the middle of the clients' chairs is one reminder.

There may be times where the individuals have such divergent values that compromise, or even agreeing to disagree, may not be possible. In this case, therapy becomes a place for the couple to explore why they are staying together, how much work each person is willing to direct toward the relationship, and how much personal sacrifice each person is willing to make for the sake of the relationship. Sometimes, couples therapy turns into relationship termination counseling, and your role becomes mediator as you help the couple to end the relationship amicably.

You also act as a role model for clients. Modeling respect for individual differences is one way to accomplish this task. Modeling cooperative behavior shows clients how to become involved in each other's decision-making process. Thus, you will actively listen to each partner, show empathy toward each person's experience and feelings, and validate each person's point of view without necessarily agreeing with it. Illuminating the process of modeling respect for clients' divergent attitudes and beliefs is helpful for couples.

Besides acting in these three capacities, it is equally important for you to help same-gender couples develop insight into the source of conflict that lies beneath ostensible problems. These issues include fearing rejection or abandonment, feeling unloved, recapitulating family of origin issues, and needing reassurance. It is useful to point out patterns that you observe. When you suggest that each person take responsibility for escalating conflict, each partner has the opportunity to uncover major issues, as we consider in Case Study 5.2.

Performing Individual Therapy in Couples Therapy

Many clinicians like to do individual therapy with one partner as the other partner observes the interaction. This method is beneficial because partners can develop more empathy for one another and can air their grievances without the usual responses from the partner. Although the emphasis of couples counseling should be on the dynamics of the relationship, individuals bring to the session their own patterns, past, internalized homophobia, and degree of openness about being out. If an individual's problems require a great deal of time or you do not prefer to do individual therapy in couples sessions, you should consider referring the client to individual therapy.

Sources of Stress and Support for Same-Gender Couples

Institutions that provide a foundation for heterosexual marriages can act as barriers to successful same-gender relationships. There is a high degree of variability regarding institutional stress and support for same-gender couples, so it is important to assess the level of support

Case Study 5.3 (Angela, continued from Case Study 4.3)

Jodi, Angela's partner, wants her parents to visit for the holidays. Angela told Jodi that she's not comfortable sleeping with Jodi during their visit. Jodi is angry because she hid the relationship when Angela's family visited them, but she doesn't feel that she should have to do this when it comes to her own family. Angela will not budge, and Jodi said that she's thinking about ending the relationship because she "doesn't want someone who is ashamed of me."

As with Jodi and Angela, many couples hide their relationships when families come for visits, and it is not uncommon for one partner to temporarily move into another bedroom. This situation can be a source of tension for couples. How would you mediate Angela and Jodi's dispute? If you feel that Angela needs to "lighten up," can you prevent this thought from influencing your neutrality? How can you reframe Jodi's belief that Angela is ashamed of *her*?

the couple receives from family of origin, friends, place of worship, and the workplace.

Pointing out problems that result from external stressors, as opposed to poor communication or inadequate coping strategies, allows couples to place some responsibility for relationship difficulties outside of their relationships. Doing so can lead to more cohesion and less relationship strain, as well as provide ways to develop coping strategies to buffer external stress.

Families of Origin

Informing individuals who are contemplating coming out to their families of origin about the risks and rewards of potential family support empowers them in terms of when to reveal the nature of the relationship. For clients whose families reject them for being lesbian or gay, you should help the couple find ways to cope with this additional challenge. A lesbian or gay couple's family of origin can be a source of antagonism between the partners. In Case Study 5.3, only one partner has come out to her family of origin, and conflict is the result.

Not uncommonly, when families of origin who live in other cities have gatherings and celebrations, they either exclude the same-gender partner altogether, have them sleep in separate beds, or ask them to stay at a hotel. Sometimes, family rules for same-gender couples are unspoken. During session discussions about family gatherings, it is important to prompt a discussion of underlying feelings, to find mutually agreeable solutions, and to help the partners respect one another's opinions and beliefs.

On the other end of the spectrum, many families of origin offer a great deal of support. For many couples, one family tends to be more supportive than the other. Thus, same-gender couples have a good chance of receiving support from some members of at least one of the families of origin.

Friends

It is important to appraise couples' support systems. Social support is not only related to relationship satisfaction, as noted previously, but it also affects the strength of each person's commitment to the relationship. One consequence is to encourage the members of same-gender couples to seek support both individually and as a couple. Referring couples to support groups in the community or on the Internet could be valuable because these this kind of support leads to greater relationship satisfaction.

Friends of same-gender couples offer varying degrees of support for their relationships. Sometimes, friends devalue same-gender relationships by failing to treat people involved as couples. However, many couples find a great deal of support for their relationships from friends, and friends attend holy union ceremonies, anniversaries, and other special occasions to honor their relationships.

Places of Worship

Another cultural influence on lesbian and gay relationships is religion. Same-gender couples who have different religious upbringings and beliefs may have difficulty finding a place of worship where they can attend openly as a same-gender couple. Other couples attend a place of worship together but hide their relationship and sexual orientation. Some couples attend lesbian- and gay-affirming places of worship, even though they may not be congruent with their own spiritual beliefs.

The Workplace

At work, lesbian or gay employees might not feel free to discuss relationship problems, stresses, joys, and celebrations. As noted in previous chapters, corporations and government municipalities offer varying degrees of support for same-gender couples in terms of benefits and protection from discrimination.

Differences of opinion can arise in terms of how out the couple wishes to be at each of their workplaces. As with the other topics in this section, negotiation remains key to finding a mutually agreeable solution, and helping the couple to communicate their needs, their fears, and their hopes in a safe environment is crucial.

Influence of Gender Role Socialization

Same-gender couples seek psychotherapy with many of the same issues as heterosexual couples, but their approach differs because of the part that gender role socialization plays. Silverstein (1990) observes that gay male couples tend to accentuate traditionally masculine traits, whereas lesbian couples tend to emphasize traditionally feminine traits. Although numerous examples of gender role nonconformity exist, many lesbians and gay men conform to their respective gender roles in relationships.

For each lesbian or gay man, having a similar gender role socialization to that of her or his partner can lead to relationship challenges. Whereas gay males tend to spurn vulnerability and try to win arguments at their partners' expense (*distancing*), lesbians tend to avoid confronting their partners because they do not want to disrupt relationship harmony (*merging*).

Men are traditionally socialized to be competitive, aggressive, and powerful; in contrast, women are traditionally socialized to be cooperative and to consider their partners first or as equally important. And while men are taught that if there is a problem, they need to fix it, women are taught that if there is a problem, they need to listen to their partners' feelings and to maintain relationship harmony.

When lesbian partners' boundaries loosen to the point where the couple becomes enmeshed, partners can lose their individual identity for the sake of the relationship. Partners who are enmeshed tend to share feelings about problems but not secure resolutions. Fusion can also lead to intolerance of differences between partners (Klinger, 1991) and a collapse of ego boundaries, which results in functioning as a single unit (Gray & Isensee, 1996). As a result, when selfhood is neglected in lesbian relationships, partners attempt to maintain relationship harmony at all costs. Continually sacrificing for the relationship gradually leads to a fissure, however, because of the strain from neglecting one's own needs and desires. And as Ramirez Barranti (1998) remarks, emotional distancing, unresolved conflict, and individual problems lead to a loss of intimacy.

Some research findings challenge these notions of fusion and enmeshment in lesbian relationships; many lesbian couples report high levels of relationship satisfaction (Ramirez Barranti, 1998). Merging can give rise to a sense of connection and create a strong bond. It can also lead to the development of women's' identities rather than suppress them. Moreover, emphasizing connectedness in the couple serves the adaptive function of supporting and protecting the relationship. Slater (1995) adds that fusion is an adaptive process resulting from lack of societal support.

When working with lesbian couples, have them differentiate between the desire for closeness and the importance of taking care of their own needs while still caring for their partners (Gray & Isensee, 1996). When couples find a balance between caring for themselves and their partners, they de-merge to the extent that each individual can assert herself and reduce resentment. You should facilitate dialogue and support each partner's attempt to assert herself, perhaps by adding assertiveness training for couples. Noting the costs to the relationship when unspoken resentments accumulate could lead to exploring ways to talk about their feelings without threatening the other person.

In contrast to lesbian couples, gay male couples are socialized toward competition, independence, and lack of emotional expression. They also tend toward stereotypical male socialization, devaluing tenderness and weakness (George & Behrendt, 1988). Vulnerability is a serious challenge for many male couples; feelings of tenderness, neediness, and hurt are unspoken due to fears of being vulnerable. In regard to sex, the stereotypical male gender role is to be ready for sex anytime. If one or both partners buy into this stereotype, this unrealistic expectation puts an additional strain on the relationship.

However, not all aspects of male socialization are harmful to gay male relationships. Independence and assertiveness, for example, are two areas of potential relationship strength. For gay male couples, part of your task is to help them understand and express their feelings. Moreover, men often funnel feelings of hurt and vulnerability into anger. Thus, one intervention is to help them decipher and express their more vulnerable feelings.

Also, for both lesbian and gay male couples, you should challenge gender role socialization. One way to approach this subject is to inform clients that the outcome of male and female socialization enhances the quality of the relationship as well as harms it. The goal for same-gender couples is to learn to balance the qualities of distancing and merging so that they enhance their relationship intimacy.

In addition to challenging gender role socialization, it is also important to ask about their current and past sex life, as well as to obtain information about sex in prior relationships. Encouraging communication between partners is of prime importance for a good sex life. Sometimes, due to its personal nature, you could recommend discussions as homework so that the couple can discuss the details at home and report on progress or whether resolution has been made in future sessions. You'll find a discussion of sexual dysfunction later in this chapter.

❖ LESBIAN AND GAY PARENTING

Lesbians and gay men face an array of issues when they decide to become parents, and these issues are at the forefront for many lesbians and gays, both individually and as couples. Many lesbians and gay men have children from previous marriages or other heterosexual relationships, and children often become a part of a newly created family headed by same-gender parents. Whether the lesbian/gay families are formed through artificial insemination, adoption, or blending, couples must consider the impact of each of their families of origin, legal issues, and societal discrimination (Baum, 1996). In the remainder of this section, we address the options available to lesbians and gay men if they wish to start a family, and we compare lesbian/gay parenting to nongay parenting. Finally, we discuss blended families.

Options for Having a Child

For lesbians and gay men who are choosing to become parents, several options are available. For lesbians, choices include artificial insemination through known or anonymous donors. Some lesbians prefer that their children know their fathers, so they enlist friends or acquaintances to donate sperm. Other lesbians, wishing to prevent potential custody battles or for other reasons, prefer the anonymity that fertility clinics provide.

Lesbian couples must decide which partner will carry the child. Many lesbian couples decide that each partner will have a child, sometimes using the same donor, thus ensuring a biological tie between mother and child, as well as providing a genetic connection between siblings. For many couples, however, one woman wants to give birth more than her partner. Occasionally, couples inseminate using creative means. For example, for some lesbian couples, one woman is the birth mother for two children, but the fertilized egg of her partner is used for the second child. This situation allows the family to have two children genetically connected by using the same donor, with each partner having a biological child. See Case Study 5.4.

Another issue of concern for lesbians involves the way the couple's family and friends perceive the role of the nonbiological mother. In both same-gender and heterosexual relationships, the focus is on the pregnant woman throughout the pregnancy. In heterosexual relationships, the soon-to-be father receives attention by having a recognizable role. In lesbian relationships, however, close friends may acknowledge the nonbiological mother's role, but others may pay little attention to her. Families of origin and others are often not supportive of the nonbiological mother, although their feelings may change over time. In the meantime, it is possible for the nonbiological mother to feel isolated. This plight is fueled in part because the nonbiological parent has little or no legal rights over the child (Kirkpatrick, 1996).

As with lesbians, gay men have several options when having children. Along with adoption, gay men may choose surrogacy, and options are available regarding which woman carries the child, the rights of the birth mother, and the level of involvement by the birth mother.

Another option is for lesbians and gay men to become coparents. A lesbian or gay man may either be single or in a couple, so there can be two, three, or four coparents. A gay man or couple can be part of the

---

Case Study 5.4 (Angela, continued from Case Study 5.3)

It has been a year since Angela stopped seeing you for individual therapy. Angela had reached most of her goals, and she had come to terms with being a lesbian. Coming out to her family and making good friends are behind her.

The other day, you received a phone call from Angela, who now wants to start couples therapy. She and Jodi are planning for their first child. In their first session, Angela and Jodi ask you for advice about some major decisions. Jodi would like her brother, Hal, to inseminate Angela so that the baby will have a biological tie to Jodi and will have a male role model. Angela would like to have an anonymous donor because she is afraid that Hal might step in to exercise his parental rights.

How would you approach this issue with Angela and Jodi? What other kinds of information would you like to obtain from the couple? If you don't want to offer advice, how would you place the responsibility back on the Angela and Jodi for their choices? If they choose Hal as the father, would you include him in any future sessions?

---

child's upbringing. There are various living arrangements possible. Some coparents live in the same household, and others live nearby or in the same city.

Regarding adoptions, joint adoptions are illegal in many states, so often only one partner can adopt a child. Many times, the adoption process for a legally unmarried individual will occur more quickly if she or he is willing to adopt a child that is an ethnic minority, physically or mentally challenged, or older. Many lesbians and gay men adopt children through international adoptions. International adoptions often require complex paperwork and an ability to travel to the country of origin for an extended period of time prior to the adoption.

Regardless of the insemination or adoption process couples choose, many lesbians and gay men spend months or years finalizing their decision to have a child. Considering the great deal of time preparing for parenthood, many individuals and couples have a dedicated emotional commitment.

Comparing Lesbian or Gay
Parenting with Nongay Parenting

Kirkpatrick (1996) notes that some theorists believe that children of lesbians and gay men experience gender role confusion, sexual identity problems, and psychological disturbances. However, a body of evidence is growing that, in spite of unique challenges, children of lesbian and gay parents are as adjusted as children of heterosexual parents. Furthermore, children of lesbian and gay couples develop in much the same way as children of heterosexual parents, with some variation in attitudes about gender roles and sexual orientation proclivities.

In a review of the literature, Patterson (1994) found support for the notion that children raised in lesbian households have more emotional reactions to stress and a greater sense of well-being than children raised in heterosexual households. One explanation for this phenomenon is that women are socialized to express emotions openly. When two women model emotional expression, this "double-socialization" leads to a better chance for their children to learn how to express emotions, which in turn leads to a greater sense of well-being.

Green and Bozett (1991) note that the most pointed observation in the literature regarding children of lesbians and gay men is that there is no significant difference in pathology rates when these children are compared with children of heterosexual couples. Moreover, in a meta-analysis examining children raised with same-gender parents, Allen and Burrell (1996) found no significant differences in emotional well-being and adjustment between children raised by same-gender parents and children raised by heterosexual parents.

In a review of existing literature, Biblarz and Stacey (2001) found that children in same-gender households, compared with those in heterosexual households, had different attitudes regarding gender roles, and they found a difference in sexual experiences. The researchers found that boys raised in lesbian households tend to be less aggressive and more sexually restrained than boys raised by heterosexuals. Conversely, girls raised by lesbians exhibit less stereotypical feminine behaviors and their play is more gender neutral, as is their later choice of occupation. They also found that children raised in lesbian or gay households had a greater tolerance for same-gender relationships and were more likely to be involved in same-gender relationships, even though they found no significant difference in terms of self-labeling as gay, lesbian, or bisexual than among children raised by heterosexuals. Many explanations for this phenomenon are possible, from genetic differences to greater honesty in self-reporting, but more research is required in this area before conclusions can be made.

Parenting in Blended Families

Blended gay or lesbian families include original two-parent families, blended families, and single-parent families, with the latter configuration occurring due to relationship dissolution or the choice to be a single parent. Two keys to providing affirmative therapy for lesbian and gay families are understanding the impact of living in a household run by same-gender parents and how societal prejudice affects parents and children (Baptiste, 1987). Understanding these issues enables you to educate the family about the challenges of being in such a household and ask how these challenges influence them. This approach includes encouraging clients to express the myriad feelings in regard to difficulties that the family encounters and facilitating authentic communication between family members.

As is the case with heterosexual parents, same-gender parents must alter their relationships to accommodate the needs of their children. Bohan (1996) notes that adjustments in the relationship bring new stressors, including less freedom, less time for intimacy and sex, and less energy for the primary relationship. The parents' level of comfort about their sexual orientation influences attitudes and beliefs of the children about having lesbian/gay parents. When parents fear discovery, they convey to children the message that being lesbian/gay is "bad." So, helping parents become more comfortable with their sexual orientation will influence the messages they send to their children.

For same-gender couples, the need to decide when to tell children about their parents' sexual orientation and the nature of the relationship arises. When children are informed after a protracted period, it is not uncommon for them to feel shame and anger about having same-gender parents.

Options for working with lesbian/gay families include working with the entire family or with only the parents, depending upon your theoretical orientation, the nature of the problems, the family's needs, and the ages of the children. Multifamily therapy is one way to provide family counseling. One advantage of counseling two or three families at the same time includes family members being given the opportunity to compare communication styles and to compare their own relationship issues to those of other families. This could have the effect of normalizing their issues and feelings about being in a lesbian/gay family. Another advantage is that the families can be a considerable source of support for one another.

An important skill in treating blended families is to be able to distinguish those challenges that relate to being in a same-gender household from those related to being in a stepfamily. It would be a mistake to assume that problems are related to having same-gender parents without thoroughly assessing the nature of the problems and eliciting responses from family members. It is a safe assumption that children in stepfamily households run by same-gender couples experience many of the same challenges as children in stepfamily households led by heterosexual parents. These issues include jealousy and competition, changed ordinal position, and feelings of rejection. Additional challenges include relationship adjustment and altered role expectations, degree of like or dislike for the new family members, and meshing into new blended families.

There are several challenges unique to families headed by same-gender couples. Both biological and nonbiological parents may fear losing parental rights due to their sexual orientation. This situation can lead couples to conceal the nature of their relationships, often putting extra strain on their families. Couples can also disagree about the level of involvement the coparent will have with school and community activities. In addition, because nonbiological parents often have no legal rights, many coparents fear having no legal recourse in some situations, such as when taking an injured child to the hospital. Moreover, nonbiological parents fear that, if the relationship dissolves, they will not have legal recourse if they want coparenting responsibilities or visitation with their children.

As children become adolescents, they become aware of their own budding sexuality, and the desire to fit in with peers becomes stronger. Many older children become increasingly uncomfortable having same-gender parents, and this discomfort manifests in various ways. For example, some adolescent children of same-gender parents become openly rebellious or are reluctant to bring home friends and dates (Baptiste, 1987). Children also experience discrimination from individuals outside the home, so you should facilitate a discussion about the impact of discrimination on the family. In family therapy, you can help children better articulate anger, fear, and concern. This intervention can serve the dual purpose of validating the child's feelings and providing a role model to parents in terms of developing supportive responses.

In many cities, you can make referrals to support groups for same-gender parents and their children, in addition to pointing clients toward numerous books for both lesbian/gay parents and their children. One example of a self-help group for children is COLAGE (Children of Lesbians and Gays Everywhere), which provides support through meetings and pen-pal programs. See the appendix for more such resources.

A Psychotherapy Model for Lesbian/Gay Families

There are many ways to approach family therapy when working with lesbian and gay heads of households. Baptiste (1987) offers a three-phase model based on a systems approach. Baptiste notes that in the first phase of therapy, it is important to gather information to understand the family system and its members.

Assessment should include intrapersonal, interpersonal, and environmental information (Livingston, 1996). *Intrapersonal* information refers to cognitive, emotional, and cultural aspects, as well as the health status of each individual. *Interpersonal* information includes communication style and behavioral patterns within the family system. *Environmental* assessment includes an evaluation of the support system, including family, friends, and support groups, in addition to issues such as communication level, financial resources, and level of external stressors. By the end of the assessment, you should have a clear understanding of the nature of the family's challenges, conflicts, and strengths. When pointing out family and individual strengths, you want to fortify existing strengths and help the family develop new ones. For example, the levels of commitment and persistence in terms of becoming parents are two strengths that you can note to clients. You can then describe how these strengths can be utilized in their current situation.

In the second phase of Baptiste's model, you offer to family members insights gained from the first phase and help the family develop goals for changing unwanted or maladaptive behaviors. Goals of therapy include having family members develop greater understanding of their motivations and behavior, establishing better relationships between family members, and effecting improved communication between family members. In the third phase of therapy, you would help the family integrate and implement interventions based on the insights gained from the first two phases. This process helps families consolidate their gains.

❖   OTHER SAME-GENDER COUPLE AND FAMILY ISSUES

Domestic Violence

Domestic violence can be defined as a systematic attempt by one person to control his or her partner through threats, intimidation, and physical force. Island and Letellier (1991) emphasize that domestic violence is not a relationship problem; rather, it is a deliberate, violent act by one person upon another. Walker (1984) proposes a cyclical model of domestic violence. The first part of the cycle is an increase in tension that may stem from, among other reasons, the batterer being unhappy with the victim's way of doing chores, cooking, etc., or from suspicions of infidelity. Next, battering occurs, followed by a time of loving attention, apologies, and promises by the batterer that he or she will never do it again. Individuals report that the period of contrition can be exceedingly convincing, which keeps the victims hopeful. Then, the tension building phase begins, and when the tension reaches the breaking point, the batterer attacks again.

Renzetti (1992) found that substance abuse, history of childhood abuse in the family of origin, dependency, and jealousy are factors in battering. As jealousy increases, batterers are more demanding and controlling. Battering tends to increase when victims try to assert their independence. Many studies have found that when abused partners threaten to leave, batterers increase threats and violence.

Klinger and Stein (1996) observe that the effects of violence on abused lesbians and gay male partners are similar to the effects for heterosexual victims. They note an additional consequence, however. If a lesbian or gay victim of domestic violence has earlier been victimized by hate crimes, feelings of self-hatred and anger following abusive episodes are exacerbated. Another difference between same-gender and heterosexual domestic violence is that society has a hard time accepting that persons of the same gender can be in domestic violence situations. This attitude contributes to the minimization of abuse. For men, society has a tendency to perceive domestic violence as a form of conflict between two equal persons. Society views women, on the other hand, as incapable of abuse. As Greene (1994) notes, some lesbians in battering relationships are unable to appropriately label the abuse as such because of the pervasive belief that "lesbians don't batter." That is, the partners in relationships where domestic violence occurs also believe these messages.

Another difference in same-gender violent relationships, compared with heterosexual violent relationships, is that the batterer can threaten to out the partner to coworkers, landlords, family, and friends. This is an especially effective weapon when the victim feels he or she has a lot to lose if other people know about his or her sexual orientation.

Couples counseling is not advised when domestic violence is present. As noted previously, any assertion of independence on the part of the victim causes the batterer to reassert control, and it increases battering. In addition, many batterers feign improvement in couples therapy and resume the violence when they drop out of therapy or when couples therapy has terminated. Couples counseling should only be considered long after the violence has ended (Klinger, 1991) and when the batterer shows a strong commitment to nonviolence through written promises from the batter to the victim to never batter again and the batterer's long-term participation in a batterers group. The violence should have ended at least 1 year before couples counseling commences, although 2 years is optimal.

Zemsky and Gilbert (1990) propose a model for working with battering lesbians in individual therapy that emphasizes accountability and responsibility. In this model, lesbian batterers are held accountable to the victim and must understand and acknowledge the full extent of the battering behaviors, admit complete responsibility for the violence and consequences to the relationship, make verbal and financial amends, and respect boundaries set by their partners.

Klinger (1991) asserts that a major part of working with batterers has more to do with addressing issues of self-esteem, expression of feelings, choice, forgiveness of self, and independence. Thus, interventions include esteem building, teaching positive self-talk, and facilitating appropriate emotional expression. Klinger also suggests that battering clients need to learn to recognize internal and external cues that would lead them to batter. This intervention involves teaching batterers behavioral cues, using self-talk to cool themselves down, and employing relaxation and stress-management techniques.

Turning to individual therapy with abused partners, the first and most essential element of therapy is personal safety. Because safety is paramount, you should first help clients develop a safety plan. Abused partners who are hesitant to leave their relationships are still amenable to incorporating safety measures and finding safe havens (Klinger & Stein, 1996). Moreover, suggesting actions such as obtaining a post office box, opening an individual bank account or secretly saving money, and mentally rehearsing leaving the relationship are beneficial interventions.

Denial and minimization are common ways to cope with being battered, so helping clients admit they are being abused can enable them to identify the situation clearly and not minimize or deny that violence is occurring. Two ways to assist clients is to give clients literature on domestic violence in same-gender relationships and to teach them about the cycle of violence. Other interventions include having battered clients write unsent letters to the batterers, encouraging clients to express feelings about the abuse, and helping clients rebuild self-esteem. Victims often take responsibility for the violence. Through educating them about the cycle of violence and giving them handouts about domestic violence, you can help them develop a more accurate picture of what is occurring.

For many reasons, trying to persuade clients to leave is a counter-therapeutic intervention. Many victims are afraid to leave and feel shame for not taking your advice. Some victims have conflicting feelings about their batterers and may not be ready to leave, and they may be persuaded by their batterers that they will not be hurt again. Often, batterers threaten their victims' lives or the lives of their loved ones, so staying in or going back to the relationship may be the safest action to take.

Because many victims develop post-traumatic stress disorder (PTSD), you need to provide interventions and referrals to address it. Signs of PTSD include hypervigilance, insomnia, flashbacks, nightmares, and anxiety. A detailed discussion of the treatment of PTSD is beyond the scope of this book. See Foa, Keane, and Friedman (2000) for further information.

To assist in reducing shame and isolation related to being a battered partner, it is important to encourage victimized clients to tell trusted friends and relatives about the abuse. You should give clients information about support groups for victims of domestic violence, if available, or urge them to call lesbian-friendly women's shelters. Referring battered men is more challenging because support groups for battered men and shelters for battered men are rare. In some cities, gay and lesbian centers offer hotel vouchers for male victims of domestic violence, but in some cases, referring clients to homeless shelters might be the only option for escape. Trauma-recovery groups are available in many cities. See the appendix of this book for a list of domestic violence resources.

Victims who have recently left their relationships are most at risk for extreme violence and homicide. One intervention at this point is having the client rehearse for chance encounters, which can include teaching self-preservation tactics, such as running into crowded areas and obtaining specially equipped 911 cell phones. In addition, you can offer clients referrals to legal aid or to an attorney to obtain information about restraining orders. If the client has filed a police report that includes violence or threats of violence, you can refer him or her to the Victim of Crime Compensation program, which pays for medical, dental, and psychotherapy expenses related to the abuse, in addition to emergency relocation expenses. You can also refer clients to victim assistance programs, which provide services ranging from court accompaniment to assistance in filing for various programs.

Monogamy

Same-gender couples deal either openly or implicitly with decisions about monogamy and level of sexual commitment. Although many couples choose monogamy, others have differing degrees of openness, and couples often attempt to seek a mutually agreeable solution. It is useful to have couples negotiate the terms of their sexual relationships, to assist them in expressing their feelings about non-monogamy, and to resist imposing your values about monogamy on clients.

One area to discuss with couples in agreements about sex outside the relationship is the degree to which each individual is comfortable with the arrangement. It may turn out, for example, that one partner is going along with the agreement to please the other partner or to avoid conflict. Another area for exploration is negotiating safety in the relationship and with outside partners. You will want to address, as part of their agreement, the type of sex they are having both inside and outside of the relationship. In addition, you should foster discussions about expectations in regard to informing the other partner of outside sexual activities.

As a final note, an area worth exploring in relation to the issue of monogamy is if internalized homophobia and gender role socialization play a part in having sex outside the relationship. If lesbians or gay men devalue themselves, that often translates into devaluing the relationship (Hall & Stevens, 1990). This devaluation can lead to sexual activities outside the relationship. Gender role socialization for men includes the belief that sex with several partners is one way to claim their manhood. Thus, it is worthwhile to help the couple discover why their sexual boundaries are where they have made them.

Sexual Dysfunction

Being lesbian or gay can impose additional layers of complexity when dealing with sexual dysfunction. After a physician rules out organic causes, it leaves clients to come to terms with sexual dysfunction being related to their past, their feelings about being sexual, or their beliefs about being lesbian or gay. Sexual dysfunction can be related to past abuse, religious teachings, cultural beliefs, and guilt about sex, all of which may be related to how they feel about their sexual orientation. We would like to highlight some of these issues here.

Lesbians and gay men often make assumptions about sexual knowledge in regard to being with members of the same sex. Anthony (1985) states that a common belief among lesbians is that women naturally know how to please other women. This belief inadvertently reinforces lack of communication. Further, some lesbian couples have inflexible sexual roles, which can give rise to both partners feeling dissatisfied.

An often-debated notion is known as *lesbian bed death*, which refers to the rapid decline of sexual activity among lesbian couples. The notion is debated because of researchers' emphasis on bed death among lesbians, even though sexual activity declines with most couples irrespective of gender or sexual orientation. Nonetheless, research by

Blumstein and Schwartz (1983) indicates that lesbians have less sex than gay male or heterosexual couples. One possible explanation is that women are socialized to be receptive partners, so initiating sex may be harder for women.

In addition to a decline in sexual activity, some lesbians experience female sexual arousal disorder (FSAD) or female orgasmic disorder (FOD). Women with FSAD have a desire for sex, but their genitals do not respond. Women with FOD are unable to reach orgasm. Although causes of FSAD and FOD include underlying physical problems or inadequate foreplay, psychological causes include poor self-image, depression, past abuse, and shame or guilt about sex, which could include internalized homophobia.

In their work with gay male couples, George and Behrendt (1988) found that the most common form of sexual dysfunction is inhibited sexual desire, which may stem from internalized homophobia or a general aversion to sex. It may also be due to not wanting to risk vulnerability in front of another man. Other forms of sexual dysfunction include impotence, erectile dysfunction, inhibited male orgasm, and inhibited sexual excitement. Impotence, erectile dysfunction, and inhibited orgasm may result from internal conflicts about homosexuality. Gay men who believe that sex with other men is wrong may have a problem relating sexually to other men. Therefore, assessing for these beliefs can help individuals link negative feelings about being lesbian or gay to sexual dysfunction. Another origin for these dysfunctions is a fear of letting go or abandoning themselves, and thus losing control. Assessing for control needs can help with determining the causes of these dysfunctions.

George and Behrendt (1988) note that gay men may develop inhibited sexual excitement if they believe the stereotypical beliefs surrounding masculinity and male sexuality. When they adopt a masculine role and feel competitive toward former partners, for example, performance anxiety can result. Moreover, inhibited sexual desire and other dysfunctions can stem from childhood sexual abuse. Consequently, you should assess clients for childhood sexual abuse. When working with clients in which one partner has been abused, it is important to stress that the previously abused partner may need to feel a sense of control over where, when, and how sex takes place.

Because gender role socialization influences sex, same-gender couples encounter the issue of sexual initiation. According to Blumstein and Schwartz (1983), for both lesbians and gay men, the more emotionally expressive partner is more likely to initiate sex. They describe the emotionally expressive partner as the one "who is more likely to begin to talk about what is troubling the couple when there is tension, and the one who is more able to give (the) partner a spontaneous hug or kiss when something good happens" (p. 217). When the person who generally initiates sex is repeatedly refused, it can lead to a decline in sexual activity. Some lesbians and gay men equate sex with power, and initiation and refusal can become symbols for dominance and can act as a substitute for ongoing, perhaps unspoken, relationship problems. Hence, sex can become a symbol for other relationship problems.

George and Behrendt (1988) recommend that gay men be educated that they don't have to have sex or ejaculate during sex unless they choose to. They further recommend that gay men should assume responsibility for how the sex goes and to not feel pressured into having unwanted kinds of sex. The same holds for lesbian couples. Moreover, gay and lesbian couples should be encouraged to talk about roles, inhibitions pertaining to initiating sex, and beliefs in relation to feeling entitled (or not entitled) to a satisfying sex life.

Finances

Laws pertaining to marriage do not apply to same-gender couples. As a result, relationship issues involving finances can be more complex and problematic for same-gender couples than for married couples. When working with same-gender couples, it is helpful to understand the challenges with respect to finances.

One challenge is when (or if) to merge finances and how and when to set financial goals (Larson, 1997). In a legal marriage, future finances become marital property. In contrast, same-gender couples merge finances at their own pace and, as noted by McWhirter and Mattison (1984), many male couples don't fully merge their finances until the 10th year or beyond. If partners have different opinions about when and how to merge finances, conflict can result. This conflict can reflect diverging levels of commitment the partners feel, or it may be due to relationship stage discrepancy. Thus, counseling requires exploration of issues with respect to finances, as well as unique and creative solutions. An increase in lesbian- and gay-friendly financial services means that a referral to a financial advisor is often available. Referring clients to a financial advisor can help couples sort through the myriad financial issues confronting them.

Another issue that can create tension involves income disparity. Generally, one partner makes more money than the other partner, and sometimes the difference between the two salaries is significant. For gay men, there is a tendency to establish relative power in terms of amount of income (Blumstein & Schwartz, 1983). Clients can also perceive income disparity in terms of competition or different levels of contribution to the relationship. Gay men in particular have a tendency to judge their own success by comparing themselves to their partners. So, one clinical task is to have clients reframe finances as simply one type of contribution to the relationship. If a couple sees financial contributions as one of the many qualities that each person brings into the relationship, partners have the opportunity to put income disparities in perspective and achieve a better balance of power in their relationship.

Lesbians, on the other hand, tend to equate income with power less then gay men. Perhaps this is because many lesbians understand the power that money bestows on men, and they do not feel they should perpetuate the male-oriented view of power (Blumstein & Schwartz, 1983).

Nonetheless, for both lesbians and gay men, financial conflict is often a symbol of other relationship problems or is a place to act out power struggles. Helping same-gender couples develop insight about these possibilities, in addition to educating them about how gender role socialization comes into play, can uncover underlying issues, such as competition and fear of abandonment. After the underlying issues surface, much of the focus in therapy will be on what money represents rather than on the money itself.

❖   HIV/AIDS, DATING, AND RELATIONSHIPS

Relationship Configurations and Impact of HIV/AIDS

Three relationship configurations in terms of HIV status for same-gender couples are possible: both partners are HIV-positive, the couple is sero-discordant, or both partners are HIV-negative. Variations exist within these scenarios. A partner may believe that he or she is HIV-negative until getting tested for HIV or developing an opportunistic infection. Another possibility is that one or both partners become infected during the course of the relationship. Or, one partner might erroneously assume that she or he is HIV-positive, get tested, and learn of a negative result.

Lesbians and gay men who are HIV-positive may limit their dating to other individuals who have HIV. This can occur for several reasons: due to an HIV-positive person's fear that she or he will be rejected by individuals who are HIV-negative, to avoid the complications surrounding sero-divergence (one partner is HIV-positive and the other is HIV-negative), or because of the desire to find someone who understands the emotional and medical issues of having HIV/AIDS (Harmon & Volker, 1995). Sometimes, people distinguish between people with AIDS and people who are HIV-positive, and persons with AIDS are often considered less desirable than persons who are HIV-positive.

Some individuals with HIV/AIDS dispense with dating and go right to the *merging* relationship stage. Clients may describe the feeling of racing against time and not having the luxury to play games. Some couples could move in together without getting to know one another well. Treatment for these couples tends to focus on issues of adjustment to the new relationship. In addition, when two people with HIV/AIDS enter a relationship, a high degree of uncertainty is inevitable. The potential looms for an extraordinary amount of stress to be placed on the individuals and on the relationship. Other issues of particular concern for couples with HIV include financial concerns, choices about employment, loss of life image, health concerns, and death and dying issues.

It is useful to facilitate a discussion about what the couple will do if one partner gets an opportunistic infection and what outside assistance and social support they can rely upon. It is important to address these and other issues that arise, because the couple may be dealing with these possibilities ineffectively or ignoring them altogether. Furthermore, the person who maintains wellness for a longer period of time could become overwhelmed if her or his HIV-infected partner becomes ill and fearful of looking at her or his own future. Therefore, you should prepare for a range of feelings and reactions if one member of the relationship develops an opportunistic infection.

As for sero-discordant couples, when individuals who are sero-discordant begin to date, the reflex of most therapists is to question the judgment of the HIV-negative person. However, your role is not to dissuade HIV-negative clients from pursuing a relationship with someone

> **Case Study 5.5 (Mark and Rick,
> continued from Case Study 5.2)**
>
> In the last several sessions, Mark and Rick have held to their
> positions until, in today's session, Mark admits that he is afraid
> Rick will leave him for Joe and, even though Mark is healthy
> now, Rick is fearful that if Mark's health declines, Rick will have
> nowhere to turn. Rick admits that he resents Mark for having
> HIV even though he knew Mark was HIV-positive when they
> got together. It also turns out that, 2 years ago, Mark talked to a
> friend who sero-converted after many years of living with his
> HIV-positive partner, and Rick is afraid of getting HIV. After
> these more vulnerable issues emerge, Rick agrees to stop seeing
> Joe and to return to the original agreement. Now, the work can
> begin to improve their relationship.

who has HIV/AIDS; rather, it is to explore the many reasons why
clients make the choices they do and to help them become more aware
of deeper motives behind these choices (Harmon & Volker, 1995). After
exploring their motives, you can assist clients by helping them express
their fears as you validate their concerns, as with Case Study 5.5.

As Harmon and Volker (1995) note, some individuals seek out
partners with the opposite sero-status. According to the researchers,
there are several reasons for this situation. HIV-negative individuals
may, for example, have a desire to rescue someone, either due to an
unconscious wish to neglect their own problems or because someone
who has HIV represents a victim, and they want to rescue them.
Similar searching occurs for people with HIV who seek exclusively
HIV-negative partners. Many people with HIV are in a practical quest
to find someone who will help them later on (Harmon & Volker, 1995).
Therefore, some people with HIV view HIV-negative people as potential rescuers. On the other hand, many HIV-positive and HIV-negative
individuals are simply open to meeting and dating other people,
regardless of HIV status. The attitude among HIV-negative persons
may be that if a potential mate is HIV-positive, they will handle it, just
like they deal with other issues that arise from being in a relationship.

Nonetheless, if one partner becomes infected or learns that she or he is HIV-positive during the relationship, it can create distress not only for the individual who is infected, but it can create turmoil for the partner and for the relationship. Furthermore, the HIV-negative partner may have survivor's guilt or be angry with the partner for contracting HIV. The HIV-negative partner may put these issues aside while the HIV-positive partner adjusts to a new set of circumstances. The HIV-negative partner must also come to terms with an evolving caregiver role, and both partners must face the pregrieving process. The HIV-positive partner may shut the partner out emotionally. Because life expectations are dramatically altered for someone diagnosed with HIV, the relationship will waver before the couple has a chance to adjust to the new situation. Moreover, the HIV-positive partner could envy the HIV-negative partner for not being infected.

A couple who has entered therapy upon learning one partner is HIV-positive often needs more support than couples therapy can offer. So, along with couples therapy, a referral to individual therapy is often a necessary adjunct. Some cities offer support groups for sero-discordant couples. In sero-discordant support groups, couples have the opportunity to have their feelings normalized, and it gives the couple an opportunity to witness other couples coping with and resolving their difficulties.

Regardless of the relationship configuration, HIV/AIDS plays a significant role in same-gender couples' lives. When both partners are HIV-negative, the couple still has fear and concern about HIV/AIDS, including fear of contracting HIV, questions of sex outside the relationship, and whether to engage in safer sex with one another. Problems related to HIV may manifest in emotional distance, fighting over unrelated issues, maladaptive forms of coping, and withdrawal or sexual dysfunction. Because these problems may be due to reasons the couple is not aware of, one task of the therapist is to ask the couple to uncover the origins of relationship difficulties.

Loss of a Partner due to AIDS-Related Illnesses

When a partner with AIDS dies, the loss to the survivor is most often devastating. Individuals who have lost their partners to AIDS are sometimes not ready to deal with their loss for months or years. As Dworkin and Pincu (1993) note, losing a loved one is like losing a part of one's own identity. The death of a partner often leads to suicidal thoughts and feelings, especially if little social support is available or if the partner relies on escapism to cope with the loss (Rosengard & Folkman, 1997). Notably, the HIV status of the surviving partner is of little consequence in terms of grief reactions, and bereavement is a vulnerable time for surviving caregivers, during which the risk for self-destructive behavior and suicide increases.

Not only is the surviving spouse grieving, but she or he has just spent months or perhaps years taking care of another person. As Irving, Bor, and Catalan (1995) state, they were not just supporting their partners, they were also coping with demands associated with the physical and emotional care for their partners, facing the terminal aspect of the illness, and confronting the premature death of their spouses. Irving et al. found that distress most often took the form of depression. Other maladies include anxiety, panic attacks, and sexual and substance abuse. If you would like to review the subject of treating bereavement, please refer to Chapter 4.

❖ SUMMARY

Although many issues for same-gender couples and families headed by lesbians and gay men are the same as those that confront hetero-sexual couples and households, treatment for same-gender couples has additional dimensions and requires varying approaches. Unique forms of pressure and discrimination that same-gender couples face lead to novel approaches to assessment and treatment.

Several myths regarding same-gender relationships are believed less than they were in the past but still persist in the culture, and it is important to be aware of them when treating same-gender couples. Furthermore, there are several stages for lesbian and gay male rela-tionships, and McWhirter and Mattison (1984) and Slater (1995) devel-oped relationship stage models for men and women, respectively. These models provide a framework for working with same-gender couples.

Issues to explore in therapy with same-gender couples and their families include the impact of gender role socialization, marginalization, and internalized homophobia on relationship conflict, sexual issues, and challenges in having and raising children. It is also important to examine the impact of stress and support from family, friends, place of worship, and the workplace on same-gender couples.

Helping couples and families develop insight into issues that lie below the surface can lead to a decrease in unhealthy patterns. To deal with this and other relationship challenges, Baptiste (1987) offers a three-stage model for treating lesbian and gay families. Irrespective of the model you choose, a therapist performs three roles when providing therapy for same-gender couples and families: educator, mediator, and role model.

Lesbians and gay men encounter several additional challenges. The first is domestic violence. Other relationship challenges include domestic violence, monogamy, sexual dysfunction, finances, and HIV/AIDS. The impact of these challenges is often a major theme in therapy with same-gender couples.

Regarding the case studies, Tom attempted his first same-gender relationship and Angela grew from being unable to see herself as a lesbian to making arrangements to have a child with her partner Jodi. Mark and Rick, a sero-discordant couple, are dealing with difficult and complex relationship issues related to HIV/AIDS.

We now move from romantic relationships to social relationships. Chapter 6 discusses therapeutic change agents for lesbian and gay male clients in group psychotherapy and offers information on facilitating group therapy and support groups. We also present models for several types of support groups.

6

Group Psychotherapy
and Support Groups
for Lesbians and Gay Men

❖ ❖ ❖

Therapists have several options for providing group psychotherapy and counseling to lesbian and gay male clients. Clients can attend commingled (mixed gay and nongay) groups or exclusively lesbian/gay groups. Within the latter option, clients can be placed in exclusively lesbian, exclusively gay male, or mixed lesbian/gay groups. Whether the groups are commingled or exclusively gay/lesbian, they can be broken down into several categories. Psychotherapy (process) groups are helpful for clients who are dealing with intimacy, communication, and other relationship issues; workplace challenges; and learning to become more comfortable as a lesbian or as a gay man. Support and recovery groups have specific aims. For example, support groups can be geared toward coming out, HIV/AIDS, or surviving childhood sexual abuse. Settings for the groups include mental health inpatient, outpatient, substance abuse treatment, agency, and private practice.

Some general guidelines exist for referring lesbian and gay clients to groups. Frost (1990) offers a model for placing gay men in groups based on the clients' stage of identity development. We feel that his model applies to lesbians as well. In the early stage of coming out, lesbians and gay men might be uncomfortable being with exclusively self-identified lesbians and gay men. Therefore, a more appropriate referral would be to a predominantly heterosexual group. In fact, placing some clients in an all-lesbian or all-gay group might be detrimental. For example, clients who are in the early stages of coming out may not be ready to confront issues related to being lesbian or gay in a group setting, which could increase maladaptive coping mechanisms.

In the middle stages of coming out, lesbian and gay clients may have a strong preference to attend exclusively lesbian/gay groups. Being in exclusive groups can help strengthen group members' lesbian or gay identity. In the latter stages of coming out, clients may still have a preference for one type of group over another, and treatment issues should influence placement. Nonetheless, Frost states that in the latter stages of coming out, either commingled or all-lesbian/all-gay groups are appropriate referrals for lesbians and gay men.

In addition to being aware of client characteristics that influence placement of lesbians and gay men into therapy groups, you should take group dynamics into account. For instance, lesbian and gay male clients who have difficulty relating to heterosexuals should be considered for a commingled group, because these clients have the opportunity to discover what they have in common with heterosexual clients. On the other hand, if group members in a predominantly heterosexual group might scapegoat or reject lesbian or gay male clients, you should strongly consider a referral to another group.

❖ GROUP PSYCHOTHERAPY

Getzel (1998) notes that group therapy helps lesbians and gay men to manage identity issues and deal with prejudice. Group psychotherapy can help clients cope with marginalization, discrimination, and the HIV/AIDS crisis. In addition, group therapy can help clients come to terms with their sexual orientation.

Yalom's Therapeutic Factors
Applied to Lesbians and Gay Men

Group settings provide many agents for change and growth for lesbians and gay men. In this section, we delineate these elements. Yalom (1995) states that there are 11 therapeutic factors that work toward the healing process across theoretical orientations. Although Yalom considered these therapeutic factors to be helpful to all clients, we emphasize the ways in which these agents are especially significant for lesbian and gay clients. Note that the therapeutic factors are interdependent and cannot facilitate healing individually; however, by separating the different factors, Yalom (1995) provides a psychological map.

The first therapeutic factor is Instillation of Hope. As Yalom (1995) notes, because hope for a good therapeutic experience correlates with a positive therapeutic outcome, clinicians who provide group counseling should attempt to increase clients' confidence by discussing possible benefits of group counseling. This intervention benefits lesbian and gay clients in a unique way. Many lesbians and gay men were ostracized and called names from the time when they didn't yet understand what "faggot" or "queer" meant. It instills hope in lesbian and gay clients when they hear that they feel wanted as group members for a therapeutic "team."

The second therapeutic factor is Universality. As Yalom (1995) notes, many clients enter therapy thinking that they are unique in having unacceptable or frightening thoughts, desires, and behaviors. They may also believe that they are the only ones who perceive themselves to be contemptible, worthless, and miserable. These feelings preclude individuals from feeling accepted by others, thus fostering a sense of isolation. This therapeutic factor affects lesbians and gay men on several levels. In a commingled group, lesbian and gay male clients may enter the group feeling somewhat distrustful and disconnected from heterosexuals. As lesbian and gay clients begin to examine their own lives and compare them to heterosexual clients' lives, they begin to realize that they are not as different from nongay people as they once thought. In addition, lesbian and gay clients receive validation and caring from nongay group members when nongay clients listen to the concerns, hopes, fears, and day-to-day life of lesbian and gay clients. The message that nongay clients send to lesbian and gay clients is that,

Case Study 6.1 (Patti, continued from Case Study 1.5)

Patti has been in individual therapy for 2 years and also attends your commingled psychotherapy group. She has been at odds with the other lesbian group member, Kathy, as well as the non-gay group members. Patti has been dissatisfied, and she has mentioned that she wants to leave the group.

In this session, Patti confronts Arthur, who is heterosexual, for an offensive joke that he told to her before the session started. Patti says, "Arthur, your joke was in poor taste." Arthur says, "It was just a joke." Patti replies, "The joke was sexist and homophobic, and it points out your way of looking at us." Turning to the other group members, she continues, "*This* is why I'm thinking about leaving the group." Arthur replies, "You are more homophobic than I am, and you threaten to leave because you're scared we'll reject you first." Patti answers, "That's not true. You have no idea what I think. And if you knew what I go through, and the stares and comments when I walk with my girlfriend, you'd never have told that joke. You can't relate to me and don't understand my problems. I want to leave because I can't relate to you and the others." Arthur angrily responds, "So, I have no idea what you go through? When I was a kid, the neighbors told me that I killed Christ because I'm Jewish. Once they threw rocks at me. Now, my wife and I have to deal with stares because I'm white and she's black. I relate to your problems more than you realize." Patti sits silently.

What intervention could you use to help turn this situation into an opportunity for Patti and Arthur to bond? How could you involve other group members in building group cohesiveness? What other therapeutic factors come into play? Would you take a here-and-now focus and encourage clients to express their feelings? At the same time, how would you prevent the group from becoming unsafe for Patti?

even though they are different in terms of sexual orientation, their thoughts, feelings, and challenges are similar to their own, as we illustrate in Case Study 6.1.

As illustrated in this case study, exploring the issue of discrimination in a commingled group has benefits because it offers gay and nongay clients the opportunity to explore their own heterosexism and to recognize that they have experiences and feelings in common. On the other hand, exclusively lesbian/gay groups can assist lesbian and gay clients in exploring the impact of discrimination from a lesbian/gay perspective. When lesbian/gay clients have stereotypical beliefs about the gay community, they have the opportunity to reduce levels of internalized homophobia, in part by seeing that they have much in common with their microcosmic "community."

The third therapeutic factor is Imparting Information, which Yalom (1995) describes as suggestions, advice, and guidance provided by the facilitator and group participants. Objectives include enlightening group participants, structuring the group, and explaining the process of therapy. Imparting information may reduce fear and anxiety for clients by normalizing various thoughts, feelings, and experiences. Further, group members who offer direct advice or suggestions show caring for one another, and the recipient feels the concern.

As noted, lesbians and gay men may believe that their experiences are unique, which can lead to feeling estranged from heterosexuals. To counter that belief, you need to impart information about similarities between them. For example, you can explain that the awkward, adolescent feelings that arise when lesbians and gay men start dating persons of the same gender are akin to the emotions that heterosexuals experience when they return to dating after leaving a marriage or long-term relationship. As another example, going back to the previous case study, you could explain to Patti that her coming out process is similar to Arthur having to tell family and friends that he is dating someone with a different ethnicity.

You may also impart information during certain situations, such as explaining typical problems that arise when people experience loss of their support system due to AIDS-related illness. Clients may be experiencing an array of feelings, so supplying information on the trauma, depression, anger, and survivor's guilt may reduce anxiety about having these feelings, as well as encourage a dialogue to facilitate the healing process.

The fourth therapeutic factor, Altruism, refers to acts of helpfulness from one client to another client. Sharing experiences and suggestions is one way group members support one another. Yalom (1995) notes that one therapeutic aspect of altruism is that clients transcend being self-absorbed by coming to the aid of others. Yalom also states that altruism is particularly valuable for individuals who feel that they have nothing to offer. When lesbian and gay clients feel worthless or inferior, they have the opportunity to feel valued when they give feedback to other group members that they subsequently learn is valuable.

The fifth therapeutic factor is Recapitulation of the Primary Family Group (Yalom, 1995). This factor refers to how early interpersonal family dynamics emerge from the group dynamics. Childhood feelings of intimacy, competitiveness, and rivalry are often re-experienced by group members. Because many lesbian and gay clients come from families that ostracized them for being themselves, lesbian and gay clients can work through childhood experiences in a group setting.

For instance, many lesbian and gay male clients have memories of growing up in homes where their parents suspected they were "different," and parents would try to force their children to change. We are aware of clients whose parents locked them in closets or beat them to toughen their sissy boys or soften their tomboys. Furthermore, adolescent peers may have belittled them, adding to their marginalized sense of self. Experiencing a "functional family" in group therapy, however, can create emotionally corrective experiences for lesbians and gay men, as we demonstrate in Case Study 6.2.

The sixth therapeutic factor is Development of Socializing Techniques. Yalom (1995) notes that, for many clients, the process of developing social skills has been inhibited. Lack of social skills can lead to offensive or off-putting qualities that undermine social relationships. For example, some gay men become "drama queens." Drama queens' lives are tumultuous, with one crisis happening after another, and they have off-putting qualities. Quite often, other people are able to tolerate them for only short periods of time. In group therapy, lesbian/gay clients have the opportunity to develop social skills by receiving feedback and by observing other members' social skills. Many lesbian and gay clients grew up socially isolated, and social isolation inhibits learning how to successfully interact with others. Moreover, clients who abused drugs and alcohol need to learn to socially interact with others without the lowered social inhibitions that drugs and alcohol can bring.

Case Study 6.2 (Patti, continued from Case Study 6.1)

In this week's session, a new group member, Darren, was supposed to come to his first group session. After 30 minutes, it is apparent to the group that he is not going to attend. Because Patti pushed back vacation plans specifically so she could meet Darren at this session, she becomes upset. Patti says, "This is the last straw. I'm giving notice that I'm leaving group in two weeks." Kathy becomes defensive in reaction to Patti and tells her, "Leave, if you want. It's not our fault that this guy didn't show up." Arthur, expressing irritation at Kathy's defensive response, says, "Kathy, why don't you let Patti say what she wants? We all know this isn't about the group. It's about Patti."

Upon exploration, Patti realized that her anger stemmed from the second-class status she received from her family of origin. Patti took Darren's no-show personally and, while processing this, she says, "Changing my vacation plans only to be blown off by a group member felt like my family blowing off my recitals and soccer games." Other group members later pointed out that Kathy's defensive response to Patti's anger was a cover-up for feeling abandoned by Patti. Kathy says, "Patti is like my mother. Even when I was little, when we'd go somewhere as a family, my mom would threaten to leave me at home unless I changed into a dress, and I would be terrified she'd leave me there. I always changed clothes, even though I hated it."

Arthur was frustrated with Kathy for taking Patti's angry remarks personally. But, he later realized, "I reacted to Kathy the same way I used to react to my sister, who is such a pleaser. I assumed Kathy was just trying to please the group by letting us know how good we are and to reassure us that Patti wanting to leave has nothing to do with us."

In this session, group participants took the opportunity to gain insight into how early childhood experiences continue to influence their relationships. Kathy and Patti also realized how their families' homophobia perpetuates their worldview that people do things "to" them because they are lesbian when, in fact, many times it is not the case. Developing these insights can help group members change long-standing beliefs and patterns that act as barriers to intimacy.

How would you continue to turn this problem into an opportunity for growth for these clients? Would you continue to explore how other members were affected by Darren's no-show? Would you illuminate the therapeutic factor of Recapitulation of the Primary Family Group? If so, when would you provide this intervention?

Overcoming long-standing maladaptive social skills can be challenging. In group therapy, clients learn to identify the off-putting qualities that perpetuate their isolation. Furthermore, they can receive feedback about the cost of their behavior. Hence, group therapy offers socially immature lesbians and gay men the opportunity to develop social skills.

One particularly useful intervention to help clients discover how they come across to others is the Johari Window (Luft, 1969). In this intervention, you ask clients to picture a window with four panes:

- ❖ *First pane:* "What I know about you and you know about you."
- ❖ *Second pane:* "What you know about you but I don't know about you."
- ❖ *Third pane:* "What I know about you but you don't know about you."
- ❖ *Fourth pane:* "What neither of us know about you."

Using the Johari Window, clients learn to develop social skills by getting feedback about how they come across to others, which is the focus of the third pane. When clients talk to each other about how they perceive one another, they learn about qualities that put others off, including arrogance, boastfulness, and belligerence. Conversely, clients can learn about qualities that others find endearing, as well as things they are saying or doing that encourages others to feel close to them.

The seventh therapeutic factor is Imitative Behavior. This notion refers to how clients learn new behaviors from imitating the facilitator and other group members. Clients can try out behaviors in group therapy before they attempt them outside of group. For example, many lesbians and gay men have not had the opportunity to share their more intimate, private thoughts with peers. In group therapy, however, they witness other people being intimate and modeling trust within the group and later "try on" these new behaviors. So, after clients observe how others relate intimately, they can start to take risks to be vulnerable with others.

The eighth therapeutic factor is Catharsis (Yalom, 1995). Catharsis, which refers to releasing emotions, leads to personal insights and increases group cohesiveness. It has been our experience that emotional release precedes insights, which is consistent with several counseling theories. Also, when other group members view a client's innermost feelings and beliefs, they develop greater empathy for and feel closer to clients who reveal deeply personal information.

The ninth therapeutic factor is what Yalom (1995) refers to as Existential Factors. He notes that clients must come to grips with the fact that they will die someday and that they are ultimately alone in this world. One outcome of an existential exploration is for clients to take more responsibility for their lives and make peace with being alone. In explaining this existential aspect of therapy to clients, you should describe the difference between aloneness and loneliness. Having been lonely for much of their lives, lesbian and gay clients may confuse loneliness, which is a result of social isolation, with aloneness, which is the condition they must live with. Many lesbian and gay clients mistakenly try to fill the latter void. To help clients make the distinction, you can explain that aloneness is a fact of life, whereas loneliness diminishes by taking action.

Interventions involving this therapeutic factor also involve encouraging clients to live more authentically. To be authentic as lesbians and gay men carries risk because an honest answer to a seemingly benign question may expose one's sexual orientation. The reward for clients being in an authentic environment can be great, but it is the therapist's task to balance the need for authenticity with the need for the emotional safety of the group. For example, revealing sexual orientation to a commingled group involves risk, and you may wish to prepare lesbian and gay clients for the range of possible responses in an individual session.

Once clients come out, you would want to facilitate genuine responses from other group members. However, if comments start to take the form of an attack, you must ensure the safety of the lesbian/gay group member by preventing escalation.

The 10th therapeutic factor is Group Cohesiveness. In citing studies that support the notion that the most healing aspect of therapy is the therapeutic relationship, Yalom (1995) states that the most critical ingredients of therapy are warmth, empathy, trust, and an accepting atmosphere in which therapy takes place. In group therapy, relationships with other members, in addition to relationships with you, become the most important curative factor. These emotionally close relationships are what Yalom refers to as group cohesiveness, adding that it also includes a sense of solidarity and the value placed on the group.

In explaining the interdependence of the therapeutic factors and how group cohesiveness plays a part, Yalom (1998) observes,

> Catharsis and universality, for example, are not complete processes. It is not the sheer process of ventilation that is important; it is not only the discovery of others' problems similar to one's own and the ensuing disconfirmation of one's wretched uniqueness that are important. It is the affective sharing of one's inner world *and then the acceptance by others* that seem of paramount importance. To be accepted by others brings into question the patient's belief that she or he is basically repugnant, unacceptable, or unlovable. (p. 27)

In an exclusively lesbian or gay male group, acceptance symbolizes becoming part of the lesbian and gay community. For commingled groups, acceptance and support by other members represents acceptance by society.

The 11th therapeutic factor is Interpersonal Learning. As Yalom (1995) observes, social outcasts have compelling social needs due to being hurt by repeated rejection. Yalom states that because maladjustment has an interpersonal basis, counseling should stress interpersonal relationships. He further observes that a shift in priorities from symptom relief to objectives of an interpersonal nature, such as learning to communicate with others and being more trusting of others, takes place in group therapy. For many lesbians and gay men, interpersonal learning means discovering how to connect with others on a more intimate level. Therefore, at nearly every opportunity, you should guide the group from talking about outside relationships to experiencing and processing the relationships with one another.

With Interpersonal Learning and the 10 other therapeutic factors, group counseling is a very powerful healing agent for lesbians and gay men. Initially, lesbian and gay clients may feel overwhelmed at the level of honesty and emotion expressed in group sessions. Over time, however, they have the opportunity to risk vulnerability and overcome fears of intimacy. Outside of group, they can use what they learned to develop greater self-acceptance, form bonds with heterosexuals and other lesbians and gay men, and replace maladaptive forms of coping with healthier ways of dealing with discrimination and other stresses related to being lesbian or gay in the culture.

❖ SUPPORT GROUPS

In addition to group psychotherapy, there are many types of support groups available for lesbians and gay men. Support groups tend to be psycho-educational, in that they have process and content oriented components. They may be time-limited, such as 8 or 10 weeks in length, or be open-ended, with clients entering and leaving when the therapist and client mutually choose. In this section, we discuss issues, present formats, and provide suggestions for facilitating (a) coming out groups, (b) sexual orientation growth groups, (c) support groups for lesbians and gay men with HIV/AIDS, and (d) HIV-negative gay men's groups. We also offer comments on bereavement groups and substance abuse treatment groups.

Coming Out Groups

Coming out groups tend to be time-limited, psycho-educational groups that are designed for lesbians and gay men who are coming to terms with their sexual orientation. Six of Yalom's (1995) therapeutic factors play a large role in coming out groups: Universality, Instillation of Hope, Imparting Information, Interpersonal Learning, Catharsis, and Group Cohesiveness.

As noted in a literature review by Morrow (1996), five issues are related to the coming out process among lesbians: lesbian identity development, homophobia and heterosexism, religious matters, career issues, and family-of-origin concerns. Morrow developed and studied a 10-week psycho-educational group format for lesbians who are coming out. This program was structured around various themes, and each week's session had a specific topic. The first half of the program included introductions and goal setting, review of research on the etiology of same-sex attraction, Cass's identity development model, a discussion on homophobia and heterosexism and their relationship to sexism and racism, and assertiveness training. The second half of the program focused on matters related to spirituality, workplace issues, family of origin and relationship issues, and the costs and benefits of living openly as a lesbian. The program also included outside speakers who presented some of the topics. For the session on spirituality, a guest speaker from a lesbian and gay affirmative church discussed religious teachings. Guest speakers who have a gay son or a lesbian daughter spoke about their experiences in coming to terms with their children's sexual orientation. Group discussions followed the lectures.

Although coming out groups tend to be time-limited, some of them have a "drop in" format. In this type of format, clients can enter at any time, select which sessions to attend, and leave when they choose to do so. New members can witness what it is like for more seasoned clients to have gone through some of their coming out process. In coming out groups, facilitators may provide "field trips," in which clients attend events, restaurants, retail stores, and bars in the gay community.

Coming out groups can greatly assist individuals in coming to terms with their sexual orientation. In her study, Morrow (1996) compared women who attended a lesbian coming out group with a control group of women who did not. For the experimental group, she measured several characteristics of individuals—including ego development, lesbian identity development, empowerment, and disclosure—before and after they participated in the coming out group. For the control group, she measured these qualities at the same times. For the lesbians in the experimental group, Morrow found increases in every area, and the gains in empowerment and disclosure were highly significant. Thus, the test group subjects felt more self-control in their lives and were coming out to a greater number of people than those in the control group. Although Morrow (1996) discussed lesbian coming out groups, the format applies to coming out groups for gay men as well. For example, regarding the impact of sexism, you could discuss the influence on gay men of living in a sexist society and how sexism relates to homophobia.

The following is a week-by-week coming out group template. Jones (2001) developed the format for the "Six-Week Coming Out Workshop Series," which are held at the Los Angeles Gay and Lesbian Center:

Week 1: Coming Out to Ourselves
Am I gay?
> ~Self-recognition as gay: Explore the thoughts and feelings about your attraction to members of the same sex.
> ~Accepting your sexuality: Discuss the fear you feel about how society, family, friends, coworkers, and members of the religious community will react to your sexuality.
> ~Support: Do you have a support system? Discuss ways in which a positive support system can be established.
> ~Start a journal: For the next 6 weeks, write down all of your feelings about being gay. Ask yourself what you expect to achieve by the end of this workshop.

Week 2: Coming Out to Friends, Family, and Children
That First Talk . . .
> ~When, where, how
> ~If you have children
> ~Are you ready?
> ~Your straight spouse
> ~Your parents
> Discuss various ways to come out in a positive and powerful way

Week 3: Coming Out at Work
Should you or should you not?
> ~Understanding the dynamics of your company
> ~Beware! Homophobic coworkers/bosses
> ~Make it fun
> ~Prepare for the worst
> Check-in: How is the journal writing?

Week 4: Dating/Meeting Other Gay People
Now the fun begins!!
> ~Where do you go?
> ~What type of person/people would you like to meet?

~Developing a family of friends
~Dating! Oh no! What to do?

Week 5: Relationships
Is it love? Is it lust?
~Sex vs. intimacy
~Play Safe
~Real Love
Safer sex presentation

Week 6: I'm Out . . . NOW WHAT?!
Being gay is being yourself. . . . Being gay is being free. . . .
~Spiritual health
~Emotional health
~Balance
~Pride
Presentation by PFLAG (Parents, Families and Friends of
Lesbians and Gays)
Check-in: Has journal writing been beneficial to your coming out
experience? Have you achieved your goals?

Sexual Orientation Growth Groups

Whereas coming out groups are designed for lesbians and gay men
who are coming to terms with their sexual orientation, sexual orientation growth groups are designed for individuals who are unsure of
their sexual orientation.

The purpose of this type of group is for individuals to participate
in exploring the meaning of their sexual attractions and experiences.
A sexual orientation growth group is time-limited and psychoeducational. A sexual orientation growth group is also a place where clients
can express their thoughts and feelings about sexual attractions and
behaviors in a supportive, nonjudgmental atmosphere.

While atteding the University of North Texas, Jeff cofacilitated
sexual orientation growth groups for undergraduate students. In the
groups, the facilitators did not label any sexual or nonsexual experiences
for clients. Many of the students labeled themselves either bisexual or

gay/lesbian during the groups, and some of them vacillated between labels. Other students experimented with various behaviors and did not label themselves in any way for the duration of the group.

Two central questions emerged in the beginning phase of each group: "Do I have to know who I am?" and "Why do I have to put a label on myself even if I know?" Addressing these and other questions led to a sense of relief for group members. It also led to rapid cohesiveness among the participants. As the groups became more cohesive, the facilitators witnessed the students opening up to one another about spirituality, friendships, and families. They also trusted one another to talk about sexual experiences and what these experiences meant to them.

Group members discussed several major themes, including how to develop sexual identities amid the confusion and emotional roller coaster of young adulthood. By the end of the sessions, some of the participants were more certain of their sexual orientation, and others came away from their experience feeling more comfortable with not labeling themselves. Although we did not pre- and post-test the participants, doing so in the future could lead to information in terms of how such a group affects self-acceptance, labeling, disclosure of sexual orientation, and identity development.

One by-product of the group was to help students develop social support. Many group members became friends outside of group, and they reported a growing sense of social connection with one another. This bonding is also a result of participating in coming out groups because clients process their experiences through others who are experiencing similar emotions and experiences.

It also became evident to the facilitators that the same therapeutic factors that play large roles in coming out groups are also major influences in sexual orientation growth groups. By coming together with a group of people who did not know or understand their own sexual orientation, participants reported great relief when they discovered that they were not alone. In this kind of atmosphere, other therapeutic factors rapidly multiply, and outside friendships develop.

Support Groups for Lesbians and Gay Men with HIV/AIDS

As Fontaine, McKenna, and Cheskin (1997) state, support groups for lesbians and gay men with HIV/AIDS often provide emotional support, practical information, and a place to explore existential issues. The researchers found that subjects in support groups developed a higher degree of perceived self-control compared with subjects who were not in support groups. Kalichman, Sikkema, and Somlai (1996) found that people in support groups have a better quality of life. People who attend HIV/AIDS support groups have less emotional distress, including depression, less reliance on avoidant coping strategies, higher self-esteem, and less loneliness than those not attending support groups.

There are many advantages to a group composed exclusively of clients with HIV/AIDS. Beckett and Rutan (1990) note that group members can expect certain shared experiences with a resulting high level of trust and support for one another. These expectations, concomitant with an elevated willingness to share personal information, lead to more rapid group cohesiveness.

In a study by Foster, Stevens, and Hall (1994), lesbian subjects with HIV/AIDS were offered a choice of two support groups. The first support group was a 12-week, closed membership, structured group; the other was an open-ended group. Goals of treatment were to reduce isolation, provide stress management and safer sex information, help women in recovery, and provide a safe place for clients to live with HIV/AIDS while remaining connected to the lesbian community. The researchers indicate that the open-ended group seemed the most promising in terms of meeting the needs of lesbians with HIV. They also note that the cohesiveness that developed among the members helped them in terms of empowerment and activism. One finding was that clinicians could increase attendance by offering low- or no-cost groups for lesbians with HIV/AIDS. Further, allowing for occasional missed sessions increased participation because many lesbians with HIV/AIDS may have unpredictable absences due to bouts of illness, child care needs, and transportation problems.

Although support groups meet many needs for clients with HIV/AIDS, clients can meet other emotional and psychological needs in a general psychotherapy group. Many people on highly active antiretroviral therapy (HAART) are restoring their health. Thus, they are renewing dating, reentering the workforce, and rebuilding friendships, and these issues are explored in more depth in psychotherapy groups than in support groups. Tunnell (1994) notes that group therapy can help clients adjust to living with HIV/AIDS. Groups provide a forum

---

Case Study 6.3 (John, continued from Case Study 4.6)

John has been in group therapy for 4 months since leaving individual therapy. In a recent session, group members mention to John that they are concerned that he has missed several group sessions without informing them ahead of time. In today's session, John did not show up again. Neither you nor any of the group members received a call from John, which violates a group rule. You raise the question of whether John, whose health is in decline due to AIDS, should be terminated from group. The clients challenge you for suggesting termination and for being unfeeling for not allowing John to miss some sessions due to his illness.

This case is symbolic of a cohesive family defending against the removal of a family member by an outside force. How would you deal with the challenge from clients? How can you enforce group rules but still be compassionate? When John returns, how will you raise the issue and promote a discussion about group members' fears of a decline in John's health?

---

for social interaction and support. In fact, Beckett and Rutan (1990) note that group therapy is a way to reduce shame, isolation, and difficulty coping with the disease.

The topic of death and dying becomes an inevitable group discussion. Because mortality is a difficult issue to discuss, you may have to broach the subject. Chipping away at the denial of mortality may motivate clients to find meaning in their lives. Examining death and dying issues can also be an enriching experience, as illustrated in Case Study 6.3.

A major challenge for any group occurs when one member's health starts to deteriorate. When a client with HIV/AIDS misses a session without prior notice, you face a choice of fostering immediacy by eliciting group members' thoughts and feelings or waiting until the client returns. If you foster a here-and-now discussion, the advantages include giving clients the opportunity to voice concerns and fears. If you wait until the client returns to group, however, the chance to process clients' initial reactions has passed. Upon the client's return, however, group members have the opportunity to express their concerns and fears. Thus, the client can learn how his or her absence affects others. It also has the advantage of potentially spurring a discussion about fears related to that client's failing health and ultimately into a discussion about death and dying.

Another subject to explore in therapy and support groups is the challenge of living in two or more life stages simultaneously. According to Tunnell (1994), lesbians and gay men with HIV/AIDS find themselves in Erikson's (1963) various stages of psychosocial development. These stages are trust versus mistrust, autonomy versus shame and doubt, initiative versus guilt, industry versus inferiority, identity versus role confusion; intimacy versus isolation, generativity versus stagnation, and integrity versus despair. You can use Erikson's stages as a framework to help clients with HIV/AIDS understand why it is difficult to trust others, rely on group members, and develop intimacy. This type of discussion can give meaning to seemingly unconnected beliefs and feelings.

Support Groups for HIV-Negative Gay Men

Support groups for HIV-negative gay men are helpful in terms of preventing the spread of HIV, building self-esteem, and developing a positive gay identity. Gay men who are HIV-negative must live with the threat of HIV infection (Johnston, 1995), and clients in these groups have the opportunity to deal with ongoing losses, receive support for safer sex choices, and meet social needs.

Those who receive a negative test result experience many emotions simultaneously, including relief, elation, and disbelief. HIV-negative clients may experience survivor's guilt and become inured to repeated, traumatic losses. Some clients react to friend's deaths as if they were mundane occurrences. On the other hand, clients may have a wish to join departed friends and partners. Still others react by developing an overwhelming fear of contracting HIV and may develop post-traumatic stress. Some survivors avoid feelings of grief by abusing substances.

Feelings of sexual guilt and internalized homophobia may surface (Johnston, 1995). Some gay men wonder if they "deserve" to remain uninfected, given their sexual histories and their belief that their behavior should be punished (a belief that may stem from internalized homophobia). To deal with these issues, Koetting (1996) created a group design for HIV-negative gay men. The model consists of a low-structure, time-limited counseling group. One goal of the group is to redirect the clients' focus away from how people with HIV/AIDS in their lives deal with their illness, to how the clients themselves feel about HIV/AIDS as HIV-negative gay men. Another aim is to help clients develop an identity as gay males who are uninfected.

The following outline is a format for an eight-week HIV-negative gay men's group (W. Johnson, personal communication, August 19, 2001):

Week 1: Introductions and Going Over the Next 8 Weeks Together
~Facilitator introduction
~Participant introductions, including what each member hopes to gain
~Going over group guidelines
~Overview of the group
~Benefits of journal writing

Week 2: Dating, Relationships, and Intimacy
(NOTE: Each week has a check-in for 15 to 30 minutes, at which time participants can bring up issues as they relate to group.)
~Where do you meet other men?
~Dealing with the fear of rejection
~Negotiating the slippery slope of dating
~Additional issues for bisexual men
Discuss: challenges and rewards of dating

Week 3: Dating, Relationships, and Intimacy, continued
~Dating men who are HIV-positive
~How to bring up the topic of testing
~How far do you go with trust?
Check-in: How is journal writing coming?

Week 4: Sex
~What is safer? What is not?
~Concerns about decision making
~How to reduce "slips"
~Negotiating safety; how to open the lines of communication

Week 5: Sex, continued
~Negotiating safety, Part II: Setting sexual boundaries
~Communication
~Assertiveness
~Role playing
Safer sex demonstration

Week 6: Good Grief
~Dealing with grief
~Losing friends and lovers
~What do you do when you feel alone or bleak about the future?
~Finding ways to celebrate in the midst of loss
Check-in: Journal writing

Week 7: Survivor's Guilt
~What is a survivor?
~Why do you feel guilty for surviving?
~How do you create meaning out of losing people?
~Developing social support

Week 8: Managing and Preventing Stress
~Unhealthy ways of coping: isolation, substance abuse, sexual
compulsion
~Managing stress: exercise
~Managing stress: relaxation (includes relaxation exercise—bring
a tape recorder!)
~Managing and preventing stress: social support
~Managing and preventing stress: spirituality
Consolidating gains: Where do we go from here?

General Comments on Bereavement Support Groups

Bereavement counseling is usually offered in a support group framework. This setting provides clients with the opportunity to benefit from relating to other people's grief, in addition to expressing their own. This may help clients begin to understand that they are not alone in their grief and that they are not the only ones who may have seemingly unusual thoughts and feelings. The format may be psychoeducational with a process component, or it may be process. In either format, facilitators generally convey information in regard to the stages of grief, emotional responses to death, stress management, and spirituality. Clients should be encouraged to define and express feelings about how their lives have changed since their loss and how to take care of themselves throughout the grieving process.

General Comments on Substance Abuse Treatment Support Groups

For substance abuse treatment utilizing a group format, there are generally educational and process components. In the educational component, facilitators offer information about sexual orientation issues combined with substance abuse information. This dual approach facilitates clients' understanding of how issues related to sexual orientation and substance abuse affect one another. For instance, running away from feeling bad about being lesbian or gay may fuel substance use. By combining a didactic component with a process component, you have a greater chance of helping clients develop a tailored relapse prevention plan. Moreover, in the process segment, clients have an opportunity to discuss feelings and reactions that result from the educational component.

Several lesbian and gay community agencies have developed a treatment program for people with HIV/AIDS who abuse substances, mostly with psycho-educational formats. The didactic component includes talks on stress, assertiveness, nutrition, relapse prevention, homophobia and heterosexism, and HIV/AIDS. The process component helps limit denial and rationalization for alcohol and drug use and bolsters support for sobriety.

These groups are generally not limited to specific topics, so there are opportunities to discuss issues ranging from the day-to-day stresses of living with HIV/AIDS to family of origin issues. With their worlds continually changing, in part due to evolving medical treatment strategies and in part due to unpredictable changes in clients' lives, these groups can provide a considerable amount of ongoing support.

❖ SUMMARY

There are an array of choices for placing lesbian and gay male clients into psychotherapy groups and support groups. Lesbians and gay men can benefit greatly from group therapy, although you must take care to ensure a good fit between prospective group members and the group.

Yalom's (1995) therapeutic factors have special significance for lesbian and gay clients. As a result, group therapy can be particularly helpful in allowing clients to develop a positive lesbian/gay identity. There is a good deal of potential for personal growth, as well as the opportunity to reduce shame related to internalized homophobia. Finally, group therapy is a training ground for lesbians and gay men to develop friendships and intimacy.

There are several types of support groups, including coming out groups, sexual orientation growth groups, groups for people with HIV/AIDS, HIV prevention groups for HIV-negative gay men, as well as bereavement groups and substance abuse treatment groups. All of these formats have advantages for clients who wish to focus on particular aspects of their lives.

Regarding the case studies, Patti, Kathy, and Arthur realized how early childhood experiences continue to influence their lives. They also appreciated how heterosexism impacts them as individuals and as a group, and they learned to relate on an emotional level to one another despite having different sexual orientations. John's health is starting to decline due to AIDS, and the other clients in his group explored the impact of his missed sessions both individually and as a group.

In this chapter and in Chapters 4 and 5, we discussed issues with respect to individual, couples, and group psychotherapy assessment and treatment. Although we have alluded to several ethical and legal guidelines in these chapters, we now turn to a more extensive discussion of legal and ethical issues in providing affirmative psychotherapy to lesbian and gay clients.

7

Ethical and Legal Considerations for Affirmative Psychotherapy

❖ ❖ ❖

A number of ethical and legal considerations emerge when you work with lesbians and gay men. As you become aware of these issues, you are better able to ensure ethical delivery of mental health services within an affirmative framework. Each professional organization established what constitutes ethical practice. One ethical standard is that you be familiar with and ascribe to the code of ethics of your profession, whether it be promulgated by the American Psychological Association, American Counseling Association, National Association of Social Workers, or Feminist Therapy Institute.

As Brown (1996) observes, professional codes delineate prohibitions about what should not be done, but less information is provided about what should be done. This situation leaves open to interpretation what constitutes ethical, affirmative practice in the hands of practitioners. Because many ethical guidelines leave room for individual interpretation, you will encounter challenges while attempting to provide ethical treatment for lesbian and gay clients. Furthermore, your worldview, beliefs, and attitudes influence your interpretation of the code. Therefore, although you are guided by several ethical principles, you will generally find more than one "proper" course of action.

This built-in ambiguity means that other sources of information—such as books, discussions with colleagues, and training that address ethical practices—are vital resources in sorting through concerns and dilemmas that arise. The purpose of this chapter is not only to highlight ethical and legal issues of particular importance in treating lesbians and gay men, but also to provoke thought about these topics and stimulate discussion. As a final note before we turn to ethical and legal considerations, we would like to point out that much of the research we cite has been done on lesbian/gay therapists and their lesbian/gay clients. As you read the chapter, however, you will see that these issues—from self-disclosure of sexual orientation to homophobia—apply to nongay as well as gay therapists.

❖ ETHICAL CONSIDERATIONS WITH RESPECT TO TREATING LESBIANS AND GAY MEN

Notions of ethical treatment for lesbians and gay men have evolved through the years, as evidenced by a resolution passed by the American Psychological Association (APA) (APA, Committee on Lesbian and Gay Concerns, 1998). The resolution, titled "Appropriate Therapeutic Responses to Sexual Orientation," states that because homosexuality is not a mental illness, it is the responsibility of all psychologists not to treat it as such.

The APA is one of several mental health associations to make pronouncements for ethical treatment of lesbians and gay men. The National Association of Social Workers passed a revised code of ethics (National Association of Social Workers, 1996). In the code, individuals with a same-gender orientation are considered a minority group on equal par with ethnic minority groups. The code specifies that clinicians should obtain the necessary training to understand and interact affirmatively with lesbians and gay men, and a stated goal for social workers is not to discriminate, dominate, or exploit any minority group.

The American Counseling Association (ACA) passed a resolution titled "Appropriate Counseling Responses to Sexual Orientation" (ACA, Human Rights Committee, 1998). This resolution states that counselors should be aware of their own values, attitudes, beliefs, and behaviors; that they should avoid imposing their values on clients; and that they should not condone or engage in discrimination based on sexual orientation. In part, the resolution states,

> [The ACA] opposes portrayals of lesbian, gay, and bisexual youth and adults as mentally ill due to their sexual orientation; and supports the dissemination of accurate information about sexual orientation, mental health, and appropriate interventions in order to counteract bias that is based on ignorance or unfounded beliefs about same-gender sexual orientation. (p. 15)

These professional associations maintain that clinicians should receive education and training necessary to ethically treat lesbians, gay men, and bisexuals. Murphy (1992) proposes that advancement of ethical treatment in the mental health field be related to training in higher-education settings. She asserts that this goal could be advanced by requiring licensing organizations to include case scenarios that involve lesbian and gay clients on licensing exams. This could motivate universities that are slow to implement teaching affirmative practice. In addition, Murphy suggests that professionals work with accreditation organizations that review educational programs to ensure that course curricula include current information on treatment for lesbians and gay men.

She further suggests that sites applying for internships should be required to provide in-service training on lesbian and gay issues. Specific methods that provide educational opportunities to encourage affirmative treatment toward lesbian and gay male clients include the use of guest speakers, dialogues, role plays, and videotapes. Moreover, because lesbian and gay male students, in addition to heterosexual students, come into contact with homophobia and heterosexism, these exercises and experiences may challenge erroneous beliefs held by lesbian/gay, as well as heterosexual, students. As Murphy (1992) states, "All mental health workers must be taught that unless they can actively affirm gay and lesbian lifestyles, they cannot ethically work with these clients" (p. 240).

❖ SEXUAL ORIENTATION OF THE THERAPIST

Experience plays a major role in providing affirmative therapy for lesbian and gay male clients. To illustrate, McDermott, Tyndall, and Lichtenberg (1989) found that therapists with little to no experience with lesbian and gay male clients scored significantly higher on scales measuring internalized homophobia than therapists who had treated lesbian and gay male clients. One implication of the study is that clinicians who develop bonds with their lesbian and gay clients are able to work through their biases and misunderstandings about lesbians and gay men. Their increased familiarity and comfort level helps ensure ethical treatment, often resulting from higher amounts of empathy and understanding for their lesbian and gay clients.

As an illustration of exemplary practice, Holahan and Gibson (1994), a heterosexual male therapist and a heterosexual female therapist, led an all-gay-male group and an all-lesbian group in a university counseling center setting. Prior to starting the groups, they learned about the developmental processes of lesbians and gay men and arranged for 5 weeks of supervision from a gay male therapist followed by 5 weeks of supervision by a lesbian therapist. Holahan and Gibson's proactive stance and continued attention to the dynamic created because they are heterosexual therapists demonstrates the amount of work required from therapists who counsel lesbians and gay men. Indeed, they received positive feedback from the participants upon termination of the groups. Case Study 7A illustrates this type of commitment from a new employee at a lesbian/gay agency.

As illustrated by this case study, nongay clinicians can provide affirmative, ethical therapy as effectively as lesbian and gay clinicians. Some clients erroneously assume that lesbian and gay male therapists have fewer biases than heterosexual therapists do. Further, these clients assume that they will more easily gain rapport and trust with lesbian/gay therapists, and that being lesbian or gay implies common experiences and even common interests. Many clients also believe that lesbian/gay therapists have a greater amount of knowledge and understanding in how to provide treatment for lesbians and gay men. The fact that clinicians are lesbian or gay, however, does not ensure that clients will receive ethical treatment.

Nonetheless, many lesbian and gay clients prefer to have lesbian or gay therapists. On the other hand, many clients have no preference,

Therapist Case Study 7A

A heterosexual intern, K. D., started working at a lesbian and gay community agency. She had no prior experience as a therapist and no prior contact with the lesbian/gay community. As a result, K. D. was unaware of the challenges she would encounter and the experience she would need to have in order to become a competent, affirmative therapist.

Within just a few weeks, however, by investing time and energy in asking questions of staff members, reading lesbian/gay books, and going into the gay community, K. D. started to become knowledgeable. Over time, she became adept at treating lesbian and gay male clients. Her comfort level with the lesbian and gay community grew to where she participated in a number of Gay Pride events with her husband and children. Because of her willingness to immerse herself in the gay community, she was able to work through many of her preconceived notions to become an affirmative clinician.

and some prefer heterosexual therapists for various reasons, such as to obtain a different point of view. McDermott, Tyndall, and Lichtenberg (1989) found that 39% of the participants in their study did not have a preference regarding sexual orientation of the therapist, whereas close to 50% preferred a lesbian or gay male therapist.

In actuality, although many lesbian and gay therapists confront their own internal biases, others have high levels of internalized homophobia. And, just because lesbian/gay therapists are open about their sexual orientation, it does not mean that they a high level of comfort and acceptance with being lesbian or gay. Nor does it indicate that they have dealt with their own issues involved with developing a positive lesbian/gay identity. Likewise, inexperienced and biased nongay therapists can be reluctant or unwilling to provide affirmative therapy. As such, both lesbian/gay and nongay clinicians can possess significant countertransference, which reduces the chances for providing ethical therapy. Countertransference is discussed in the next section.

❖ COUNTERTRANSFERENCE

Developing *countertransference*, which can be defined as projected feelings and beliefs toward clients, is a possibility in treating any client. With respect to lesbian and gay clients, however, there is a high likelihood to have countertransference reactions. This potential for countertransference arises partly from therapists' heterosexist bias, of which they are often unaware. Therapists may inadvertently avoid topics that are uncomfortable to them, especially when they have unresolved emotions or conflict regarding those issues (Frost, 1998). For example, lesbian and gay male clients who have sexual dysfunction and want to explicitly talk about sexual acts can stir up feelings of discomfort in clinicians.

As Rudolph's (1990) study (noted in Chapter 3) suggests, many heterosexual therapists are comfortable with lesbian and gay issues on an intellectual level but, once the topic of eroticized activity is brought up, they may experience inner conflicts. The same holds true for lesbian and gay clinicians who are uncomfortable with their sexual orientation. When therapists have difficulty with their own their sexual orientation, countertransference can have deleterious effects on lesbian or gay male clients. Cabaj (1996) indicates that these effects include reducing the therapeutic pace, failing to address and commend client progress, and projecting their own situation onto the client's circumstances.

Furthermore, countertransference may lead therapists to underidentify or overidentify with their clients. Therapists who underidentify with lesbian and gay clients may overdiagnose pathology. These clinicians may play down the effects of various situations lesbians and gay men encounter and instead attribute clients' actions to mental illness.

Another result of underidentifying with clients is for therapists to become impatient with the coming out process. For instance, some clinicians may pressure clients to come out because of their belief that "It's difficult now but, after you come out, things will be better." Clinicians with this attitude may have friends and relatives who have come out and had positive outcomes from supportive families and friends, or they had a positive experience coming out themselves. They may therefore minimize clients' struggles, wishing for clients to "get on with it." As a result, these therapists may underestimate potential harmful consequences, such as the loss of friendships and family relationships, financial consequences, and job-related problems, including fears of being terminated or hitting a glass ceiling.

On the other hand, overidentification with clients may lead to downplaying the benefits of coming out, joining clients in their anger at prejudice, and feeling overly protective of lesbian or gay clients. As a result, these therapists may offer suggestions to clients based on their own experiences, use explanations to rationalize behavior, and underdiagnose mental illness. Clinicians who overidentify with lesbian and gay clients may also convey the message that clients are pacing the coming out process too quickly, and they may attempt to slow them down. These clinicians may recall the difficulty of their friends or family members who have come out, or their own difficulty when coming out, and they may use those experiences as a way to justify warnings and exaggerate the harmful effects of coming out.

Frost (1998) indicates that the potential for countertransference points to the need for supervision and peer consultation for therapists working with lesbian and gay clients. Fortunately, as the number of affirmative therapists for lesbians and gays increases, it becomes easier to find the peer support necessary to establish and maintain ethical treatment.

❖ BOUNDARIES

One consequence of countertransference is a blurring of boundaries. Boundaries that are too rigid or too flexible can result from discomfort with oneself due to internalized homophobia or heterosexism. Heyward (1993) illustrates the consequences of the abuse of power that can result from rigid boundary setting. Heyward describes how the patriarchal bent of traditional psychotherapy and the resulting dispassionate professional role can be harmful when therapists hide behind professional personae and use boundary setting as a way to manipulate clients. Likewise, boundaries that are too loose can lead to unethical situations and relationships. For example, therapists with loose boundaries may ask clients to do favors for them, encourage individual therapy clients to talk to each other out of session, and barter therapy for services.

In her study, Lyn (1995) reported on guidelines that lesbian, gay, and bisexual therapists employed in their practice. Types of guidelines include contact initiation outside of session, unallowable topics for discussion between sessions, negotiating introductions, discussing social interactions in the next session, and whether socializing can take place after termination. Other considerations include self-disclosure and gift giving.

According to professional codes of ethics, dual relationships are to be avoided whenever possible. These relationships should be avoided whether the individuals are current or former clients, but it is not always possible to avoid them. In her research, Lyn (1995) set out to document and describe experiences of lesbian, gay, and bisexual therapists who practice in their communities. She found that although social encounters occurred with high frequency, social relationships occurred with less frequency, and sexual activity was even less frequent.

Social encounters and interactions often lead to ethical dilemmas. Lyn (1995) defines a dilemma as "a situation in which a clear course of action is not evident" (p. 199). Gartrell (1994), who also delineated boundary issues for lesbian therapists, indicates that unclear therapeutic boundaries lead to inappropriate contact between therapists and clients. Most lesbian therapists reported feeling discomfort due to social encounters in the community.

When you work in the gay community, there is a greater possibility of chance meetings than in the general community. Therapists may unexpectedly discover that they are at the same place of worship, restaurant, or retail establishment or are attending the same function, celebration, or charity event where clients are present. We discuss this "small town" aspect of working in the gay community in the next section. Although situations involving unexpected meetings cannot be predicted, Gartrell (1994) maintains that setting boundaries clarifies expectations about what to do when this happens. To reduce the possibility of awkward or embarrassing situations, one option for boundary setting includes finding a mutually agreeable solution with clients at the outset of therapy. Doing so allows clients to develop a sense of security by having a clear picture of each person's role. When both therapists and clients acknowledge the guidelines, therapists are providing an atmosphere in which clients feel freer to question interventions and the purpose of exercises and dialogue, thus indirectly promoting the establishment of good boundaries. In spite of good boundary setting, you should be prepared to have some awkward moments, as we discuss in Case Study 7B.

Therapist Case Study 7B

It is Saturday night, and you are sitting at a popular coffee shop with some friends. A client, Debbie, spots you through the picture window and hurriedly approaches you to have a private discussion. Debbie says, "I have to talk to you about something urgent, and it can't wait until the next session." She says this in front of your friends, creating an awkward situation.

Would you agree to talk to her? What if you agreed to talk to her, but it turns out that the "urgent" issue could have waited until the next session? Would you ask Debbie to wait until the following session to talk about it?

The choices you have to make in Case Study 7B are similar to those you have to make when you have any chance meeting with clients in public places. To illustrate, if introductions are not made when you greet clients when their friends are present, it is natural for their friends to wonder why they are not being introduced to you. If introductions are made, however, it could lead to being asked how you and your clients know each other. For this reason, you may wish to explain to clients that you will not approach them in public places. You can inform clients that you will leave the decision up to them in each situation as to whether to greet you. This reduces the possibility of placing clients in a potentially embarrassing situation, while at the same time not leaving them to feel rejected when you do not approach them in public.

With respect to contact with former clients, your first consideration should be to use ethical guidelines for the professional association(s) in which you are a member as the minimum standard. Another consideration, as Gartrell (1994) suggests, is that it is exceedingly difficult to be well acquainted with former clients because of the imbalance of power. You know a wealth of intimate details about former clients, whereas ex-clients have limited, if any, personal information about you. There are also difficulties in removing the therapeutic framework from these relationships, and ex-clients may desire informal therapy, and the therapeutic relationship may habitually continue. As a result, you may consider having a "once a client, always a client" guideline, which is a conservative approach that helps ensure proper boundaries with former (who may also be future) clients.

Moreover, this decision eliminates the possibility that social relationships with former clients turn into sexual ones. Because sexual contact between therapists and their current clients is the most deleterious form of boundary violation, all ethical codes prohibit it. Although the APA and ACA permit sexual contact under some circumstances with former clients after 2 years beyond termination, the National Association of Social Workers takes a stronger prohibition, and the Ethical Guidelines for Feminist Therapists (1999) prohibits all sexual contact with former clients.

Benowitz (1995) studied female therapists who sexually exploit clients. She found that abusing therapists share certain characteristics, including a difference in age from abused clients (11 years older, on average) and a discomfort with their sexual orientation. A little more than half of the therapists had a major relationship change (mostly breakups) immediately before the abuse began. Surprisingly, she found that the sexual orientation was not uniform; 20% were heterosexual, and 33% were legally married.

Benowitz also distinguishes between covert and overt sexual exploitation. Covert sexual activity includes flirting, sexualized talk, and physical contact, such as prolonged hand holding or hugging. Covert sexual activity usually precedes overt sexual contact. Sexual contact and other major boundary violations are sometimes the endpoint of several smaller boundary violations.

There are certain signs along the way to serious violations. One sign is the therapist becoming social isolated. Gonsiorek (1995) notes that other risk factors for gay male therapists include becoming depressed, experiencing stress or major disappointments in their lives, or making major life changes. Gay male psychotherapists, especially those with overlapping ties to their own communities, may blur distinctions among their social and therapeutic roles. If they do, they may be tempted to view clients as peers or a support system. Thus, they may attempt to get their own needs met at the expense of those of their clients. Naturally, these notions apply to lesbian therapists.

In regard to self-disclosure, limiting information to basic demographics and generalized responses to specific questions helps keep therapeutic boundaries appropriate. Unfortunately, moving away from

---

Therapist Case Study 7C

A client with dependency issues asks you about your relationship status. To this point, you have not revealed whether you were in a relationship because the subject has never come up. In today's session, however, the client states that she is deciding whether to leave her partner for someone else. She lists qualities in her ideal partner, which happen to be many of the qualities that she sees in you.

Would you answer her question? Would you consider maintaining boundaries to be more important than answering the question fully and truthfully? How can you turn this question into grist for the therapeutic mill?

---

the balance, by offering too much or too little information, has an impact on treatment. At times, it is difficult to find a balance, as we discuss in Case Study 7C.

Gift giving and receiving, which is also addressed by Gartrell (1994), can be problematic. Acknowledging a special event with a card or small gift is appropriate but, under most circumstances, giving and receiving gifts carries therapeutic risk. Gartrell indicates that it is inevitable that some clients will attempt to give gifts to their therapists and, as long as this is infrequent and incidental, it probably will not affect therapy. As noted in Chapter 4, with respect to pro bono or low fee clients, small tokens of appreciation may be a way to maintain a sense of dignity through reciprocity.

When therapists find themselves along the continuum of possible ethical violations, Lyn (1995) recommends that, in order to resolve, negotiate, or prevent potentially harmful boundary situations, therapists must perceive that the situation is an ethical dilemma in the first place. This leads to determining how to proceed in an ethical manner. An important consideration is to have ongoing consultation and supervision. The more isolated you become, the easier it is to lose perspective or to take inappropriate courses of action. Peer consultation and supervision provides you with the opportunity to have a realistic appraisal of boundary challenges (Gonsiorek, 1995).

Gonsiorek (1995) has several other recommendations, including maintaining a personal support system and creating an identity separate from your professional one. He also notes that it is important to monitor your life stresses and consider breaks in treating clients when major life events occur. Also, Gonsiorek states that it is important to seek consultation for prolonged countertransference reactions and to develop at least one other area of professional competence. Possibilities include having a part-time position in teaching or consulting. Following these recommendations may help avoid the frustration and burnout associated with the "small town" aspect of working in the lesbian and gay community, which is discussed in the next section.

❖ THE "SMALL TOWN" PHENOMENON

Clinicians, whether nongay or lesbian/gay, often experience the impact of living and working in what feels like a small town. Therapists are often visible in the lesbian and gay community, and their behavior may be under scrutiny. Lyn (1995) notes that many therapists feel conscious of social interaction issues and inhibited at social gatherings. As a result, many clinicians limit attendance at social gatherings, live outside of the lesbian/gay community, and travel on a regular basis. Dating may be particularly problematic. Single lesbian and gay clinicians who are dating may find it exceedingly difficult, as in Case Studies 7D and 7E.

In addition to the challenges of dating, attendance at lesbian and gay functions, where therapists are placed in the position of public role models, can be awkward. For example, therapists can become acutely aware of their public behavior when they are alone or with friends and romantic partners. In general, when clinicians feel watched and evaluated, they may limit friendships and curb activities in the lesbian and gay community, and some therapists feel resentful at having to do so. As a result, these feelings may result in countertransference.

Kranzberg (1998) states that it is important for therapists to realize that the role model position creates an overlapping relationship with clients. This predicament may place a strain on authenticity because needing to have a "public face" causes therapists to feel disingenuous.

Although being a therapist in the lesbian and gay community has its drawbacks, lesbian therapist Anthony (1985) argues that once you

Therapist Case Study 7D

A client reports that she is dating someone new. During the course of the session, the client mentions that her name is Monica. After the client tells you what Monica does for a living and her age, among other qualities she has, you realize that you and the client are dating the same person.

Although this example appears to be extreme, it can happen. There is no right or wrong answer to any of our examples but, as with several dilemmas, the choices are few. In this instance, would you stop dating Monica, or would you refer your client to another therapist? If you talked to Monica about the situation, you would be violating your client's right to confidentiality. So, there appear to be only two choices: Stop dating Monica immediately or, if you choose not to stop dating her, refer the client to another therapist.

Neither course of action is ideal. If you choose the former, you will continue therapy with a client who may have heard information about you that you would ordinarily not reveal. If you choose the latter, you have interrupted the course of therapy, and you are dating someone who is dating a newly terminated client.

accept your role in the community, you provide opportunities for client growth through being a role model. This is particularly true when you value and accept your lesbian (or gay) identity. As Anthony (1985) states,

I participate in and enjoy gay and lesbian community activities for the same reasons I encourage my clients to participate; to enjoy feeling free from hiding and passing, to be with other gay men and lesbians in a relaxed atmosphere, and to enjoy the feeling of community and confirmation of my lifestyle. (p. 53)

Therapist Case Study 7E

You are a well-known therapist in the gay community. Over the years, you have limited your contact with organizations, preferring to participate by donating money to various causes and limiting attendance to large community events.

You have a small circle of friends who are aware of your situation. Last week, you and your partner attended a small dinner party. Your friend Jill brings her date Susan with her to dinner. Susan is a current client. You learn at the dinner party that Jill started dating Susan several weeks ago.

Susan ordinarily talked about her dating life in therapy, but she failed to mention that she was seeing Jill. And Jill never told you about Susan, even though the two of you generally talk about personal information.

What are your options? You could limit your friendship with Jill, but there would still be occasions where you will see Jill and Susan together. You would be very uncomfortable hearing about your client from Jill, and you couldn't comment on Susan or the relationship with either of them. It is likely that your client Susan would limit information about Jill and the relationship when speaking to you, and you would clearly be uncomfortable when you hear information about Susan from your friend Jill.

It may be that in this particular situation, the only ethical course of action would be to terminate therapy with Susan and refer her to another therapist. Your ability to help Susan has diminished, and the possibility for triangulation is high.

❖ COUNTERTRANSFERENCE
   WITH RESPECT TO HIV/AIDS

Countertransference often arises when treating clients with HIV/AIDS. As an example, finding a balance between approaching and distancing from clients to maintain therapeutic boundaries is challenging when working with clients who have HIV/AIDS. In this section, we discuss sources of countertransference, including feelings of helplessness, anxiety about death and dying, and anger at real and perceived injustices.

Feelings of Helplessness

The first source of countertransference is clinicians' feelings of helplessness. One coping mechanism is to take credit for situations outside of their control, imagining that they are keeping clients from illness or death. Therapists may convince themselves that if clients continue to come to therapy, they will remain healthy.

Another way to cope is to attempt to rescue clients. Rather than sitting with clients' pain, therapists may feel compelled to push clients into action, whether or not the clients are ready for such action and regardless of its appropriateness. Bernstein and Klein (1995) state that when therapists intervene by telling clients what actions to take, clients become dependent on their therapists for answers. And telling clients what to do interferes with the therapeutic process by taking away clients' responsibility. The third reaction to helplessness is joining with clients in catastrophizing, blaming, and feeling depressed or emotionally drained. When these feelings arise, therapists can lose objectivity, causing clients' opportunities to process their issues to diminish.

Fears About Death and Dying

The second source of countertransference that arises when working with clients who have HIV/AIDS is anxiety about death and dying. Feelings that come up with respect to mortality are particularly distressing because of the early age of onset of the disease and the potential for premature death. Gay male therapists are especially vulnerable to this kind of countertransference due to the possibility that they may have HIV or may fear contracting the disease.

Therapists employ several coping strategies to contend with mortality. When clinicians feel overwhelmed, they may compensate by assuming an emotionally detached posture. This stance is an attempt to mitigate the impact of clients' impending or actual deaths and to curtail thoughts about their own mortality. Unfortunately, emotional detachment leads to several problems in therapy, including clients being emotionally abandoned and curtailed from fully exploring their own fears about dying.

A natural way to deal with anxiety about death and dying is denial, which serves a useful function because it gives people the opportunity to live life without the threat of anxiety becoming overwhelming. When therapists employ denial as a defense, however, they tend to steer around issues related to death and dying. If therapists take care of their own needs at the expense of clients' needs, therapists can attempt to gloss over death-and-dying issues, such as clients' fear of death, funeral arrangements, and other challenges.

Anger at Real and Perceived Injustice

In reaction to the third source of countertransference, anger at real and perceived injustice, therapists may join their clients in directing their anger at hospitals, government agencies, and other institutions. When clinicians become angry along with clients, they inhibit clients' emotional responses. Joining can also stave off exploring clients' underlying issues with respect to their anger.

When clients' anger is directed at their therapists, countertransference can lead therapists to employ strategies to restrain clients' anger, such as becoming defensive and withdrawing. However, Bernstein and Klein (1995) suggest that when therapists resist their countertransferance impulses, clients benefit by being in a permissive atmosphere where they can express their feelings.

❖ DUTY TO WARN AND HIV/AIDS

Ethicists and psychologists applied the concept of confidentiality to the field so clients could feel free to disclose information without the threat of repercussion from outsiders. Some interpretations of confidentiality uphold that all client information is confidential, and it is clinicians' ethical responsibility to ensure it (Stanard & Hazler, 1995).

Legal Considerations

Today, however, there are legal mandates to break confidentiality. One legal requirement to violate confidentiality is the reporting of certain information when the lives of potential victims are at stake. Although statutory considerations are beyond the scope of this book, we would like to make some general comments in regard to the complexity involving the legal duty to warn for clients with HIV/AIDS.

For states that apply the Tarasoff case, as decided in Tarasoff v. Regents of California (see Keith-Spiegel & Koocher, 1985), therapists have a duty to protect known intended victims of homicide. There are three conditions that are required to legally breach confidentiality by warning a potential homicide victim. These conditions are having a special relationship, foreseeing that future behavior could be harmful, and the existence of a known victim.

The duty to warn potential victims of clients with HIV/AIDS is a gray area partly because it is difficult to assess potential lethality. For example, the identified "victim" may already be HIV-positive or be aware of clients' HIV status prior to having sex. Another uncertainty includes the use of condoms. Condoms reduce the possibility of infection but, if a condom breaks, an individual is at much greater risk of infection (Stanard & Hazler, 1995). So, is there a duty to warn when clients use condoms because of the possibility of breakage? Does a client's self-report of condom use with sexual partners still not preclude therapists' duty to warn? In terms of our most fundamental ethical duty to do no harm, do you report if, as Pais, Piercy, and Miller (1998) observe, there is the possibility of severe discrimination and emotional harm to a third party?

Yet another complication, as Schlossberger and Hecker (1996) point out, is that therapists have no duty to intervene when people engage in activities that are legal, such as mountain climbing and skydiving. They conclude that, unless state law directly or indirectly requires HIV-positive clients to warn partners of risk of infection, therapists have no legal duty to warn. To determine whether you must inform a third party about clients' HIV status, consultation with colleagues, professional associations, and attorneys familiar with these issues is essential.

As a final note about legal issues, you should include the limits of confidentiality in your informed consent form and review your consent form with clients prior to starting therapy. As a result, clients can make an informed decision before entering therapy with you.

Ethical Considerations

Turning from legal to ethical considerations for duty to warn, as Stanard and Hazler (1995) note, there is no blanket answer to solve any ethical dilemma. So, if laws in your state do not directly or indirectly address the issue of duty to warn for clients with HIV, ethical and therapeutic considerations take precedence. Schlossberger and Hecker (1996) observe that whether you violate confidentiality or keep "guilty" secrets, each course of action has ethical and therapeutic ramifications.

In general, in determining whether to breach confidentiality, therapists should consider the ethical principles of fidelity, autonomy, nonmalfeasance, beneficence, and justice (Stanard & Hazler, 1995). By applying each of these principles to the situation, you can assess whether clients' rights are infringed upon, whether there will be repercussions to breaking confidentiality that could harm clients or third parties, and whether it is in clients' or others' best interests.

In regard to the principles of fidelity and autonomy, Schlossberger and Hecker (1996) maintain that informing partners without clients' consent violates these principles by depriving clients of their de facto legal right to keep their HIV status private. However, HIV-positive clients who decline to reveal their status to partners violate others' autonomy. Thus, as a matter of ethical practice under these principles, for clients who refuse to reveal their HIV status to partners, you should encourage, cajole, and urge clients to disclose their HIV status on their own, rather than violating their confidentiality.

In regard to the ethical principles of nonmalfeasance and beneficence, you should consider to what degree disclosure to third parties would possibly harm them or your clients socially, personally, and economically. Then, you should determine if the potential benefits would outweigh the harmful impact, including a breach of trust.

In regard to the last principle, justice, you must weigh your options carefully before deciding whether to reveal a client's HIV status to another party. Have you done enough to persuade the client to reveal his or her HIV status? Do the ends justify violating confidentiality, especially if AIDS moves from a "deadly disease" to a "manageable disease"?

To come to an ethical conclusion for a course of action, you should examine each of these issues, along with other therapeutic and ethical considerations relevant to the each case. When deciding on the most ethical course of action, you must consider the ethical principles involved, discuss the situation with colleagues, contact your professional association and legal counsel, and compare it to similar cases.

❖ RESEARCH

We discussed the selection and use of assessment instruments in Chapter 3. In this section, we present issues related to research subjects. Researchers should provide a comfortable environment and be sensitive to specific issues with respect to lesbian and gay subjects. Considerations regarding research subjects include research methods, sampling techniques, use of instruments, treatment of research subjects, and collection of normative data.

Herek, Kimmel, Amaro, and Melton (1991) designed a series of questions to help practitioners become aware of the potential effects of research on lesbians and gay men. We adapted the questions as follows for developing inclusive and affirmative research design:

1. Does the research question . . .
   * ❖ assume the presence of lesbians and gay men?
   * ❖ equate heterosexuality with homosexuality as normal sexual variations?
   * ❖ refuse to propagate lesbian or gay stereotypes?
   * ❖ assume that the individual's sexual orientation is unrelated to the behavior observed?

2. Is the sample . . .
   * ❖ representative of the population to which it will be generalized?
   * ❖ collected from a diversified sample across the group that is being researched?
   * ❖ appropriate for the research question?

3. Is sexual orientation . . .
   * ❖ the variable of interest?
   * ❖ assessed appropriately?
   * ❖ the parameter to use in determining comparison groups?

❖ not assumed to be heterosexual based on questions asked?
❖ an issue for the researcher, and may it influence the participants?

4. Does the research . . .
  ❖ maintain confidentiality?
  ❖ mitigate potentially harmful effects for lesbian and gay male subjects?
  ❖ not reinforce stereotypes or prejudicial beliefs?
  ❖ use recruitment and research techniques that respect subjects' privacy?
  ❖ mitigate potential embarrassment with questions regarding sexuality?

5. In the results of the study . . .
  ❖ are the findings not assumed to reflect pathology?
  ❖ is the language inclusive?
  ❖ are limitations noted and discussed?
  ❖ have the findings been presented in a way to reduce misinterpretations by the general public?
  ❖ have the findings been reported to the participants and, if appropriate, to the lesbian and gay community?

As a final comment, there is a need for continuing research on subjects with respect to counseling and psychotherapy with lesbians and gay men. When you address these research issues related to the needs of lesbians and gay men, there is a greater potential for affirmative and inclusive research activities. Moreover, when you obtain training and information on counseling lesbians and gay men based on the latest research, you are taking care to provide ethical treatment.

❖ REPARATIVE THERAPY

Although the American Psychiatric Association removed homosexuality and ego-dystonic homosexuality (a struggle with being lesbian or gay) from the *Diagnostic and Statistical Manual* (DSM) in 1973, Brown (1996) indicates, from a survey review, that some clinicians still believe that homosexuality is pathological and would treat it as such in their

---

Case Study 7.1 (Tom, continued from Case Study 5.1)

You notice that Tom was guarded in last week's session when he talked about growing up. You remark to Tom that he seems slow to develop trust for you. He talks about former therapy, even though on the intake form he indicated otherwise.

Tearfully, Tom states, "When I was 17, my parents took me to a psychiatrist because I told them that I was gay. The psychiatrist recommended that my parents put me in a hospital for conversion therapy. I had no choice." Tom pauses for a moment, adding, "They did terrible things to me. Every day, I had a device attached to my penis that detected swelling, and they showed me pictures of naked men. When I got aroused, I got a shock. It wasn't as painful as it was humiliating. They had a one-way mirror, and people were watching me."

Tom continues, "They also told me to fantasize about women when I was ready to ejaculate, and they told me I needed to play football, if you can believe that. I wanted to change, but I couldn't. A week before I left the hospital, they told my parents I was hopeless. I spent 6 months in that place. Right after I left the hospital, I tried to kill myself. A few months later, I met and decided to marry Elizabeth. I dated her for 2 months, and I thought I could at least pretend to be straight."

---

practice. One form of treatment is reparative therapy, which refers to attempting to convert people from homosexuality to heterosexuality. Techniques vary, but practitioners generally adopt a behavioral approach, which includes pressure to leave same-gender relationships, associate solely with heterosexuals, discontinue same-gender sex, and move away from the lesbian/gay community.

The APA passed a resolution stating that reparative therapy is not in the best interests of lesbian and gay male clients. The APA resolution, "Appropriate Therapeutic Responses to Sexual Orientation" (APA, Committee on Lesbian and Gay Concerns, 1998), states that reparative therapy is not desirable or appropriate. The APA stated that it is questionable to conduct therapy to change something that is not considered pathological. Because it is the APA's commitment to recognize and respect individual differences, treating lesbian and gay male clients in any way other than in an affirmative setting is considered unethical.

Nonetheless, one argument for offering reparative therapy is the large number of individuals who enroll in reparative therapy programs. However, nearly all lesbians and gay men go through a period of time where they are uncomfortable with their sexual orientation. Because this time period often includes a desire to change to heterosexuality, it makes lesbians and gay men vulnerable to attempts to change their sexual orientation. Many "repaired" lesbians and gay men temporarily disavow same-gender attraction while mimicking heterosexuality. Their fantasies continue to be same-gender in nature, even though they may not act upon them (Haldeman, 1994).

For many lesbians and gay men, the negative impact of such therapy on clients is long lasting. Practitioners override the ethical principle of nonmalfeasance, and examples abound of clients who, as a result of taking the blame for being unable to change, feel despair while undergoing reparative therapy or thereafter, as Case Study 7.1 illustrates.

Many lesbians and gay men who have undergone reparative therapy have little trust for the mental health field. Even if they know you are lesbian, gay, or gay-friendly, these clients were traumatized by their former therapists, and their scars may never completely heal.

❖   SELF-AWARENESS

Mallon (1998) notes that when society considers an individual or group to be outside the norm, it is easier to marginalize individuals and the group's importance to the culture. Although we are all products of a heterosexist culture, we can overcome these thoughts and beliefs by first developing awareness of introjected beliefs. As you attain greater self-awareness, you experience more empathy and understanding for lesbian and gay clients, especially in regard to feeling marginalized or discriminated against. However, providing lesbian- and gay-affirming therapy requires that you evaluate your belief system on an ongoing basis. Case study 7F illustrates one way to evaluate therapists' belief systems.

Therapist Case Study 7F

You are attending a breakout session at a conference. The facilitator asks the participants to wear name tags that indicate that you are all lesbian or gay. However, written on some of the name tags is a slang word—such as *fag, dyke,* or *sissy*—that is usually considered derogatory. The facilitator announces that you have a 15-minute break, and she asks you to keep the name tags on during the break. Later in the session, she asks you to discuss your feelings about wearing the labels.

Even though other people attending the conference might assume your name tag is related to the breakout session, would you feel uncomfortable having the word attached to your shirt? Would you remove the name tag prior to leaving the room for a break in spite of her instructions? Reactions and feelings generated by this kind of exercise can be enlightening.

To aid in self-awareness on the part of heterosexuals, Rochlin (1972) developed the "Heterosexual Questionnaire." This instrument turns the tables on heterosexuals by changing questions often asked of lesbians and gay men into those that heterosexuals can answer. When they do, they realize just how absurd these questions sound to lesbians and gay men. Questions include, "When did you first realize that you were heterosexual?" Also, "Why do you have to flaunt your sexuality by touching or kissing in public?" And finally, "How do you really know that you are heterosexual when you've never had a good same-gender relationship?"

❖ SUMMARY

There are myriad ethical and legal considerations when providing affirmative treatment for lesbians and gay men. Although your own sexual orientation influences the treatment of lesbian and gay clients, your attitude and willingness to monitor your evolving feelings and attitudes have a much greater impact. The issues of countertransference, boundaries, consequences of working and living in the gay community, and HIV/AIDS pertain equally to lesbian and gay therapists and heterosexual therapists.

In this chapter's case studies, a therapist who was naive when she started working at a lesbian/gay agency became knowledgeable in her work with lesbian and gay clients in a short amount of time. Other case studies included therapists encountering ethical dilemmas, some of which arise out of the "small town" aspect of working in the gay community.

As a final note, you are continually in a position to make choices about providing a valuable therapeutic experience for lesbian and gay male clients. In addition to providing therapeutic interventions based on your theory or theories of choice, building blocks for affirmative practice include addressing biases against lesbians and gay men; providing warmth, empathy, and support; focusing on clients' strengths and adaptive coping strategies; and sharing your knowledge of community resources. Becoming skilled at working with lesbian and gay clients is a continuous process of growth. And it is the professional responsibility of all of us to provide a supportive, nonjudgmental environment in which we have the willingness, attitude, and knowledge to successfully carry out the task.

Appendix

Resources for Lesbian and Gay Male Clients

❖ ❖ ❖

❖ SEARCH ENGINES AND DATABASES

- ❖ Bi/Gay/Lesbian Search Portal: www.bglad.com
- ❖ Freeality Queer Resources: www.freeality.com/queer
- ❖ Gayscape search engine: www.jwpublishing.com/gayscape
- ❖ Lesbian.org—Promoting Lesbian Visibility on the Internet: www.lesbian.org

❖ NATIONAL AND INTERNATIONAL GAY AND
LESBIAN ORGANIZATIONS AND PUBLICATIONS

- ❖ Gay and lesbian studies information: www.lib.washington. edu/subject/GayLesbianStudies
- ❖ Gay-Straight Alliance Network: 160 14th St., San Francisco, CA 94103, 415-552-4229, www.gsanetwork.org
- ❖ A lesbian and gay bibliography: www.growing.com/accolade/ viol/gaylesb.htm
- ❖ Queer Reads (a database of LGBT books): www.queerreads.com
- ❖ Rainbow Directory: www.rainbowquery.com

Note: If you would like updated links to the Web sites listed in this appendix, please contact Jeff Chernin at JNChernin@aol.com.

❖ SELF-HELP AND HOTLINE REFERRALS

- ❖ Gay and Lesbian National Hotline: www.glnh.org, 888-843-4564. Provides local hotline numbers, plus peer counseling and shelter referrals.
- ❖ National Association of Lesbian and Gay Community Centers: www.lgbtcenters.org. An international listing of LGBT centers by location.
- ❖ The Trevor Project: www.thetrevorproject.org, 800-850-8078. A hotline for LGBT and questioning youth.

❖ AGING

Organizations and Online Resources

- ❖ The Gay and Lesbian Association of Retiring Persons: 10940 Wilshire Blvd., Ste. 1600, Los Angeles, CA 90024, 310-966-1500, www.gaylesbianretiring.org
- ❖ Golden Threads: P.O. Box 1688, Demorest, GA 30535 america.net/~wildiris/goldenthreads.html. A network for senior lesbians.
- ❖ Lesbian and Gay Aging Issues Network (of the American Society on Aging): 833 Market St., Ste. 511, San Francisco, CA 94103, 415-974-9600, www.asaging.org/lgain.html
- ❖ Pride Senior Network: 356 W. 18th St., New York, NY 10011, 212-271-7288, www.pridesenior.org
- ❖ Senior Action in a Gay Environment: 305 Seventh Ave., 16th Floor, New York, NY 10001, 212-741-2247, email: sageusa.com
- ❖ Senior Health Resources: Temple Heights Station, P.O. Box 53453, Washington, DC 20009, 202-388-7900, www.seniorhealthresources.org

Books

Berger, R. M. (1996). *Gay and gray: The older homosexual man* (2nd ed.). New York: Harrington Park Press.

Ellis, A. L. (Ed.). (2001). *Gay men at midlife: Age before beauty.* New York: Harrington Park Press.

Kehoe, M. (1989). *Lesbians over 60 speak for themselves.* New York: Haworth Press.
Schoonmaker, C.V. (1993). *Aging lesbians: Bearing the burden of triple shame.* New York: Haworth Press.

❖ YOUTH

Organizations and Online Resources

- ❖ Financial Aid for Lesbians, Gay and Bisexual Students: P.O. Box 81620, Pittsburgh, PA 15217, www.finaid.org/otheraid/gay.phtml
- ❖ Gay, Lesbian, and Straight Educators Network: 121 West 27th St., Ste. 804, New York, NY 10001, 212-727-0135, www.glsen.org
- ❖ Lambda GLBT Community Services: P.O. Box 31321, El Paso, TX 79931, 915-329-GAYS, www.lambda.org
- ❖ National Youth Advocacy Coalition (NYAC): 1638 R St., NW, Ste. 300, Washington, DC 20009, 202-319-7596, www.nyacyouth.org
- ❖ Outproud, the National Coalition for Gay, Lesbian, Bisexual and Transgender Youth: 369 Third St., Ste. B-362, San Rafael, CA 94901, 415-460-5452, www.outproud.org
- ❖ Project 10: 15 W. California Blvd., #116, Pasadena, CA 91105, 626-577- 4553, www.project10.org
- ❖ Queer Resources Directory: www.qrd.org
- ❖ Youth Assistance Organization: www.youth.org

Books

Gray, M. L. (1999). *In your face: Stories from the lives of queer youth.* New York: Haworth Press.
Heron, A. (Ed.). (1994). *Two teenagers in twenty: Writings by gay and lesbian youth.* Boston: Alyson.
Howard, K., & Stevens, A. (Eds.). (2000). *Out and about on campus: Personal accounts by lesbian, gay, bisexual, and transgendered college students.* Boston: Alyson.
Jennings, K. (1994). *Becoming visible: A reader in gay and lesbian history for high school and college students.* Boston: Alyson.
Pollack, R., & Schwartz, C. (1995). *The journey out: A guide for and about gay and lesbian teens.* New York: Viking Children's Books.
Windmeyer, S. L., & Freeman, P. W. (Eds.). (1998). *Out on fraternity row: Personal accounts of being gay in a college fraternity.* Boston: Alyson.
Windmeyer, S. L., & Freeman, P. W. (Eds.). (2001). *Secret sisters: Stories of being lesbian and bisexual in a college sorority.* Boston: Alyson.

❖ COMING OUT

Organizations and Online Resources

- ❖ Coming Out to Parents, Relatives and Straight Friends: www.geocities.com/WestHollywood/3188/coming_out_straight.html
- ❖ Empty Closets—The Online Guide to Coming Out: www.empty-closets.com
- ❖ Lavender Visions: www.lavendervisions.com. For lesbians and bisexual women.
- ❖ National Coming Out Project: www.hrc.org/ncop/index.asp
- ❖ Outpath—Start Your Journey: www.outpath.com

Books

Curtis, W. (Ed.). (1988). *Revelations: A collection of gay male coming out stories.* Boston: Alyson.

Eichberg, R. (1990). *Coming out: An act of love.* New York: Plume.

Ford, M. T. (1996). *The world out there: Becoming part of the lesbian and gay community.* New York: New Press.

Isensee, R. (1997). *Reclaiming your life: The gay man's guide to love, self-acceptance, and trust.* Los Angeles: Alyson.

Johnson, B. K. (1997). *Coming out every day: A gay, bisexual, or questioning man's guide.* Oakland, CA: New Harbinger Publications.

Kaufman, G., & Raphael, L. (1996). *Coming out of shame: Transforming gay and lesbian lives.* New York: Doubleday.

McNaught, B. (1997). *Now that I'm out, what do I do?* New York: St. Martin's.

Vargo, M. E. (1998). *Acts of disclosure: The coming-out process of contemporary gay men.* New York: Harrington Park Press.

❖ ETHNIC AND OTHER MINORITIES

Organizations and Online Resources

- ❖ Audre Lorde Project, a Center for LGBT People of Color: 85 S. Oxford St., 3rd Floor, Brooklyn, NY 11217, 718-596-0342, www.alp.org
- ❖ Blackberri Café: www.blackberricafe.com/homepage.htm. For lesbians of color.

❖ The Blackstripe: 1714 Franklin St., Ste. 100-140, Oakland, CA 94612, 510-302-0930, www.blackstripe.com For LGBT individuals of African descent.

❖ Deaf Queer Resource Center: www.deafqueer.org

❖ Gay and Lesbian Arabic Society: www.glas.org

❖ Gay Asian Pacific Alliance: P.O. Box 421884, San Francisco, CA 94142, 415-282-4272, www.gapa.org

❖ Gay Men of African Descent: New York, NY, 212-828-1697 www.gmad.org

❖ Men of All Colors Together (MACT): P.O. Box 73796, Washington, DC 20056-3796, 800-624-2968, www.nabwmt.com

❖ LLEGÓ: The National Latina/o Lesbian, Gay, Bisexual, and Transgender Organization: 1420 K St., NW, Ste. 200, Washington, DC 20005, 202-408-5380, www.llego.org

❖ Passing Twice: A Proud Network of Queer Stutterers and their Allies: P.O. Box 91267, Durham, NC 27708, www.geocities.com/ West Hollywood/3323/

❖ The Two-Spirit Tradition in Native American Experience: www. androphile.org/preview/culture/NativeAmerica/amerindian. htm

❖ Utopia—Asian Gay and Lesbian Resources: www.utopia-asia.com

Books

Boykin, K. (1996). *Respecting the soul: Daily reflections for Black lesbians and gays.* New York: Avon.

Boykin, K. (1998). *One more river to cross: Black and gay in America.* New York: Anchor.

Constantine-Simms, D. (Ed.). (2000). *The greatest taboo: Homosexuality in Black communities.* Boston: Alyson.

Eng, D. L., & Hom, A. Y. (Eds.). (1998). *Q&A: Queer in Asian America.* Philadelphia: Temple University Press.

Greene, B. (Ed.). (1997). *Ethnic and cultural diversity among lesbians and gay men.* Thousand Oaks, CA: Sage.

Jacobs, S. E., Wesley, T., & Lang, S. (1997). *Two-spirit people: Native American gender identity, sexuality, and spirituality.* Urbana: University of Illinois Press.

Ratti, R. (Ed.). (1993). *A lotus of another color: An unfolding of the South Asian gay and lesbian experience.* Boston: Alyson.

Smith, C. M. (1999). *Fighting words: Personal essays by Black gay men.* New York: Avon.

❖ BISEXUAL AND TRANSGENDER

Organizations and Online Resources

- ❖ BiNet: 1800 Market St., Ste. 405, San Francisco, CA 94102, 415-865-5628, www.binetusa.org
- ❖ The Bisexual Foundation: www.bisexual.org
- ❖ The Bisexual Resource Center: P.O. Box 1026, Boston, MA 02117, 617-424-9595, www.biresource.org
- ❖ Female-to-Male International, Inc.: 1360 Mission St., Ste. 200, San Francisco, CA 94103, 415-553-5987, www.ftm-intl.org
- ❖ The Harry Benjamin International Gender Dysphoria Association, Inc.: 1300 South Second St., Ste. 180, Minneapolis, MN 55454, 612-625-1500, www.hbigda.org
- ❖ Intersex Society of North America: P.O. Box 301, Petaluma, CA 94953, 707-636-0420, www.isna.org
- ❖ Transgender Forum's Community Center: www.transgender.org

Books

Carlisle, D. B. (1998). *Human sex change and sex reversal: Transvestism and transsexualism.* New York: Edwin Mellon.

Feinberg, L. (1997). *Transgender warriors.* Boston: Beacon.

Hutchins, L., & Ka'ahumanu, L. (Eds.). (1991). *Bi any other name: Bisexual people speak out.* Boston: Alyson.

Kirk, S., & Rothblatt, M. A. (1996). *Medical, legal and workplace issues for the transsexual: A guide for successful transformation.* Blawnox, PA: Together Lifeworks.

Klein, F. (1993). *The bisexual option* (2nd ed.). New York: Harrington Park Press.

Lee, V. (2001). *The tranny guide.* Wayout Publishing.

❖ FRIENDSHIPS AND SOCIAL RELATIONSHIPS

Books

Adelman, M. R. (Ed.). (2000). *Midlife lesbian relationships: Friends, lovers, children, and parents.* New York: Haworth.

Nardi, P. M. (1999). *Gay men's friendships: Invincible communities.* Chicago: University of Chicago Press.

Signorile, M. (1997). *Life outside—The Signorile report on gay men: Sex, drugs, muscles, and the passages of life.* New York: HarperCollins.

Van Gelder, L., & Brandt, P. R. (1996). *Girls next door: Into the heart of lesbian America.* New York: Simon & Schuster.

Weinstock, J. S., & Rothblum, E. D. (Eds.) (1996). *Lesbian friendships: For ourselves and each other.* New York: New York University Press.

❖ WORKPLACE ISSUES

Organizations and Online Resources

- ❖ Holland's Self-Directed Search online: www.self-directed-search. com/index.html
- ❖ Lesbian/gay employment: www.gaywork.com
- ❖ Strong Interest Inventory online: www.careers-by-design.com/ strong_interest_inventory.htm

Books

Baker, D. B. (1995). *Cracking the corporate closet: The 200 best (and worst) companies to work for, buy from, and invest in if you're gay or lesbian—and even if you aren't.* New York: HarperBusiness.

Diamont, L. (Ed.). (1993). *Homosexual issues in the workplace.* Washington, DC: Taylor & Francis.

Gelberg, S., & Chojnacki, T. (1996). *Career and life planning with gay, lesbian, and bisexual persons.* Alexandria, VA: American Counseling Association.

Mickens, E. (1994). *100 best companies for gay men and lesbians.* New York: Pocket Books.

Rasi, R., & Rodriguez-Nogues, L. (Eds.). (1995). *Out in the workplace: The pleasures and perils of coming out on the job.* Los Angeles: Alyson.

Woods, J. D., & Lucas, J. H. (1993). *The corporate closet: The professional lives of lesbians and gay men in America.* New York: Free Press.

Zuckerman, A.J., & Simons, G. F. (1995). *Sexual orientation in the workplace: Gay men, lesbians, bisexuals, and heterosexuals working together.* Thousand Oaks, CA: Sage.

❖ SPIRITUALITY

Organizations and Online Resources

- ❖ Dignity/USA: www.dignityusa.org. For gay, lesbian, bisexual, and transgendered Catholics.
- ❖ Evangelicals Concerned, Inc.: www.ecinc.org. National network of gay and lesbian Evangelical Christians and friends.

- ❖ Gays for God: www.gaysforgod.org
- ❖ Honesty: Support and Education for Gay, Lesbian Southern Baptists: www.rainbowbaptists.org/honesty.html
- ❖ Lesbian/gay-friendly places of worship: accnet.org/where.htm
- ❖ Twice Blessed: The Jewish GLBT Archives Online: www.usc. edu/isd/archives/oneigla/tb/
- ❖ UFMCC (Universal Fellowship of Metropolitan Community Churches) World Center: 8704 Santa Monica Blvd., West Hollywood, CA 90069, 310-360-8640, www.ufmcc.com

Books

Balka, C., & Rose, A. (Eds.). (1989). *Twice blessed: On being lesbian, gay and Jewish.* Boston: Beacon.

Boswell, J. (1980). *Christianity, social tolerance, and homosexuality: Gay people in Western Europe from the beginning of the Christian era to the fourteenth century.* Chicago: University of Chicago Press

Comstock, G. D. (2001). *A whosoever church: Welcoming lesbians and gay men into African American congregations.* Louisville, KY: Westminster John Knox Press.

De La Huerta, C. (1998). *Coming out spiritually: The next step.* Los Angeles: Jeremy P. Tarcher.

Hekniniak, D. A. (1994). *What the Bible really says about homosexuality: Recent findings by top scholars offer a radical new view.* San Francisco: Alamo Square Press.

Johnson, E. C. (2000). *Gay spirituality: The role of gay identity in the transformation of human consciousness.* Boston: Alyson.

Leyland, W. (Ed.). (1998). *Queer dharma: Voices of gay Buddhists.* San Francisco: Gay Sunshine Press.

O'Neill, C., and Ritter, K. (1992). *Coming out within: Stages of spiritual awakening for lesbians and gay men.* San Francisco: Harper.

Pennington, S. (1989). *Ex-gays? There are none!* Hawthorne, CA: Lambda Christian Fellowship.

White, M. (1995). *Stranger at the gate: To be gay and Christian in America.* New York: Plume.

❖ GENERAL HEALTH

Organizations and Online Resources

- ❖ Gay and Lesbian Health: www.gayhealth.com
- ❖ Gay and Lesbian Medical Association: 459 Fulton Ave., Ste. 107, San Francisco, CA 94102, 415-255-4547, www.glma.org
- ❖ National Center for Lesbian Health Research: www. lesbianhealthinfo.org

Books

Delaney, M., Goldblum, P., & Brewer, J. (1987). *Strategies for survival: A gay men's health manual for the age of AIDS.* New York: St. Martin's.

Penn, R. E. (1998). *The gay men's wellness guide: The National Lesbian and Gay Health Association's complete book of physical, emotional, and mental health and well-being.* Gordonsville, VA: VHPS.

Shernoff, M., & Scott, W. A. (1988). *The sourcebook on lesbian/gay health care* (2nd ed.). Washington, DC: National Lesbian/Gay Health Foundation.

Solarz, A. L. (1999). *Lesbian health: Current assessment and directions for the future.* Washington, DC: National Academy Press.

White, J., & Martinez, M. C. (1997). *The lesbian health book: Caring for ourselves.* Seattle, WA: Seal Press.

Wolfe, D. (2000). *Men like us: The GMHC complete guide to gay men's sexual, physical, and emotional well-being.* New York: Random House.

❖ HIV / AIDS AND GRIEF / LOSS

Organizations and Online Resources

- ❖ AIDS Education Global Information System: P.O. Box 184, San Juan Capistrano, CA 92693, 949-248-5843 www.aegis.com
- ❖ Glossary of HIV/AIDS terms: www.virology.net/ATVHIV-Glossary.html
- ❖ Immunet: 7985 Santa Monica Blvd., #99, West Hollywood, CA 90046, 323-656-0699 www.aids.org

Books

Bartlett, J. G., & Finkbeiner, A. K. (1998). *The guide to living with HIV infection: Developed at the Johns Hopkins AIDS clinic.* Baltimore, MD: Johns Hopkins University Press.

Herek, G. M., & Greene, B. (1995). *AIDS, identity, and community: The HIV epidemic and lesbians and gay men.* Thousand Oaks, CA: Sage.

Levine, M. P., Nardi, P. M., & Gagnon, G. H. (Eds.) (1997). *In changing times: Gay men and lesbians encounter HIV/AIDS.* Chicago: University of Chicago Press.

Nord, D. (1997). *Multiple AIDS-related loss: A handbook for understanding and surviving a perpetual fall.* Washington, DC: Taylor & Francis.

Rofes, E. *Dry bones breathe: Gay men creating post-AIDS identities and cultures.* Binghamtom, NY: Haworth.

Shernoff, M., & Picano, F. (Eds.). (1998). *Gay widowers: Life after the death of a partner.* Harrington Park Press.

❖ SUBSTANCE ABUSE AND RECOVERY

Organizations and Online Resources

- ❖ International Advisory Council of Homosexual Men and Women in Alcoholics Anonymous: www.iac-aa.org
- ❖ National Association of Lesbian and Gay Addiction Professionals: 901 N Washington St., #600, Alexandria, VA 22314, 703-465-0539 www.nalgap.org
- ❖ National Clearinghouse for Alcohol and Drug Information: www.health.org/features/lgbt/index.htm
- ❖ Pride Institute: 800-547-7433 www.pride-institute.com Has inpatient, intensive outpatient, and partial hospital programs in several cities
- ❖ Women in recovery for substance abuse: www.soberdykes.org

Books

Kettlehack, G. (1999). *Vastly more than that: Stories of lesbians & gay men in recovery.* Center City, MN: Hazeldon Information Education.

Kominars, S. B., & Kominars, K. D. (1996). *Accepting ourselves and others: A journey into recovery from addictive and compulsive behaviors for gays, lesbians and bisexuals.* Center City, MN: Hazelden Information Education.

Kus, R. J. (Ed.). (1995). *Addiction and recovery of gay and lesbian persons.* New York: Haworth.

Milton, A. *Lavender light: Meditations for gay men in recovery.* New York: Berkley.

Weinberg, T. S. (1994). *Gay men, drinking, and alcoholism.* Carbondale: Southern Illinois University Press.

❖ COUPLES, PARENTING, AND FAMILIES

Organizations and Online Resources

- ❖ COLAGE, Children of Lesbians and Gays Everywhere: 3543 18th St., #1, San Francisco, CA 94110, 415-861-4537, www.colage.org
- ❖ Couples National Network, Inc.: P.O. Box 66886, St. Pete Beach, FL 33736, 800-896-0717, www.couples-national.org
- ❖ Families Like Ours: P.O. Box 3137, Renton, Washington 98056, 425-793-7911, www.familieslikeours.org

❖ Family Pride Coalition: P.O. Box 65327, Washington, DC 20035, 202-331-5015, www.familypride.org
❖ Gay and Lesbian Family Values: www.angelfire.com/co/ GayFamilyValues
❖ *Gay Parent* magazine online: www.gayparentmag.com
❖ Partners Task Force for Gay and Lesbian Couples: P.O. Box 9685, Seattle, WA 98109, 206-935-1206, www.buddybuddy.com

Books

Barrett, R. L., & Robinson, B. E. (2000). *Gay fathers: Encouraging the hearts of gay dads and their families.* (rev. ed.). San Francisco: Jossey Bass.

Berkery, P. M. (1996). *Personal financial planning for gays and lesbians: Our guide to prudent decision making.* Chicago: Irwin Professional Publications.

Berkery, P. M. (1998). *J. K. Lasser's gay finances in a straight world: A comprehensive financial planning handbook.* New York: Macmillan.

Berzon, B. (1988). *Permanent partners: Building gay and lesbian relationships that last.* New York: Dutton.

Clunis, D. M. (1995). *The lesbian parenting book: A guide to creating families and raising children.* Seattle, WA: Seal Press.

Clunis, D. M., & Green, G. D. (2000). *Lesbian couples: A guide to creating healthy relationships.* Seattle, WA: Seal Press.

Isensee, R. (1990). *Love between men: Enhancing intimacy and keeping your relationship alive.* Boston: Alyson.

Johnson, S. M., & O'Connor, E. (2001). *For lesbian parents: Your guide to helping your family grow up happy, healthy, and proud.* Elizabeth, NY: Guilford.

Marcus, E. (1992). *The male couple's guide: Finding a man, making a home, building a life.* New York: HarperCollins.

Martin, A. (1993). *The lesbian and gay parenting handbook: Creating and raising our families.* New York: HarperCollins.

McDaniel, J. (1995). *The lesbian couples' guide.* New York: HarperPerrenial.

McWhirter, D. P., & Mattison, A. M. (1984). *The male couple: How relationships develop.* Englewood Cliffs, NJ: Prentice Hall.

Newman, L. (1989). *Heather has two mommies.* Boston: Alyson.

Slater, S. (1994). *The lesbian family life cycle.* New York: File Free Press.

Tessina, T. (1990). *Gay relationships.* Los Angeles: Jeremy P. Tarcher.

Toevs, K., & Brill, S. (2002). *The essential guide to lesbian conception, pregnancy, and birth.* Boston: Alyson.

Uhrig, L. J. (1984). *The two of us: Affirming, celebrating and symbolizing gay and lesbian relationships.* Boston: Alyson.

Willhoite, M. (1991). *Daddy's roommate.* Boston: Alyson.

❖ SUPPORT FOR FAMILIES OF ORIGIN

 ❖ For Parents of Gay Children—Can We Understand? www. outproud.org/brochure_for_parents.html
 ❖ My Child is Gay! Now What Do I Do? www.bidstrup.com/parents.htm
 ❖ Parents, Families and Friends of Lesbians and Gays (PFLAG): 1726 M St., NW Ste. 400, Washington, DC 20036, 202-467-8180, www.pflag.org

Books

Clark, D. (1997). *The new loving someone gay* (rev. ed.). Millbrae, CA: Celestial Arts.

Day, F. A. (2000). *Lesbian and gay voices: An annotated bibliography and guide to literature for children and young adults.* Westport, CT: Greenwood.

Fairchild, B., & Hayward, N. (1998). *Now that you know: What every parent should know about homosexuality* (3rd ed.). New York: Harcourt Brace.

Griffin, C. W., Wirth, M. J., & Wirth, A. G. (1996). *Beyond acceptance: Parents of lesbians and gays talk about their experiences* (rev. ed.). Englewood Cliffs, NJ: Prentice Hall.

Marcus, E. (1993). *Is it a choice? Answers to 300 of the most frequently asked questions about gays and lesbians.* San Francisco: Harper.

❖ DOMESTIC VIOLENCE

Organizations and Online Resources

 ❖ Gay Men's Domestic Violence Project: 955 Massachusetts Avenue, Cambridge, MA 02139, 617-354-6056. Hotline: 800-832-1901 www.gmdvp.org
 ❖ The Network La/Red (National Lesbian Domestic Violence Network): P.O. Box 6011, Boston, MA 02115, 617-695-0877. Hotline: 617-423-7233 www.thenetworklared.org

Books

Island, D., & Letellier, P. (1991). *Men who beat the men who love them: Battered gay men and domestic violence.* New York: Harrington Park Press.

Kaschak, E. (Ed.). (2002). *Intimate betrayal: Domestic violence in lesbian relationships.* New York: Haworth.

Leventhal, B., & Lundy, S. E. (Eds). (1999). *Same-sex domestic violence: Strategies for change.* Thousand Oaks, CA: Corwin Press.

Lobel, K. (Ed.). (1986). *Naming the violence: Speaking out about lesbian battering.* Seattle, WA: Seal Press.

Renzetti, C. (1992). *Violent betrayal: Partner abuse in lesbian relationships.* Thousand Oaks, CA: Sage.

❖ SPORTS AND RECREATION

Organizations and Online Resources

- ❖ Gay Golf: www.gaygolf.com
- ❖ Gay Outdoors: 149 Orange St., #3, Manchester, NH 03104, 603-669-1936, www.gayoutdoors.com
- ❖ International Frontrunners: www.frontrunners.org
- ❖ International Gay and Lesbian Aquatics: P.O. Box 190134, Atlanta, GA 31119, www.igla.org
- ❖ Outsports: www.outsports.com

❖ POLITICAL

Organizations and Online Resources

- ❖ Gay/Lesbian Politics and Law: www.gaypoliticsandlaw.com
- ❖ Gay Vote: www.gayvote.com
- ❖ Human Rights Campaign: 919 18th St., NW, Ste. 800, Washington, DC 20006, 202-628-4160 www.hrcusa.org
- ❖ A listing of Gay Pride celebrations around the world: www.planetout.com/pno/splash.html
- ❖ Log Cabin Republicans: 1607 17th St., NW, Washington, DC 20009, 202-347-5306, www.lcr.org
- ❖ National Gay and Lesbian Task Force: 1700 Kalorama Rd., NW, Washington, DC 20009, 202-332-6483, www.ngltf.org
- ❖ National Stonewall Democrats: P.O. Box 9330, Washington, DC 20005, 202-625-1382, www.nationalstonewalldemocrats.org

❖ LEGAL AND IMMIGRATION ISSUES

Organizations and Online Resources

- ❖ American Civil Liberties Union, Lesbian and Gay Rights: 1400 20th St., NW, Ste. 119, Washington, DC 20036, 202-457-0800, www.aclu.org/issues/gay/hmgl.html
- ❖ Center for Lesbian and Gay Civil Rights: 1211 Chestnut St., Ste. 605, Philadelphia, PA 19107, 866-542-8519, www.center4-civilrights.org
- ❖ Lambda Legal Defense and Education Fund: 120 Wall St., Ste. 1500, New York, NY 10005, 212/809-8585, www.lambdalegal.org
- ❖ Lesbian and Gay Immigration Rights Task Force: 350 West 31st St., Ste. 505, New York, NY 10001, 212-714-2904, www.lgirtf.org
- ❖ National Center for Lesbian Rights: 870 Market St., Ste. 570, San Francisco, CA 94102, 415-392-6257, www.nclrights.org
- ❖ National Lesbian and Gay Law Association: 200 East Lexington St., Ste. 1511, Baltimore, MD 21202, 508-982-8290, www.nlgla.org
- ❖ Servicemembers Legal Defense Network: P.O. Box 65301, Washington DC 20035-5301, 202-328-3247, www.sldn.org

Books

Clifford, D., Curry, H., & Leonard, R. (1996). *A legal guide for lesbian and gay couples.* (10th ed.). Berkeley, CA: Nolo Press.

Holt, F. (1998). *Legal affairs: Essential advice for same-sex couples.* New York: Henry Holt.

Rubenstein, W. B. (Ed.). (1993). *Lesbians, gay men, and the law.* New York: New Press.

❖ LESBIAN AND GAY PRESS

Organizations and Online Resources

- ❖ *The Advocate* Online: www.advocate.com
- ❖ Gay and Lesbian Alliance Against Defamation: 1825 Connecticut Ave, NW, 5th Floor, Washington, DC 20009, 800-429-6334, www. glaad.org
- ❖ Gay Netscape: www.gay.netscape.com

❖ Gayellow Pages: www.gayellowpages.com
❖ Gip Plaster: www.gayscribe.com. A comprehensive listing of local and regional LGBT publications.
❖ Planet Out: www.planetout.com

References

Adler, A. (1964). *Social interest: A challenge to mankind*. New York: Capricorn Books.

Allen, M. A., & Burrell, N. (1996). Comparing the impact of homosexual and heterosexual parents on children: Meta-analysis of existing research. *Journal of Homosexuality, 32*(2), 19-35.

American Counseling Association, Human Rights Committee. (1998). *Appropriate counseling responses to sexual orientation*. Alexandria, VA: Author.

American Psychiatric Association. (1973). *Diagnostic and statistical manual of mental disorders* (2nd ed.). Washington, DC: Author.

American Psychological Association, Committee on Lesbian and Gay Concerns. (1998). *Appropriate therapeutic responses to sexual orientation*. Washington, DC: Author.

Anthony, B. D. (1985). Lesbian clients—lesbian therapists: Opportunities and challenges in working together. In J. C. Gonsiorek (Ed.), *A guide to psychotherapy with gay and lesbian clients* (pp. 45-58). New York: Harrington Park Press.

Aura, J. (1985). Women's social support: A comparison of lesbians and heterosexuals (Doctoral dissertation, University of California, Los Angeles, 1985). *Dissertation Abstracts International, 46-12B*, 4389.

Avery, A. M., Hellman, R. E., & Sudderth, L. K. (2001). Satisfaction with mental health services among sexual minorities with major mental illness. *American Journal of Public Health, 91*(6), 159-162.

Baptiste, D. A., Jr. (1987). Psychotherapy with gay/lesbian couples and their children in "stepfamilies": A challenge for marriage and family therapists. *Journal of Homosexuality, 14*(1/2), 223-239.

Baum, M. I. (1996). Gays and lesbians choosing to be parents. In C. J. Alexander (Ed.), *Gay and lesbian mental health: A sourcebook for practitioners* (pp. 115-126). Binghamton, NY: Harrington Park Press.

Beatty, R. (1983). *Alcoholism and adult gay male populations of Pennsylvania*. Unpublished master's thesis, Pennsylvania State University, University Park, PA.

Beckett, A., & Rutan, J. S. (1990). Treating persons with ARC and AIDS in group psychotherapy. *International Journal of Group Psychotherapy, 40*(1), 19-29.

Bell, A. P., & Weinberg, M. S. (1978). *Homosexualities: A study of diversity among men and women.* New York: Simon and Schuster.

Bell, A. P., Weinberg, M. S., & Hammersmith, S. K. (1981). *Sexual preference: Its development in men and women.* Bloomington: Indiana University Press.

Benowitz, M. (1995). Comparing the experiences of women clients sexually exploited by female versus male psychotherapists. In J. C. Gonsiorek (Ed.), *Breach of trust: Sexual exploitation by health care professionals and clergy* (pp. 213-224). Thousand Oaks, CA: Sage.

Berger, R. M. (1996). *Gay and gray: The older homosexual man* (2nd ed.). New York: Harrington Park Press.

Berger, R. M., & Kelly, J. (1996). Gay men and lesbians grown older. In R. P. Cabaj & T. S. Stein (Eds.), *Textbook of homosexuality and mental health* (pp. 305-318). Washington, DC: American Psychiatric Press.

Bergeron, B. (2000). *The incredible bulk: Understanding steroid use.* Retrieved July 15, 2002, from www.gayhealth.com/templates/0/image?record=287

Bernstein, G., & Klein, R. (1995). Countertransference issues in group psychotherapy with HIV-positive and AIDS patients. *International Journal of Group Psychotherapy, 45*(1), 91-100.

Betz, N. E. (1991). Implications for counseling psychology training programs: Reactions to the special issue. *The Counseling Psychologist, 19,* 248-252.

Biblarz, T. J., & Stacey, T. (2001). (How) does the sexual orientation among parents matter? *American Sociological Review, 66*(2), 159-183.

Blumstein, P., & Schwartz, P. (1983). *American couples: Money, work, and sex.* New York: William Morrow.

Bohan, J. S. (1996). Psychology and sexual orientation: Coming to terms. New York: Routledge.

Bouton, R. A., Gallagher, P. E., Garlinghouse, P. A., Leal, T., Rosenstein, L. D., & Young, R. K. (1987). Scales for measuring fear of AIDS and homophobia. *Journal of Personality Assessment, 51*(4), 606-614.

Brown, L. S. (1996). Ethical concerns with sexual minority patients. In R. P. Cabaj & T. S. Stein (Eds.), *Textbook of homosexuality and mental health* (pp. 897-916). Washington, DC: American Psychiatric Press.

Cabaj, R. P. (1992). Substance abuse in the gay and lesbian community. In J. Lowinson, P. Ruiz, & R. Millman (Eds.), *Substance abuse: A comprehensive textbook* (pp. 852-860). Baltimore, MD: Williams and Wilkins.

Cabaj, R. P. (1996). Sexual orientation of the therapist. In R. P. Cabaj & T. S. Stein (Eds.), *Textbook of homosexuality and mental health* (pp. 513-524). Washington, DC: American Psychiatric Press.

Cass, V. C. (1979). Homosexual identity formation: A theoretical model. *Journal of Homosexuality, 4,* 219-235.

Cassens, B. J. (1985). Social consequences of the Acquired Immunodeficiency Syndrome. *Annals of Internal Medicine, 103,* 768-771.

Centers for Disease Control. (June 1, 2001). HIV incidence among young men who have sex with men. *Weekly Morbidity and Mortality Weekly Report (50)*21, 440-444.

Chan, C. S. (1995). Issues of sexual identity in an ethnic minority: The case of Chinese American lesbians, gay men, and bisexual people. In A. R. D'Augelli & C. J. Patterson (Eds.), *Lesbian, gay, and bisexual identities over the lifespan* (pp. 87-101). New York: Oxford Press.

Chernin, J. N. (June, 2001). What does gay pride mean to you? G-street, p. 21.

Chernin, J. N., Holden, J. M., & Chandler, C. (1997). Bias in psychological assessment: Heterosexism. *Measurement and Evaluation in Counseling and Development, 30*(2), 68-76.

Clark, D. (2000). Counseling. In G. E. Haggerty (Ed.), *Gay histories and cultures: An encyclopedia* (pp. 217-219). New York: Garland Publishing.

Clausen, J. & Duberman, M. (1995). *Beyond gay or straight: Understanding sexual orientation*. Philadelphia: Chelsea House.

Coleman, E. (1987). Assessment of sexual orientation. *Journal of Homosexuality, 14*(2), 9-24.

Corsini, R. J., & Wedding, D. (Eds.). (2000). *Current psychotherapies*. Itasca, IL: F. E. Peacock.

Cox, S., & Gallois, C. (1996). Gay and lesbian development: A social identity perspective. *Journal of Homosexuality, 30*(4), 1-30.

Darsey, J. (2000). Coming out. In G. E. Haggerty (Ed.), *Gay histories and cultures: An encyclopedia* (pp. 209-213). New York: Garland Publishing.

D'Augelli, A. R. (1996). Lesbian, gay, and bisexual development during adolescence and young adulthood. In R. P. Cabaj & T. S. Stein (Eds.), *Textbook of homosexuality and mental health* (pp. 267-288). Washington, DC: American Psychiatric Press.

D'Augelli, A. R. (1998). Developmental implications of victimization of lesbian, gay, and bisexual youths. In G. M. Herek (Ed.), *Stigma and sexual orientation: Understanding prejudice against lesbians, gay men, and bisexuals* (pp. 187-210). Thousand Oaks, CA: Sage.

D'Augelli, A. R., & Hershberger, S. L. (1993). Lesbian, gay, and bisexual youth in community settings: Personal challenges and mental health problems. *American Journal of Community Psychology, 21*, 421-448.

Dawson, K. (1982, November). Serving the older community. *SIECUS report*, pp. 5-6. New York: Sex Education and Information Council of the United States.

Diaz, R. M., Ayala, G., Bein, E., Henne, J., & Marin, B. V. (2001). The impact of homophobia, poverty, and racism on the mental health of gay and bisexual Latino men: Findings from 3 U.S. cities. *American Journal of Public Health, 91*(6), 927-932.

DiPlacido, J. (1998). Minority stress among lesbians, gay men, and bisexuals: A consequence of heterosexism, homophobia, and stigmatization. In G. M. Herek (Ed.), *Stigma and sexual orientation* (pp. 138-159). Thousand Oaks: Sage.

Dworkin, S. H., & Pincu, L. (1993). Counseling in the era of AIDS. *Journal of Counseling and Development, 71*, 275-281.

Eliason, M. J. (1996). Identity formation for lesbian, bisexual, and gay persons: Beyond a 'minoritizing' view. *Journal of Homosexuality, 30*(3), 31-58.

Eliason, M. J. (2000). Substance abuse counsellor's attitudes regarding lesbian, gay, bisexual, and transgendered clients. *Journal of Substance Abuse, 12*(4), 311-328.

Ellis, A., & Riggle, E. (1995). The relation of job satisfaction and degree of openness about one's sexual orientation for lesbians and gay men. *Journal of Homosexuality, 30,* 75-85.

Erikson, E. H. (1963). *Childhood and society* (3rd ed.). New York: WW Norton.

Ernst, F., Francis, R., Nevels, H., & Lemeh, C. (1991). Condemnation of homosexuality in the Black community: A gender-specific phenomenon. *Archives of Sexual Behavior, 20,* 579-585.

Espin, O. M. (1993). Issues of identity in the psychology of Latina lesbians. In L. D. Garnets & D. C. Kimmel (Eds.), *Psychological perspectives on lesbian and gay male experiences* (pp. 348-363). New York: Columbia University Press.

Esterberg, K. G. (1996). From lesbian nation to lesbian sex/from clone culture to queer nation. In R. C. Savin-Williams and K. M. Cohen (Eds.), *The lives of lesbians, gays, and bisexuals: Children to adults* (pp. 377-392). Fort Worth, TX: Harcourt Brace.

Exner, J. E., Jr. (1969). Rorschach responses as an index of narcissism. *Journal of Projective Techniques and Personality Assessment, 33,* 324-330.

Falco, K. L. (1996). Psychotherapy with women who love women. In R. Cabaj & T. S. Stein (Eds.), *Textbook of homosexuality and mental health* (pp. 397-412). Washington, DC: American Psychiatric Press.

Fassinger, R. E. (1991). The hidden minority: Issues and challenges in working with lesbian women and gay men. *Counseling Psychologist, 19*(2), 157-176.

Feminist Therapy Institute. (1999). *Ethical guidelines for feminist therapists* (rev. ed.). Denver, CO: Author. (Original work published 1987)

Finnegan, D., & McNally, E. (1987). *Dual identities: Counseling chemically dependent gay men and lesbians.* Center City, MN: Hazelden.

Foa, E. B., Keane, T. M., & Friedman, M. J. (2000). *Effective treatment for PTSD: Practice guidelines from the International Society for Traumatic Stress Studies.* New York: Guilford.

Fontaine, K. R., McKenna, L., & Cheskin, L. J. (1997). Support group membership and perceptions of control over health in HIV+ men. *Journal of Clinical Psychology, 53*(3), 249-252.

Foster, S. B., Stevens, P. E., & Hall, J. M. (1994). Offering support group services to lesbians living with HIV. *Women and Therapy, 15*(2), 69-83.

Friend, R. (1988). The individual and social psychology of aging: Clinical implications for lesbians and gay men. In E. Coleman (Ed.), *Integrated identity of gay men and lesbians* (pp. 307-331). New York: Harrington Park Press.

Frost, J. C. (1990). A developmentally keyed scheme for the placement of gay men into psychotherapy groups. *International Journal of Group Psychotherapy, 40*(2), 155-167.

Frost, J. C. (1998). Countertransference considerations for the gay male when leading psychotherapy groups for gay men. *International Journal of Group Psychotherapy, 48,* 3-23.

Fung, R. (1998). Looking for my penis: The eroticized Asian in gay video porn. In Eng, D., & Hom, A. (Eds.), *Q & A: Queer in Asian America.* Philadelphia: Temple University Press.

Gale, D. (June, 2001). Love Danny. *A & U,* p. 20.

Garnets, L. D., & Kimmel, D. C. (Eds.). (1993). *Psychological perspectives on lesbian and gay male experiences.* New York: Columbia University Press.

Gartrell, N. (1994). Boundaries in lesbian therapist client relationships. In B. Greene & G. M. Herek (Eds.), *Lesbian and gay psychology: Theory, research, and clinical applications* (pp. 176-205). Thousand Oaks, CA: Sage.

Gelberg, S., & Chojnacki, J. T. (1996). *Career and life planning with gay, lesbian, and bisexual persons.* Alexandria, VA: American Counseling Association.

George, K. D., & Behrendt, A. E. (1988). Therapy for male couples experiencing relationship problems and sexual problems. In E. Coleman (Ed.), *Integrated identity for gay men and lesbians: Psychotherapeutic approaches for emotional well-being* (pp. 77-88). New York: Harrington Park Press.

Getzel, G. S. (1998). Group work practice with gay men and lesbians. In G. P. Mallon (Ed.), *Foundations of social work practice with lesbian and gay persons* (pp. 131-144). Binghamton, NY: Harrington Park Press.

Glaser, C. (1994). The love that dare not pray its name: The gay and lesbian movement in America's churches. In J. Siker (Ed.), *Homosexuality in the church: Both sides of the debate* (pp. 150-160). Louisville, KY: Westminster John Knox Press.

Goddard, H. H. (1917). Mental tests and the immigrant. *Journal of Delinquency, 2,* 243-277.

Gonsiorek, J. C. (1995). Boundary challenges when both therapist and client are gay males. In J. C. Gonsiorek (Ed.), *Breach of trust: Sexual exploitation by health care professionals and clergy* (pp. 225-233). Thousand Oaks, CA: Sage.

Gonzalez, F., & Espin, O. (1996). Latino men, Latina women, and homosexuality. In R. P. Cabaj & T. S. Stein (Eds.), *Textbook of homosexuality and mental health* (pp. 583-602). Washington, DC: American Psychiatric Press.

Gramick, J. (1983, March/April). Homophobia: A new challenge. *Social Work, 28(2),* 137-141.

Gray, D., & Isensee, R. (1996). Balancing autonomy and intimacy in lesbian and gay relationships. In C. J. Alexander (Ed.), *Gay and lesbian mental health: A sourcebook for practitioners* (pp. 95-114). Binghamton, NY: Harrington Park Press.

Green, G. (1995). AIDS and euthanasia. *AIDS Care, 7(2),* S169-S173.

Green, G., & Bozett, F. (1991). Lesbian mothers and gay fathers. In J. C. Gonsiorek & J. Weinrich (Eds.), *Homosexuality: Research implications for public policy* (pp. 197-214). Newbury Park, CA: Sage.

Greene B. (1994). Lesbian and gay sexual orientation. Implications for training, practice, and research. In B. Greene & G. M. Herek (Eds.), *Lesbian and gay psychology: Theory, research, and clinical applications* (pp. 1-24). Thousand Oaks, CA: Sage.

Grimes, D. E., & Cole, F. L. (1996). Self-help and life quality in persons with HIV disease. *AIDS Care, 8*(6), 691-699.

Gutierrez, F. J. (1997). Culturally sensitive HIV treatment. In M. F. O'Connor (Ed.), *Treating the psychological consequences of HIV* (pp. 165-193). San Francisco: Jossey-Bass.

Haldeman, D. (1994). The practice and ethics of sexual orientation conversion therapy. *Journal of Consulting and Clinical Psychology, 62,* 221-227.

Hall, J., & Stevens, P. (1990). The coupled lesbian. In R. J. Kus (Ed.), *Keys to caring: Assisting your gay and lesbian clients* (pp. 215-223). Boston: Alyson.

Han, S. (2000). Asian American gay men's (dis)claim on masculinity. In P. M. Nardi (Ed.), *Gay masculinities* (pp. 206-223). Thousand Oaks, CA: Sage.

Harmon, L., & Volker, M. (1995). HIV-positive people, HIV-negative partners. *Journal of Sex and Marital Therapy, 21*(2), 127-140.

Hatfield, E., & Sprecher, S. (1986). *Mirror, mirror: The importance of looks in everyday life.* New York: SUNY Press.

Hays, R. B., Magee, R. H., & Chauncey, S. (1994). Identifying helpful and unhelpful behaviours of loved ones: The PWA's perspective. *AIDS Care, 6*(4), 379-392.

Heffernan, K. (1996). Eating disorders and weight concern among lesbians. *International Journal of Eating Disorders, 19,* 127-138.

Herdt, G. H. (1997). Same sex, different cultures: Gays and lesbians across cultures. Boulder, CO: Westview.

Herdt, G. H., & Boxer, A. (1993). Children of Horizons: How gay and lesbian teens are leading a new way out of the closet. Boston: Beacon.

Herek, G. M. (1984). Beyond "homophobia": A social psychological perspective on attitudes toward lesbians and gay men. *Journal of Homosexuality, 10,* 1-21.

Herek, G. M., Kimmel, D. C., Amaro, H., & Melton, G. B. (1991). Avoiding heterosexual bias in psychological research. *American Psychologist, 46*(9), 957-963.

Hersch, P. (1991, January/February). Secret lives. *Family Therapy Networker,* 37-43.

Herzog, D., Newman, K., & Warshaw, M. (1991). Body image dissatisfaction in homosexual and heterosexual males. *Journal of Nervous and Mental Disease, 179,* 356-359.

Herzog, D., Norman, D., Gordon, C., & Pepose, M. (1984). Sexual conflict and eating disorders in 27 males. *American Journal of Psychiatry, 141,* 989-990.

Heyward, C. (1993). *When boundaries betray us.* San Francisco: HarperCollins.

Holahan, W., & Gibson, S. (1994). Heterosexual therapists leading lesbian and gay therapy groups: Therapeutic and political realities. *Journal of Counseling and Development, 72,* 591-594.

Holden, J. M., & Holden, G. (1995). Sexual identity profile: A multidimensional bipolar model. *Individual Psychology, 51,* 102-113.

Hom, A. (1996). Stories from the homefront: Perspectives of Asian American parents with lesbian daughters and gay sons. In R. Leong (Ed.), *Asian*

American sexualities: Dimensions of the gay and lesbian experience (pp. 37-50). New York: Routledge.

Hong, W., Yamamoto, J., & Chang, D. (1993). Sex in a Confucian society. *Journal of the American Academy of Psychoanalysis, 21,* 405-419.

Hudson, W., & Ricketts, W. (1980). A strategy for the measurement of homophobia. *Journal of Homosexuality, 5,* 357-372.

Human Rights Watch. (2001). *Hatred in the hallways: Violence and discrimination against lesbian, gay, bisexual and transgender students in U.S. schools.* New York: Author.

Humphrey, J. C. (1999). To queer or not to queer a lesbian and gay group? Sexual and transgendered politics at the turn of the century. *Sexualities, 2*(2), 223-246.

Iasenza, S. (1989). Some challenges of integrating sexual orientations into counselor training. *Journal of Counseling & Development, 68,* 73-76.

Irving, G., Bor, R., & Catalan, J. (1995). Psychological distress among gay men supporting a lover or partner with AIDS: A pilot study. *AIDS Care, 7*(5), 605-617.

Island, D., & Letellier, P. (1991). *Men who beat the men who love them.* New York: Haworth.

Johnston, W. I. (1995). HIV-negative: How the uninfected are affected by AIDS. New York: Insight Books.

Jones, B., & Hill, M. (1996). African-American lesbians, gay men, & bisexuals. In R. P. Cabaj & T. S. Stein (Eds.), *Textbook of homosexuality and mental health* (pp. 549-562). Washington, DC: American Psychiatric Press.

Jones, M. (2001). Coming out format. Los Angeles, CA: Los Angeles Gay and Lesbian Center.

Kalichman, S. C., Kelly, J. A., Morgan, M., & Rompa, D. (1997). Fatalism, current life satisfaction, and risk for HIV infection among gay and bisexual men. *Journal of Consulting and Clinical Psychology, 65*(4), 542-546.

Kalichman, S. C., Sikkema, K. J., & Somlai, A. (1996). People living with HIV infection who attend and do not attend support groups: A pilot study of needs, characteristics, and experiences. *AIDS Care, 8*(5), 589-599.

Kallimachos, A. (2000). The two spirit tradition in Native American Experience. Retrieved July 14, 2001, from www.androphile.org/preview/culture/nativeAmerica/amerindian.htm

Karina, W. (1998). Negotiating conflicts in allegiances among lesbians and gays of color: Reconciling divided selves and communities. In G. Mallon (Ed.), *Foundations of social work practice with lesbian and gay persons.* New York: Harrington Park Press.

Katz, M. H., Douglas, J. M., Jr., Bolan, G. A., Marx, R., Sweat, M., Park, M., et al. (1996). Depression and use of mental health services among HIV-infected men. *AIDS Care, 8*(4), 433-442.

Katz, P. A., & Ksansnak, K. R. (1994). Developmental aspects of gender role flexibility and traditionality in middle childhood and adolescence. *Developmental Psychology, 30,* 272-282.

Kaufman, G., & Raphael, L. (1996). *Coming out of shame: Transforming gay and lesbian lives.* New York: Doubleday.

Keith-Spiegel, P., & Koocher, G. (1985). *Ethics in psychology: Professional standards and cases*. New York: Random House.

Kirkpatrick, M. (1996). Lesbians as parents. In: R. P. Cabaj & T. S., Stein (Eds.), *Textbook of homosexuality and mental health* (pp. 353-370). Washington, DC: American Psychiatric Press.

Klein, F., Sepekoff, B., & Wolf, T. (1985). Sexual orientation: A multi-variable dynamic process. *Journal of Homosexuality, 11*, 35-49.

Klinger, R. (1991). Treatment of a lesbian batterer. In C. Silverstein (Ed.), *Gays, lesbians, and their therapists* (pp. 126-142). New York: W. W. Norton.

Klinger, R., & Stein, T. S. (1996). Impact of violence, childhood sexual abuse, and domestic violence and abuse on lesbians, bisexuals, and gay men. In R. P. Cabaj & T. S. Stein (Eds.), *Textbook of homosexuality and mental health* (pp. 801-818). Washington, DC: American Psychiatric Press.

Koetting, M. E. (1996). A group design for HIV-negative gay men. *Social Work, 41*(4), 407-415.

Kranzberg, M. B. (1998). Comments on "countertransference considerations." *International Journal of Group Psychotherapy, 48*(1), 25-30.

Kurdek, L. (1988). Perceived social support in gays and lesbians in cohabiting relationships. *Journal of Personality and Social Psychology, 54*, 504-509.

Kus, R. J. (Ed.). (1990). *Keys to caring: Assisting your gay and lesbian clients*. Boston: Alyson.

Larsen, K., Reed, M., & Hoffman, S. (1980). Attitudes of heterosexuals toward homosexuality: A Likert-type scale and construct validity. *Journal of Sex Research, 16*, 245-257.

Larson, P. (1997). Gay money: Your personal guide to same-sex strategies for financial security, strength, and success. New York: Dell.

Laumann, E. O., Gagnon, J. H., Michaels, R. T., & Michaels, S. (1994). *The social organization of sexuality: Sexual practices in the United States*. Chicago: University of Chicago Press.

Linde, R. (1994). Impact of AIDS on adult gay male development: Implications for psychotherapy. In S. A. Cadwell, R. A. Burnham, Jr., & M. Forstein (Eds.), *Therapists on the front line: Psychotherapy with gay men in the age of AIDS* (pp. 25-51). Washington, DC: American Psychiatric Press.

Lips, H. (2000). *Sex and gender: An introduction* (4th ed.). Mountain View, CA: Mayfield.

Livingston, D. (1996). A systems approach to AIDS counseling for gay couples. In M. Shernoff (Ed.), *Human services for gay people: Clinical and community practice* (pp. 83-93). Binghamton, NY: Harrington Park Press.

Logan, C. R. (1996). Homophobia? No, homoprejudice. *Journal of Homosexuality, 31*(3), 31-53.

Loiacano, D. (1993). Gay identity issues among Black Americans. In L. D. Garnets & D. C. Kimmel (Eds.), *Psychological perspectives on lesbian and gay male experiences* (pp. 364-375). New York: Columbia University Press.

Luft, J., (1969). *Of human interaction*. Palo Alto, CA: National Press.

Luhtanen, R., & Crocker, J. (1992). A collective self-esteem scale: Self-evaluation of one's social identity. *Personality and Social Psychology Bulletin, 18*, 302-318.

Lyn, L. (1995). Lesbian, gay, and bisexual therapists' social and sexual interactions with clients. In J. C. Gonsiorek (Ed.), *Breach of trust: Sexual exploitation
by health care professionals and clergy* (pp. 193-212). Thousand Oaks, CA:
Sage.

MacDonald, A. P., Huggins, J., Young, S., & Swanson, R. A. (1973). Attitudes
toward homosexuality: Preservation of sexual morality or the double
standard? *Journal of Consulting and Clinical Psychology, 40*(1), 161.

Mallon, G. P. (1998). Knowledge for practice with gay and lesbian persons. In
G. Mallon (Ed.), *Foundations of social work practice* (pp. 1-30). Binghamton,
NY: Harrington Park Press.

Manalansan, M. (1996). Searching for community: Filipino gay men in
New York City. In R. Leong (Ed.), *Asian American sexualities: Dimensions of
the gay and lesbian experience* (pp. 51-64). New York: Routledge.

Mangaoang, G. (1996). From the 1970s to the 1990s: Perspective of a gay Filipino
American activist. In R. Leong (Ed.), *Asian American sexualities: Dimensions
of the gay and lesbian experience* (pp. 101-111). New York: Routledge.

Markowitz, J. C., Klerman, G. L., Clougherty, K. F., Spielman, L. A.,
Jacobsberg, L. B., Fishman, B., et al. (1995). Individual psychotherapies
for depressed HIV -positive patients. *American Journal of Psychiatry,
152* (10), 1504-1509.

Markus, F. (2000). Neighborhoods: Gay neighborhoods in the United States.
In G. E. Haggerty (Ed.), *Gay identities and cultures: An encyclopedia*
(pp. 636-637). New York: Garland.

Martin, A. (1982). Some issues in the treatment of gay and lesbian patients.
Psychotherapy: Theory, Research, and Practice. 19, 341-348.

Martin, J. I., & Knox, J. (1997). Loneliness and sexual risk behavior in gay men.
Psychological Reports, 81, 815-825.

Maslow, A. H. (1968). *Toward a psychology of being* (2nd ed.). Princeton, NJ: Van
Nostrand.

Mattison, A. M., & McWhirter, D. P. (1987). Stage discrepancy in male couples.
Journal of Homosexuality, 14(1/2), 89-99.

Mayne, T. J., Acree, M., Chesney, M. A., & Folkman, S. (1998). HIV sexual
risk behavior following bereavement in gay men. *Health Psychology, 17*(5),
403-411.

Mays, V., Cochran, S., & Peplau, L. (1986, August). *The Black women's relationship project: Relationship experiences and the perception of discrimination.* Paper
presented at the 94th annual convention of the American Psychological
Association, Washington, DC.

Mays, V., Cochran, S. D., & Rhue, S. (1993). The impact of perceived discrimination on the intimate relationships of Black lesbians. *Journal of Homosexuality,
25*, 1-14.

McDermott, D., Tyndall, L., & Lichtenberg, J. (1989). Factors related to counselor preference among gays and lesbians. *Journal of Counseling and
Development, 68*, 31-35.

McDougall, G. H. (1993). Therapeutic issues with gay and lesbian elders.
Clinical Gerontologist, 14(1), 45-57.

McKirnan, D. J., Ostrow, D. G., & Hope, B. (1996). Sex, drugs, and escape: A psychological model of HIV-risk sexual behaviours. *AIDS Care, 8*(6), 655-669.

McKirnan, D. J., & Peterson, P. L. (1989). Alcohol and drug use among homosexual men and women: Epidemiology and population characteristics. *Addictive Behaviors, 14*(5) 545-553.

McWhirter, D. P., & Mattison, A. M. (1984). *The male couple: How relationships develop.* Englewood Cliffs, NJ: Prentice Hall.

Meyer, I. H., & Dean, L. (1998). Internalized homophobia, intimacy, and sexual behavior among gay and bisexual men. In G. M. Herek (Ed.), *Stigma and sexual orientation* (pp. 160-186). Thousand Oaks, CA: Sage.

Millham, J., San Miguel, C. L., & Kellogg, R. (1976). A factor analytic conceptualization of attitudes toward male and female homosexuals. *Journal of Homosexuality, 2,* 3-10.

Morin, S. F., & Charles, K. A. (1983). Heterosexual bias in psychotherapy— heterosexism. In J. Murray & P. R. Abramson (Eds.), *Bias in psychotherapy* (pp. 309-338). New York: Praeger.

Morris, J. F. (1997). Lesbian coming out as a multidimensional process. *Journal of Homosexuality, 33*(2), 1-22.

Morrow, D. F. (1996). Coming out for adult lesbians: A group intervention. *Social Work, 41*(6), 647-656.

Murphy, B. (1992). Educating mental health professionals about gay and lesbian issues. *Journal of Homosexuality, 22,* 229-246.

Nakajima, G., Chan, Y., & Lee, K. (1996). Mental health issues for gay and lesbian Asian-Americans. In R. P. Cabaj & T. S. Stein (Eds.), *Textbook of homosexuality and mental health* (pp. 563-582). Washington, DC: American Psychiatric Press.

Nardi, P. M. (1999). *Gay men's friendships: Invincible communities.* Chicago: University of Chicago Press.

National Association of Social Workers. (1996). *Code of Ethics of the National Association of Social Workers.* Washington, DC: Author.

Nord, D. (1997). Threats to identity in survivors of multiple AIDS-related losses. *American Journal of Psychotherapy, 51*(3), 387-402.

O'Connor, M. F. (Ed.). (1997). *Treating the psychological consequences of HIV.* San Francisco: Jossey-Bass.

Ostrow, D. G. (1997). Disease, disease course, and psychiatric manifestations of HIV. In M. F. O'Connor (Ed.), *Treating the psychological consequences of HIV* (pp. 33-71). San Francisco: Jossey-Bass.

Pagtolun-An, I., & Clair, J. (1986). An experimental study of attitudes toward homosexuals. *Deviant Behavior, 7,* 121-135.

Pais, S., Piercy, F., & Miller, J. (1998). Factors related to family therapists' breaking confidence when clients disclose high-risk-to-HIV/AIDS sexual behaviors. *Journal of Marital and Family Therapy, 24*(4), 457-472.

Páres-Avila, J. A., & Montano-López, R. M. (1994). Issues in the psychosocial care of Latino gay men with HIV infection. In S. A. Cadwell, R. A. Burnham Jr., & M. Forstein (Eds.), *Therapists on the front line:*

Psychotherapy with gay men in the age of AIDS (pp. 339-362). Washington, DC: American Psychiatric Press.

Patterson, C. J. (1994). Children of the lesbian baby boom: Behavioral adjustment, self-concepts, and sex role identity. In B. Greene & G. M. Herek (Eds.), *Lesbian and gay psychology: Theory, research, and clinical applications* (pp. 156-175). Thousand Oaks, CA: Sage.

Paul, J. P., Hayes, R. B, & Coates, T. J. (1995). The impact of the HIV epidemic on U.S. gay male communities. In A. R. D'Augelli & C. J. Patterson (Eds.), *Lesbian, gay, and bisexual identities over the lifespan* (pp. 347-397). New York: Oxford University Press.

Peplau, L. A. (1993). Lesbian and gay relationships. In L. D. Garnets & D. C. Kimmel (Eds.), *Psychological perspectives on lesbian and gay male experiences* (pp. 395-419). New York: Columbia University Press.

Peplau, L. A., & Cochran, S. D. (1980, September). *Sex differences in values concerning love relationships.* Paper presented at the annual meeting of the American Psychological Association, Montreal, Canada.

Perlstein, M. (1996). Integrating a gay, lesbian, or bisexual person's religious and spiritual needs and choices into psychotherapy. In C. Alexander (Ed.), *Gay and lesbian mental health: A sourcebook for practitioners* (pp. 173-188). Binghamton, NY: Harrington Park Press.

Perry, M. J., & Barry, J. F. (1998). The gay male client in sexual addiction treatment. *Sexual Addiction and Compulsivity, 5,* 119-132.

Pilkington, N. W., & D'Augelli, A. R. (1995). Victimization of lesbian, gay, and bisexual youth in community settings. *Journal of Community Psychology, 23,* 34-56.

Pillard, R. C. (1991). Masculinity and femininity in homosexuality: "Inversion" revisited. In J. C. Gonsiorek & J. D. Weinrich (Eds.), *Homosexuality: Research implications for public policy* (pp. 32-43). Newbury Park, CA: Sage.

Plummer, K. (1975): *Sexual stigma: An interactionist account.* London: Routledge & Kegan Paul.

Purcell, D., & Hicks, D. (1996). Institutional discrimination against lesbians, gay men, and bisexuals: The courts, legislature, and the military. In R. P. Cabaj & T. S. Stein (Eds.), *Textbook of homosexuality and mental health* (pp. 763-782). Washington, DC: American Psychiatric Press.

Rabkin, J. G., Goetz, R. R., Remien, R. H., Williams, J. B., Todak, G., & Gorman, J. M. (1997). Stability of mood despite HIV illness progression in a group of homosexual men. *American Journal of Psychiatry, 154*(2), 213-238.

Rabkin, J. G., Remien, R. H., Katoff, L., & Williams, J. (1993). Suicidality in AIDS long-term survivors: What is the evidence? *AIDS Care, 5,* 401-411.

Ramirez Barranti, C. C. (1998). Social work practice with lesbian couples. In G. P. Mallon (Ed.), *Foundations of social work practice with lesbian and gay persons* (pp. 183-207). Binghamton, NY: Harrington Park Press.

Raphael, S., & Robinson, M. (1980). The older lesbian: Love relationships and friendship patterns. *Alternative Lifestyles, 3,* 207-229.

Ratner, E. F. (1993). Treatment issues for chemically dependent lesbians and gay men. In L. D. Garnets & D. C. Kimmel (Eds.), *Psychological perspectives on lesbian and gay male experiences* (pp. 567-578). New York: Columbia University Press.

Raychaudhuri, M., & Mukerji, K. (1971). Homosexual and narcissistic reflections on the Rorschach: An examination of Exner's diagnostic Rorschach signs. *Rorschachiana Japonica, 12,* 119-126.

Renzetti, C. (1992). *Violent betrayal: Partner abuse in lesbian relationships.* Newbury Park, CA: Sage.

Rochlin, M. (1972). The heterosexual questionnaire. In M. S. Kimmel & M. A. Messner (Eds.), *Men's lives* (4th ed.) (p. 472). Boston: Allyn and Bacon.

Rodriguez, R. (1996). Clinical issues in identity development in gay Latino men. In C. Alexander (Ed.), *Gay and lesbian mental health: A sourcebook for practitioners* (pp. 127-157). Binghamton, NY: Harrington Park Press.

Rosengard, C., & Folkman, S. (1997). Suicidal ideation and bereavement, HIV serostatus, and psychosocial variables in partners of men with AIDS. *AIDS Care, 9*(4), 373-384.

Ross, M. W., Hunter, C. E., Condon, J., Collins, P., & Begley, K. (1994). The mental adjustment to HIV scale: Measurement and dimensions of response to AIDS/HIV disease. *AIDS Care, 6*(4), 407-411.

Rowden, T. (2000). African American Gay Culture. In G. E. Haggerty (Ed.), *Gay histories and cultures: An encyclopedia* (pp. 19-20). New York: Garland Publishing.

Rudolph, J. (1990). Counselors' attitudes toward homosexuality: Some tentative findings. *Psychological Reports, 66,* 1352-1354.

Russell, S. T., & Joyner, K. (1998, August). *Adolescent sexual orientation and suicide risk: Evidence from a national study.* Paper presented at the annual meeting of the American Sociological Association, San Francisco, CA.

Savin-Williams, R. (1994). Verbal and physical abuse as stressors in the lives of lesbian, gay male, and bisexual youths: Associations with school problems, running away, substance abuse, prostitution, and suicide. *Journal of Consulting and Clinical Psychology, 62,* 261-269.

Savin-Williams, R. (2001). Suicide attempts among sexual-minority youths: Population and measurement issues. *Journal of Consulting and Clinical Psychology, 69*(6), 983-991.

Schlossberger, E., & Hecker, L. (1996). HIV and family therapists' duty to warn: A legal and ethical analysis. *Journal of Marital and Family Therapy, 22*(1), 27-40.

Schneider, J., & Agras, W. (1987). Bulimia in males: A matched comparison with females. *International Journal of Eating Disorders, 6,* 235-242.

Schwanberg, S. (1993). Attitudes toward gay men and lesbian women: Instrumentation issues. *Journal of Homosexuality, 93,* 99-136.

Shidlo, A. (1994). Internalized homophobia: Conceptual and empirical issues in measurement. In B. Greene & G. M. Herek (Eds.), *Lesbian and gay psychology: Theory, research, and clinical applications* (pp. 176-205). Thousand Oaks, CA: Sage.

Siegel, R. J. (1985). Beyond homophobia: Learning to work with lesbian clients. In L. B. Rosewater & L. E. A. Walker (Eds.), *Handbook of feminist therapy: Women's issues in psychotherapy* (pp. 183-190). New York: Springer.

Siever, M. (1996). The perils of sexual objectification: Sexual orientation, gender, and socioculturally acquired vulnerability to body dissatisfaction and eating disorders. In C. Alexander (Ed.), *Gay and lesbian mental health: A sourcebook for practitioners* (pp. 223-247). Binghamton, NY: Harrington Park Press.

Silverstein, C. (1990). The coupled gay. In R. J. Kus (Ed.), *Keys to caring: Assisting your gay and lesbian clients* (pp. 204-214). Boston: Alyson Publications.

Slater, S. (1995). *The lesbian family life cycle.* New York: The Free Press.

Slater, S., & Mencher, J. (1991). The lesbian family lifecycle: A contextual approach. *American Journal of Orthopsychiatry, 61*(3), 372-382.

Stanard, R., & Hazler, R. (1995). Legal and ethical implications of HIV and duty to warn for counselors: Does Tarasoff apply? *Journal of Counseling and Development, 73,* 397-400.

Stein, T. S. (1996). Lesbian, gay, and bisexual families. In R. P. Cabaj & T. S. Stein (Eds.), *Textbook of homosexuality and mental health* (pp. 503-512). Washington, DC: American Psychiatric Press.

Stein, T. S., & Cabaj, R. P. (1996). Psychotherapy with gay men: Issues in psychotherapy. In R. P. Cabaj & T. S. Stein (Eds.), *Textbook of homosexuality and mental health* (pp. 413-432). Washington, DC: American Psychiatric Press.

Strommen, E. (1989). Hidden branches and growing pains: Homosexuality and the family tree. *Marriage and Family Review, 14,* 9-34.

Strong, E. K. (1927). The Strong Interest Inventory. Palo Alto, CA: Consulting Psychologists Press.

Tafoya, T. (1996). Native two-spirit people. In R. P. Cabaj and T. S. Stein (Eds.), *Textbook of homosexuality and mental health* (pp. 603-620). Washington, DC: American Psychiatric Press.

Takagi, D. Y. (1996). Maiden voyage: Excursion into sexuality and identity politics in Asian America. In R. Leong (Ed.), *Asian American sexualities: Dimensions of the gay and lesbian experience.* (pp. 21-35). New York: Routledge.

Thomas, W., & Medicine, B. (2000). American Indian/Alaskan Native gender identity and sexuality. In G. E. Haggerty (Ed.), *Gay histories and cultures: An encyclopedia* (pp. 49-50). New York: Garland.

Troiden, R. R. (1988). Gay and lesbian identity: A sociological analysis. New York: General Hall.

Tunnell, G. (1994). Special issues in group psychotherapy for gay men with AIDS. In S. A. Cadwell, R. A. Burnham, Jr., & M. Forstein (Eds.), *Therapists on the front line: Psychotherapy with gay men in the age of AIDS* (pp. 237-291). Washington, DC: American Psychiatric Press.

UFMCC. (2002). *Who MCC Is . . . What We Do.* Retrieved July 17, 2002, from www. ufmcc.org

Van den Boom, F. (1995). AIDS, euthanasia, and grief. *AIDS Care, 7*(2), S175-S185.

Walker, L. (1984). *The battered woman syndrome.* New York: Springer.

Wat, E. C. (1996). Preserving the paradox, stories from a Gay-Loh. In R. Leong (Ed.), *Asian American sexualities: Dimensions of the gay and lesbian experience* (pp. 71-80). New York: Routledge.

Weinberg, G. (1972). *Society and the healthy homosexual.* New York: Anchor.

Weinberg, T. S. (1978). On "doing" and "being" gay: Sexual behavior and homosexual male self-identity. *Journal of Homosexuality, 4*(2), 143-156.

Weinberg, T. S. (1983). *Gay men, gay selves: The social construction of homosexual identities.* New York: Irvington.

Weinrich, J., & Williams, W. (1991). Strange customs, familiar lives: Homosexualities in other cultures. In J. C. Gonsiorek & J. Weinrich (Eds.), *Homosexuality: Research implications for public policy* (pp. 44-59). Newbury Park, CA: Sage.

Weiss, J. J. (1997). Psychotherapy with HIV-positive gay men: A psycho-dynamic perspective. *American Journal of Psychotherapy, 51*(1), 31-44.

Whitam, F., & Mathy, R. (1986). *Male homosexuality in four societies.* Westport, CT: Praeger.

Williams, W. L. (1996). Two-spirit persons: Gender nonconformity among Native American and Native Hawaiian youths. In R. C. Savin-Williams and K. M. Cohen (Eds.), *The lives of lesbians, gays, and bisexuals: Children to adults* (pp. 416-435). Fort Worth, TX: Harcourt Brace.

Wolf, D. G. (1980). *Life cycle change of older lesbians and gay men.* Paper presented at the annual meeting of the Gerontological Society, San Diego, CA.

Wolf, D. G. (1982). *Growing older: Lesbians and gay men.* Berkeley, CA: University of California Press.

Woods, J. & Lucas, J. (1993). *The corporate closet: The professional lives of gay men in America.* New York: Free Press.

Worden, J. (1991). *Grief counseling and grief therapy: A handbook for the mental health practitioner.* New York: Springer.

Wright, L. (Ed.). (1997). *The bear book: Readings in the history and evolution of a gay male subculture.* New York: Harrington Park Press.

Yalom, I. D. (1995). *The theory and practice of group psychotherapy* (4th ed.). New York: Basic Books.

Yalom, I. D. (1998). *The Yalom reader: Selections from the work of a master therapist and storyteller.* New York: Basic Books.

Zemsky, B., & Gilbert, L. (1990, July). *Gay and lesbian domestic violence.* Paper presented at the annual National Lesbian and Gay Health Conference, Washington, DC.

Index

About the Authors

Jeffrey N. Chernin, Ph.D., is the Clinic Director for Campion Counseling Center, a project of Ocean Park Community Services, in Santa Monica, California. He began a psychotherapy internship in Dallas in 1992, became a Licensed Professional Counselor (LPC) in 1994, and earned a Ph.D. in Counseling and Student Services from the University of North Texas in 1996. After moving to California in 1998, he obtained a Marriage and Family Therapist license in 2001. Jeff has led workshops on counseling lesbians and gay men, cultural diversity, communication, conflict resolution, stress management, and crystal methamphetamine use among gay and bisexual men. He has facilitated psychotherapy groups and several kinds of support groups on subjects related to coming out, chemical dependency, having HIV/AIDS, and being HIV-negative. His published work includes professional journal articles on psychotherapy and columns and articles on health-related topics for LGBT periodicals.

Melissa R. Johnson received her Ph.D. in School and Counseling Psychology from Texas Woman's University in 1996. She has conducted workshops and presentations for local, state, and national conferences focusing on topics such as parenting, HIV and addiction, relationships, and identity issues of lesbians and gay men. Previously the Director of Counseling for a nonprofit counseling center serving lesbians and gay men in Dallas, Melissa developed and implemented a chemical dependency treatment program for HIV positive individuals with substance abuse issues. She currently works as the Director of General Studies and Academic Services for the Art Institute of Dallas. She continues to teach psychology and has been working in private practice since 1994.